7/24

Inflation and labour markets

Studies in inflation

This is the second volume in a
series of studies in inflation
under the general editorship
of D. Laidler and M. Parkin

The first volume is *Incomes Policy
and Inflation*, edited by M. Parkin
and M. T. Sumner

Further titles in prospect

Edited by D. Laidler
and D. Purdy

Inflation and labour markets

Manchester University Press

University of Toronto Press

Published by
Manchester University Press
Oxford Road
Manchester M13 9PL

ISBN 0 7190 0568 X

Canada and the United States:
First published in 1974 by
University of Toronto Press
Toronto and Buffalo

ISBN 0 8020 2163 8

Made and printed in Great Britain by
William Clowes & Sons, Limited
London, Beccles and Colchester

Foreword to the series

In July 1971 a group of some twenty economists, econometricians and accountants, financed by the Social Science Research Council began work at the University of Manchester on a three year research programme, on the problem of inflation. The research consists largely of a series of self-contained investigations of various aspects of the inflationary process. In order to ensure that our own work does not develop in isolation from that being carried out elsewhere, it is the policy of the Manchester-S.R.R.C. Inflation Programme regularly to invite scholars from other Universities in the United Kingdom and elsewhere to present papers at Manchester. Though our own work, and that of our colleagues at other institutions, consists of self-contained projects, certain common themes continue to emerge as research progresses.

The purpose of this series of volumes is to bring together in a convenient form papers on related aspects of inflation so that other research workers and students will have easy access to a relatively integrated body of material. Though each volume will contain a large proportion of previously unpublished work, previous publication in a learned journal will not disqualify an otherwise relevant paper from being included in this series.

In promoting a wider understanding of the inflationary process original research is vital, but the dissemination of the results of that research is just as vital. It is our hope that this series of volumes will enable the results of our own work at Manchester, and that of our colleagues elsewhere, to reach a wide audience.

David Laidler and Michael Parkin

Contents

Introduction   *page* ix

Chapter 1 **Trade unions and wage inflation in the U.K.: a re-
appraisal.** D. L. Purdy and G. Zis (University of
Manchester)   1

Chapter 2 **On the concept and measurement of union militancy.**
D. L. Purdy and G. Zis   38

Chapter 3 **A model of wage determination under bilateral monopoly.** J. Johnston (University of Manchester)   61

Chapter 4 **Empirical tests of a bargaining theory of wage rate
determination.** J. Johnston and M. Timbrell (University of Manchester)   79

Chapter 5 **Excess demand for labour, unemployment and the
Phillips curve: a theoretical and empirical study.**
G. C. Archibald (University of British Columbia)
Robyn Kemmis (*Time Out* magazine) and J. W.
Perkins (University College of Wales, Aberystwyth) 109

Chapter 6 **The relationship between unemployment and vacancies
in Great Britain (1958–72): some further evidence.**
J. I. Foster (University of Manchester)   164

Chapter 7 **Wage inflation and the structure of regional unemployment.** F. P. R. Brechling (Northwestern University, Illinois)   197

Chapter 8 **Wage inflation in the U.K.—a multi-market approach.**
R. L. Thomas (University of Manchester Institute
of Science and Technology)   227

Author index   255
Subject index   257

Introduction

The seminal papers of Phillips [5] and Lipsey [4] established the labour market as a central focus of interest in the study of inflation. Their work drew attention to the apparent existence of a stable negative relationship between the level of unemployment and the rate of wage inflation, a relationship which had first been noted in postwar literature by Brown [2]. Economists are now universally agreed that this simple relationship is indeed too simple to capture accurately the reality with which policy makers have to deal. Nevertheless, the problems of labour market behaviour which currently perplex inflation theorists, and which underly all the essays in this volume, have their origins in these two early papers.

The problems in question may be divided into two broad groupings. There is first the set of problems involved in identifying the causes of inflation. Considered as a purely empirical construct, the Phillips curve is consistent with both demand-pull and cost-push theories of inflation. Moreover, Phillips himself said little about the theoretical basis for the relationship between unemployment and the rate of change of money wages, whilst Lipsey explicitly claimed that the relationship was neutral as between cost-push and demand-pull explanations of inflation. Despite the agnosticism of those whose work initially led inflation theorists to study the labour market with particular care, the Phillips curve frequently came to be associated—particularly in elementary text books—with the view that the causes of inflation were to be found in the labour market. Thus, Samuelson [7] in his 5th edition referred to the relationship as a 'modified cost-push model', while Reynolds [6] explicitly related the greater rapidity of wage inflation at low levels of unemployment to the greater bargaining strength of trade unions in such circumstances.

At the same time, Hines [3], responding to Lipsey's inability to find any relationship between measures of trade union strength and the rate of wage inflation, argued that the rate of change of the density of union membership could be used as a proxy for union militancy, and seemed to find strong evidence of a close correlation between this variable and the rate of change of money wages. In short, the stimulus provided by the Phillips and Lipsey papers to the analysis of labour market behaviour gave rise to quite widely held views that the root cause of inflation was to be found in the labour market, and in particular in the practices of trade unions.

The other strand in the literature has more continuity with the work of Phillips and Lipsey. For them, whatever the reasons for the existence of a negatively sloped Phillips curve, it presented a menu for policy choice, a trade-off between the desirable policy goals of price stability and full employment. This approach naturally leads to questions about what determines the slope and location of the curve and what causes the curve to shift. Answers to these questions are clearly valuable for in principle they would enable policy makers to shift the curve, to choose, as it were, their policy menu. Lipsey himself laid the ground for much subsequent work with his suggestion that, since the national labour market was in fact the aggregate of a set of micro markets, and since each market was likely to be characterised by a non-linear Phillips curve of its own, changes in the distribution of unemployment between individual markets would shift the aggregate curve. As to the slope of the curve, Lipsey suggested that it was determined by two relationships: one between the excess demand for labour and the level of unemployment, and the other between the level of excess demand for labour and the rate of change of wages.

The essays in this volume follow up both strands in the literature. We have chosen to concentrate on recent work here and have not reprinted the basic papers of Lipsey, Phillips and Hines because they are readily available elsewhere. Moreover, every essay in this volume has been written by a member of the S.S.R.C. Manchester Inflation Programme, or has been read to a meeting of that programme's weekly workshop.

On the theme of trade union militancy as a source of wage inflation, two essays by David Purdy and George Zis call much received wisdom into question. First, they show that a careful scrutiny and reworking of Hines's studies seriously weaken both the stability and the strength of the relationship between the rate of change of union density and wage inflation. This variable is of course only one of the possible proxies for trade union aggressiveness, but the same authors proceed in their next essay to analyse the concept of 'militancy' and show not only that there are serious difficulties with any of the proxy measures which have been suggested for it in the literature, but, more fundamentally, that the very concept of militancy is difficult to determine with any precision in the context of economic analysis.

Two essays, one by Jack Johnston alone, and one by him and Martin Timbrell, take up the theme of trade union monopoly power, a concept which, unlike 'militancy', has a precise meaning in economics. Johnston notes that the market theory underlying the Phillips curve is essentially competitive and argues that there is no *a priori* reason to suppose that competition is a more accurate characterisation of labour markets than bilateral monopoly. He then constructs a model of wage determination under conditions of bilateral monopoly, in which the level of unemployment does not figure but in which the difference between workers' gross pay and net take home pay has an important role to play. This theoretical work is then tested by Johnston and Timbrell with promising results.

The paper by Archibald, Kemmis and Perkins follows up some preliminary work by Archibald [1] on the effects of the regional dispersion of unemployment on the location and stability of the aggregate Phillips curve. This paper is an extremely thorough study of this problem in the context of the British economy, but still, unfortunately, leaves many questions unanswered, finding considerable instability both over time and across regions in the conventional Phillips curve.

One feature of the approach adopted by Archibald *et al* is their clear distinction between variables which alter the transformation from excess demand to unemployment and variables which alter either the slope or intercept of the reaction function $\dot{w}/w$ on excess demand. The paper by John Foster bears on the former of these issues. It is not directly concerned with wage inflation but is addressed to the problem of explaining the much-noted shift in the relationship between unemployment and vacancies in the U.K. since 1966. His careful examination of the evidence suggests that employers' hiring policies have been affected by demographic changes in labour supply and by Redundancy Payments legislation. Moreover this demand side explanation of the $U-V$ shift clearly implies that the

xii Introduction

paradox of high levels of unemployment combined with rapid rates of wage inflation cannot be resolved by postulating an upward shift of the supply curve of labour associated with an increase in voluntary unemployment.

The essays by Frank Brechling and Leighton Thomas explore some further aspects of disaggregated models of wage determination. Brechling, using a multi-market model of wage behaviour, follows up the implications of assuming interdependence between the wage adjustment processes in different sectors. On the basis of U.S. data he tentatively constructs a theory of regional wage inflation leadership. Archibald *et al* ignore such interdependence across markets by explicitly assuming that the matrix of adjustment coefficients is diagonal, and it would certainly be worthwhile replicating Brechling's study in a British context. In Thomas's multi-market model of wage inflation the assumption of identical $\dot{w}/w$—excess demand relationships in each micro-market is abandoned. The suggestion is made that the parameters of the market adjustment function are systematically related to the degree to which the market is organised, as reflected in the level of unionisation within the market. Thomas produces evidence that is certainly consistent with this hypothesis and it surely merits further serious investigation. It begins, after all, to provide a link between the heretofore separate strands in the literature with which this volume deals.

One final note: though the issue is by no means neglected, none of the essays in this volume takes as its central topic the role of expectations of price inflation in generating wage inflation. This important question will be dealt with in a subsequent volume in this series on the role of expectations in the inflationary process.

David Laidler and David Purdy

References
[1] Archibald, G. C., 'The Phillips Curve and the Distribution of Unemployment', *American Economic Review, Papers and Proceedings*, Vol. LIX, No. 2 (May 1969).
[2] Brown, A. J., *The Great Inflation, 1939–51*, London (1955).
[3] Hines, A. G., 'Trade Unions and Wage Inflation in the United Kingdom 1893–1961', *Review of Economic Studies*, Vol. 31 (1964).
[4] Lipsey, R. G., 'The Relation Between Unemployment and the Rate of Change of Money Wage Rates in the United Kingdom 1862–1957: A Further Study', *Economica* (Feb. 1960).
[5] Phillips, A. W., 'The Relation Between Unemployment and the Rate of Change of Money Wage Rates in the United Kingdom', *Economica* (Nov. 1958).
[6] Reynolds, L. G., *Economics* (revised edition), Homewood, Ill. (1966).
[7] Samuelson, P. A., *Economics*, 5th edition (1961).

D. L. Purdy
and G. Zis[1]

Chapter 1 Trade unions and wage inflation in the U.K.: a reappraisal[2]

I Introduction

Prominent amongst attempts to explain inflation is the view that trade union pressure on wage rates is a significant independent cause of rising prices. The recent 'wages explosion', coinciding in the U.K. with a relatively high level of unemployment and an incomes 'policy off' phase, has further stimulated interest in this view. The aim of this paper is to subject to critical scrutiny the empirical work in favour of this hypothesis developed in a series of articles by A. G. Hines [6, 7, 8, 9].[3]

Hines argues that other writers either dismiss the possibility that unions may affect the rate of change of money wages independently of demand [13], or use unsatisfactory methods of identifying trade union pressure [11, 3]. He proposes as an index of union pushfulness the rate of change in the proportion of the labour force belonging to trade unions, ΔT_t ($= T_t - T_{t-1}$, where T_t denotes the unionised percentage of the labour force, or union density, in year t). His basic hypothesis is that ΔT_t is an indicator of union activity which simultaneously manifests itself in pressure on wage rates and in increased union membership and density. This hypothesis is tested at the aggregate and disaggregated levels by regressions of the rate of increase of money wage rates, ΔW, on the militancy variable, ΔT, for various periods since 1893 and in both simple and multiple regression analyses.

---

[1] We are indebted to all members of the Inflation Workshop, University of Manchester, and would like to express our special appreciation to M. Gray, D. Laidler, M. Parkin and D. Rose for their helpful comments and guidance. Also, we are grateful to Mr. J. Foster for his assistance. The responsibility for any errors is ours.

[2] Reprinted with permission, from M. Parkin (ed.), *Essays in Modern Economics*, London, Longmans (1973).

[3] Numbers in square brackets relate to references listed at ends of chapters.

The general conclusion which Hines draws from his findings is that since the period before world war one unemployment, taken as a proxy for excess demand, has become progressively less, and 'institutional' forces progressively more important in determining the rate of change of money wage rates. In particular, union pushfulness, measured by ΔT has emerged in the post-war period as a key factor in determining the pace of wage inflation.

We find the Hines hypothesis unsatisfactory on both *a priori* and empirical grounds. Other writers have been similarly dissatisfied (see [5]), and have proposed alternative indicators of union militancy such as strike frequency or the number of working days lost through strikes. None, however, has presented a systematic critique of Hines. The present study is an attempt to mount such a critique. In the next section we consider a number of qualitative objections to Hines's hypothesis, which is shown to be lacking in theoretical foundation, to be of doubtful relevance to actual union-employer bargaining in the U.K. and in any case to be incorrectly specified. In Section II, we report on the consequences of adjusting the data used by Hines in his empirical work so as to put them on a basis which is both consistent and more closely in conformity with Hines's hypothesis. These adjustments make little difference to Hines's post-war results, but substantially affect his inter-war findings. In Section IV we reconsider the explanatory power of the union militancy variable and show, contrary to Hines, that the contribution of this variable to the explanation of money wages is significant, but relatively unimportant.

In Section V, we investigate the assumption that changes in union militancy are adequately reflected by changes in union density. In particular we show how the existence of the closed shop and changes in the structure of employment may affect recorded changes in union density. We construct a more satisfactory measure of the change in aggregate union density which abstracts from the process of labour force reallocation, and conclude that Hines's unadjusted measure has been a poor index of union militancy in the post-war period. We further suggest how some of the observed association between ΔW and ΔT can be explained in terms of changes in the structure of employment. In section VI we present our general conclusions. The upshot of our argument is that the case for the cost-push view of inflation remains to be proven.

II   A critique of the Hines hypothesis

In this section we subject to critical scrutiny the arguments adduced by Hines to justify the use of ΔT as an index of militancy.

Hines claims several merits for ΔT as an index of militancy. It is objective and is uncorrelated with the demand for labour measured in various ways.[4] He also argues that as the T series is not dominated by its time trend, ΔT escapes Lipsey's objections [13] to the 'cost push via union strength' thesis that any such index would display a secular upward trend, implying that if union strength were an important determinant of wage changes there would have been a steady acceleration of wage and price movement over time. It should be noted that Lipsey referred to indices of union *strength*. Hines, on the other hand, speaks of the *activity* or *militancy* of unions, which is reflected in their year to year changes in membership density. It remains to be shown that a high or low degree of union *activity* is the same thing as a high or low degree of union *strength*. We deal below with the arguments adduced to support such an equivalence.

Further, Hines claims that ΔT is sensitive to all the 'considerable annual variation in the strength of the independent pressure which unions bring to bear on the rate of change of money wages'. In fact during the post-war period the level of unionisation, T, has remained on a plateau at between 39 and 41 per cent of the labour force. On Hines's own definitions and data the ΔT series cannot be said to have exhibited considerable annual variation. Between 1949 and 1961 its range was between -0.95 and $+0.60$. Even small changes in union density which are brought about by factors other than Hines-type militancy will have a marked effect on a series with such a minor degree of variability.[5]

The proposition that ΔT is an index of militancy which simul-

----

[4] The tests which Hines employs to demonstrate this lack of correlation, namely the simple regression of ΔT on U, current and lagged, on the Dow–Dicks-Mireaux index of excess demand pressure, and on the deviation of the index of industrial production around a straight line time trend, may be too crude to pick up the relationship between unionisation and labour market pressure. There is considerable unanimity amongst labour historians that a relationship of some sort exists between labour movement activity and both short term cyclical fluctuations and the longer periods of economic change with which economic historians are mainly concerned. See Hobsbawm [10] 'Economic fluctuations and some social movements since 1800'.

[5] A large part of the work reported in the present paper is devoted to an investigation of the impact of some of these other factors on Hines's results; see section V.

taneously manifests itself in increased union membership and in upward pressure on wage rates is not derived from any formal model of union behaviour. Nowhere does Hines spell out the objectives of the union and indicate the relative priorities which the union attaches to conflicting objectives. There is a presumption in his theory that unions aim to drive up their members' real wages by exerting pressure on money wages; that unions aim to extend the organised proportion of the labour force lying within their jurisdiction, and that the rate at which they succeed in carrying out this latter objective is a major determinant of their success in pursuing the former. Beyond this all that we have is a number of *ad hoc* rationalisations and supporting assertions, which, moreover, differ slightly in each of the papers. What follows is a compendium of all the reasons proffered by Hines to support the basic proposition that the unions' bargaining power is reflected by the rate of change of union density in any period. It should be stressed, however, that these in no way add up to a theory of union behaviour, and that without such a theory the sense in which Hines's hypothesis can be said to have contributed to the explanation of post-war inflation is at best extremely attenuated.

Hines argues that an increased rate of recruitment will make officials feel stronger and encourage them to adopt a more intransigent negotiating stance. At the same time the morale of shopfloor workers will be raised and they will become more willing to support a tougher stand by their officials, thus enhancing the potency of the strike threat. It is further argued that more intense organising activity will communicate the union's greater militancy to the employers. Then too, an extension of the union's control over a larger section of the labour force will directly reduce the danger that non-union competition may undermine the union's ability to support its demands by a strike or the threat of a strike.

The last reason mentioned appears to relate to the *level* rather than the *rate of change* of union density. Thus, even if non-union competition is an important factor affecting union bargaining power, which may be doubted on the grounds that the legal right of peaceful picketing is of greater value in preventing strike-breaking than the level of union density, the correct formulation of Hines's wage determination hypothesis should include T as well as ΔT. Hines confines the role of T in explaining ΔW to inter-period comparisons only, and excludes T from his regression estimates for the inter-war and post-war periods considered separately.[6] An additional reason for including T as well as ΔT in the wage determination hypothesis follows from Hines's argument that more intensive union recruitment will communicate the union's greater militancy to the employers. A given value of ΔT will presumably carry more weight with employers the higher the already achieved level of union density. Hines himself suggests at one point that there may be diminishing returns to recruitment effort, so that a given ΔT indicates more militancy at high than low levels of T.

Hines justifies the omission of employer resistance to union wage claims as an independent force in wage bargaining on the grounds that employer resistance will be permanently reduced to insignificance by the combination of a régime of administered prices with universal knowledge of the 'wage round'. Hence there is no need to qualify the evidence of increased union pressure on wage rates by reference to the state of employer resistance. It may well be the case that the employer's ability to pass on increased labour costs in higher prices without fear of losing sales has been a constant factor throughout the post-war period making for a lower *average* level of employer resistance than hitherto. It does not, however, follow that there has been no variation in the degree of employer resistance around this low average level,[7] and there is no *a priori* reason to assume that employer resistance has varied inversely with union militancy, making it unnecessary to give separate consideration to this factor.

The upshot of these assertions as to the role of the militancy variable, ΔT, is according to Hines [8], that 'a successful membership drive' is 'a necessary accompaniment of success in the wage bargain'. Hence, unions seek to increase their membership immediately before and during wage negotiations. In strict logic this conclusion does not follow. None of the reasons mentioned for associating the size of an increase in union density with an increase in bargaining strength entails that a membership drive is a *necessary* condition of success in wage negotiations. At most they imply that

[6] This omission is further considered in section III below.
[7] Taking the length of time elapsing between the date of filing and the date of settlement of wage claim as a crude index of the degree of employer resistance, the fifteen separate sets of national wage rate negotiations between the Engineering Employers Federation and the Confederation of Shipbuilding and Engineering Unions which occurred between the end of the war and the conclusion of the three-year package deal in 1964, took between two months and twelve months with a mean time taken of six months.

increased unionisation will be a *sufficient* condition of success in wage negotiations. Hines fails to show that there are no other ways of improving bargaining strength.

Apart from their logical coherence the relevance of Hines's *ad hoc* rationalisations may also be questioned. Where a closed shop is in operation the arguments concerning the role of ΔT are inapplicable. An effective closed shop means that employees must become members of one of a number of specified unions, either as a condition of obtaining employment in the first place, or as a condition of retaining it once obtained. McCarthy [15] estimated that some 3·75 million workers were employed in closed shop establishments, whilst a further 1,350,000 workers were in open shops within trades where the closed shop practice predominated, and which were, therefore, likely to be subject to the 'semi-closed shop' enforced by informal sanctions. Twenty-two per cent of manual workers were covered by closed shop arrangements and these constituted 49 per cent of trade unionists in manual groups. The extensiveness of the closed shop in British industry not only limits the applicability of the Hines hypothesis; it may also seriously affect the recorded changes in aggregate ΔT.[8]

Equally, as recently as 1964 it was estimated that only 54·3 per cent of the labour force in Great Britain was employed in industries which generally do not have a union recognition problem; 27 per cent of the labour force was located in areas in which employers generally refuse to recognise trade unions; a further 11 per cent in areas with a partial recognition problem; and 7 per cent in areas in which unions have not generally tried to organise, but in which recognition problems would arise if they did [1, pp. 72–3]. Of course, unions do seek to organise in establishments where they are not recognised. One of the prime purposes of building up membership in such establishments is precisely to elicit eventual recognition. Often employers explicitly agree to grant recognition if the union or unions concerned succeed in organising a majority of their employees. As with the closed shop, the existence of a substantial recognition problem limits the applicability of Hines's arguments concerning the role of union militancy in wage bargaining. Again

[8] The impact of changes in the proportion of the total labour force employed in the closed shop sector on recorded changes in union membership and density is examined in section V below.

since one of the determinants of the worker's decision to join a union is precisely whether or not the union is recognised by the employer, the extensiveness of the recognition problem and the discontinuous jump in union membership which is likely to follow the granting of recognition, may seriously affect recorded changes in union membership and density.

A final limitation to the applicability of Hines's hypothesis is the fact that some unions do not engage in industrywide bargaining over standard or minimum wage rates but prefer to rely instead on plant and company level bargaining. The leading white-collar unions, Draughtsmen and Allied Technicians Association (DATA) and the Association of Scientific, Technical and Managerial Staffs (ASTMS) for instance, are in this position. The Amalgamated Union of Engineering Workers (AUEW) has recently jettisoned industrywide bargaining in favour of plant bargaining. It is not clear whether a model of wage-related union militancy which is explicitly cast in terms appropriate to industrywide negotiations, can be applied without modification to cases such as these. Moreover, it is a commonplace of the literature on labour economics and industrial relations that the post-war period has seen the emergence of a substantial gap between minimum or standard wage rates agreed in official industrywide negotiations, and actual earnings in the workplace throughout many leading sectors of the economy. There are many other methods available to most unions of raising their members' effective real wages besides increasing their bargaining strength in industrywide negotiations.

It may be objected that these doubts as to the relevance of Hines's hypothesis apply to the microbehaviour of unions, whereas Hines's main empirical case is conducted at the aggregate level. Without entering the methodological controversy over the independence of macro and micro theory, the reply to this objection is simply that Hines's own supporting arguments relate to individual bargaining units. None of the above qualitative considerations is decisive against Hines. They do, however, weaken the cogency of his case. In sections IV and V below we attempt to quantify some of the objections raised in this section. First, however, we must reconsider the data which Hines used to test the significance of his union militancy variable.

III   Adjustments of the data appropriate to testing Hines's hypothesis
In his initial investigations of the wage rate/union militancy relationship, Hines measured union density as the ratio of trade union

membership in the U.K. to the labour force in Great Britain. His labour force series was the total working population, which includes on the one hand the employers, self-employed and armed forces, and on the other hand the unemployed. We re-estimated the simple regression of ΔW or ΔT after adjusting the labour force data in various ways.

Equation (1) in Table 1 is the equation estimated by Hines for the period 1949–61. Equation (2) places the denominator of the ratio used to measure union density on the same U.K. basis as the numerator. Equation (3) excludes from the denominator the employers, self-employed and armed forces, who can hardly be considered as potential candidates for unionisation. Equation (4) additionally excludes the unemployed.

The place of unemployed workers in the union militancy/wage negotiations mechanism outlined in section II is unclear. If unions undertake recruitment drives with a view to increasing their bargaining strength during wage negotiations, it seems more plausible to postulate that they will concentrate their energies on recruiting those who are actually in employment. Unemployed workers are dispersed and have little obvious motivation to join unions. On the other hand, in so far as unions direct their efforts towards reducing the rate of dropout from membership, then the unemployed do

Table 1   Period 1949–61 = Equation estimated $\Delta W_t = a + b\,\Delta T_t$

No.	a	b	$\bar{R}^2$	DW	Description
(1)	5·392	4·219 (0·975)	0·562	n.a.	Hines's results $L = TWP$ for G.B.
(2)	5·539 (0·545)	4·336 (1·283)	0·465	2·071*	$L = TWP$ for U.K.
(3)	5·599 (0·488)	3·974 (0·889)	0·613	2·239*	TWP for U.K. minus employers, self-employed and armed forces
(4)	5·880 (0·533)	3·482 (0·908)	0·533	2·104*	TWP for U.K. minus employers etc. and the unemployed

L = Labour Force
TWP = Total working population
Standard errors are given in parentheses.
* Indicates that the test showed no autocorrelation at the 1 per cent level.

become an important focus of any membership drive since the unions will want to persuade workers to maintain their membership even when they are out of work. Indeed, it is only by postulating this latter type of membership effort that any sense can be made of the Hines hypothesis as applied to the inter-war period when the militancy index, ΔT, registered severe falls. For this period (when, incidentally the explanatory performance of ΔT is better than in any other period), the Hines hypothesis must presumably be that wage rates fell more or less rapidly according to the degree to which unions were successful in maintaining their membership against the prevailing downward trend. Because of this lack of clarity about the place of the unemployed, we decided to see whether it makes any difference when the potentially unionisable labour force is defined so as to exclude them.

The data adjustments described above do not seriously upset Hines's results. The estimated constant term and slope coefficient are not significantly different from those estimated by Hines. Indeed, the explanatory power of the militancy variable is considerably improved when we remove the employers, self-employed and armed forces (equation 3). This is probably due to the fact that the various labour force concepts used to compute ΔT in these regressions moved in sympathy over the period in question. Suppose that the series for the 'true' labour force variable differs from Hines's series by some constant proportion α (where α may be $\gtrless 0$). Then we shall have:

$$\Delta T_t = T_t - T_{t-1} = \left(\frac{T^*}{L}\right)t - \left(\frac{T^*}{L}\right)t - 1$$

so that

$$\left[\frac{T^*}{L(1+\alpha)}\right]t - \left[\frac{T^*}{L(1+\alpha)}\right]t - 1 = \frac{1}{1+\alpha}\,\Delta T_t = \Delta T_t'$$

say, for $\alpha > 0$. A regression of ΔW on $\Delta T'$ would give estimates of a' and b' in the equation: $\Delta W_t = a' + b'\Delta T_t'$ where $b' = b/1 + \alpha$. We should therefore, expect Hines's estimated slope coefficient to be upwardly or downwardly biased according as the 'true' labour force series is proportionally greater or less than the series used by Hines. The results shown in Table 1 indicate that the bias introduced by Hines's mis-specification of the labour force variable is negligible in the post-war period.

When we turn to the inter-war period we find that Hines's mis-specification of the labour force is more serious. His labour force series is based on interpolation from a straight line time trend fitted to just two observations in the total occupied population taken from the 1921 and 1931 censuses. The derivation by linear interpolation of a series for a variable known to be influenced by fluctuations in the level of economic activity is a most dubious procedure. Moreover, the definition of the 'total occupied population' altered between these two censuses in a way which affected the recorded change in total occupied population.[9] The concept is in any case unsatisfactory for Hines's hypothesis. It includes the unemployed and, more importantly, employers and managers and members of the armed forces. A far more satisfactory labour force statistic is provided by the series for numbers insured under the unemployment insurance scheme.[10] Equation (2) in Table 2 is based on a labour force variable defined as total insured employees (employed plus unemployed). Equation 3 excludes the unemployed from this total.

In contrast to our findings for the post-war period, the respecification of the labour force variable makes a considerable difference to the regression estimates. The slope coefficients in 2 and 3 are significantly lower than those obtained by Hines. When the unemployed are included in the labour force series (equation 2) there is auto-correlation in the residuals, whilst when they are excluded the auto-correlation disappears but the proportion of variance explained by ΔT drops to less than a third of the level explained by Hines's militancy index.

What emerges from these findings is that within certain limits if one wants to use ΔT as an index of union militancy then it does not greatly matter whether the labour force series used to compute ΔT

[9] In 1921 total occupied population was defined as total population aged twelve and over minus persons retired or not gainfully employed, whereas in 1931 the age was raised to fourteen and over owing to the institution of a break between primary and secondary education in 1926 which effectively made secondary education up to fourteen universal.

[10] 'Throughout the period following the beginning of the insurance scheme in 1911, the scheme excluded employers and workers on their own account, and also certain classes of employees, the principal of which were indoor private domestic servants, teachers with pension rights, female professional nurses, established civil servants, and permanent employees in national and local government and in railway service. After 1920 the scheme covered the very great majority of manual workers and a large proportion of non-manual workers.' Ralph B. Ainsworth, 'Labour statistics' in *Sources and Nature of the Statistics of the U.K.*, ed. M. G. Kendall, vol. i, Royal Statistical Society, 1952.

Table 2   Inter-war period 1924–38 = Equation estimated
$$\Delta W_t = a + b\,\Delta T_t$$

No.	a	b	$\bar{R}^2$	DW	Description
(1)	0·098 (0·902)	2·488 (0·061)	0·902	1·479*	Hines's results, period 1921–38
(2)	0·697 (0·239)	0·882 (0·126)	0·774	0·626	L = Total insured employees in the U.K.
(3)	0·534 (0·428)	0·473 (0·193)	0·265	1·120*	L = Total insured employees in employment in the U.K.

* Indicates that the test showed no autocorrelation at the 1 per cent probability level. For other values the test showed positive autocorrelation.

is truly representative of the potentially unionisable labour force, provided that whatever series is used is internally consistent. If Hines's hypothesis is interpreted as depending crucially on the *direction* and *rate of change* of union density, then, within limits, no great significance attaches to the precise calculation of the *level* of density at any given point in time. On the other hand if T as well as ΔT should be included in the wage determination equation as we argued in section II, then the correct specification of the labour force becomes a matter of some importance.[11]

Moreover, even if we adopt Hines's interpretation of the militancy hypothesis the limits within which mis-specification of the labour force is irrelevant are illustrated by our findings for the inter-war period. The labour force series which we used moved far less in sympathy with that used by Hines in the inter-war period than in the post-war period. Thus, Hines's results are only moderately

---

[11] One of the defects of Hines's disaggregated study [8] is that the calculations of union density by industry are notoriously unreliable since there exists no accurate breakdown of union membership by industry. Thus, according to our calculations the level of union density in group 4 of Hines's twelve broad industry groupings, the general workers group (comprising chemicals and allied industries, other manufacturing, bricks, pottery, glass and cement, gas, water and electricity, and transport and communications—in all nearly 20 per cent of total employees) exceeds 100 per cent in some post-war years and is unrealistically high throughout. This evident absurdity is due to the practice of including the *whole* of the membership of the two large general unions in this industry grouping together with the membership of the other unions which recruit therein.

robust in the face of modifications designed to make the data used to compute ΔT more conformable to his hypothesis.

It is also worth noting the contrasting results which follow the exclusion of the unemployed from the unionisable labour force in the two periods. One conclusion which might be drawn from this contrast is that the focus of union concern over membership is different at different levels of employment. During the large scale unemployment of the inter-war period union efforts to maintain their membership among the unemployed had an importance which they have since lost in the full employment conditions of the post-war period. If this is so then the correct specification of the labour force is one which includes the unemployed.

It is worth while investigating the consequences of respecifying the labour force in the way outlined above. In Table 3 we present Hines's regression estimates for three variants of the unionisation

Table 3

Equation estimated	a	b	c	$\bar{R}^2$	D.W.	Description and period
(1) $\Delta W_t = a + bT_t$						
Hines	25·032	−1·191		0·497	n.a.	1921–38
	(0·497)	(0·295)				L = estimated *TOP*
P & Z	−6·238	0·164		0·086	0·576	1924–38
	(4·373)	(0·108)				L = U.K. insured employees
(2) $\Delta W_t = a + b\,\Delta T_t$						
Hines	0·098	2·488		0·913	1·479*	1921–38
	(0·902)	(0·061)				L as in (1)
P & Z	0·691	0·882		0·774	0·626	1924–38
	(0·239)	(0·126)				L as in (1)
(3) $\Delta W_t = a + b\,\Delta T_t + cT_t$						
Hines	0·757	2·454	−0·027	0·913	1·59*	1921–38
	(0·895)	(0·285)	(0·176)			L as in (1)
P & Z	−6·253	0·891	0·172	0·950	2·309*	1924–38
	(1·027)	(0·060)	(0·025)			L as in (1)

L = Labour force
TOP = Total occupied population
Standard errors are shown in parentheses.
* Indicates that the test showed no autocorrelation at the 1 per cent probability level. For other values the test showed positive autocorrelation.

hypothesis together with our own estimates based on modified labour force data for the inter-war period. For Hines's post-war period 1949–61 the parameter estimates yielded by our regressions for each of these variants do not differ significantly from those obtained by Hines. They are not, therefore, shown separately here.

Like Hines, we found that the *level* of unionisation alone offered no explanation of ΔW (equation 1). Unlike Hines, however, we found that the level of unionisation did contribute significantly to the explanation of ΔW when both the level and the rate of change of unionisation were included together as independent variables (equation 3). Moreover, the autocorrelation found in the regression of ΔW on ΔT alone is removed when T is added as a regressor. This strongly suggests that if the unionisation hypothesis is true, the correct formulation of it is one which includes the size as well as the activity of unions, notwithstanding Hines's statements to the contrary. Hines is prepared to assign an explanatory role to T only in inter-period comparisons of wage movements, arguing that the increase in the level of union density post-war compared with pre-war has been responsible for an upward shift of the ΔW–ΔT relationship. This interpretation is convenient for the militancy hypothesis and the view that unions have acquired progressively more importance in determining the rate of change of money wages, since the insignificance of T within the post-war period cannot then be taken as contrary evidence. If, however T *ought* to be included in the correct formulation of the militancy hypothesis, then its insignificance within the post-war period, which, of course, is due to its extremely small variability, weakens the view that union militancy has been an important independent cause of wage inflation.

Moreover, Hines's arguments concerning the role of T in comparisons of wage movements between the post-war and inter-war periods can be questioned. He found that the regression line for a simple regression of ΔW on ΔT was both steeper and higher in the post-war period than in the inter-war period. He offers two alternative explanations for the increase in the slope coefficient. The first is that there is an upper limit to the extent of unionisation and the more closely this limit is approached the smaller are the returns in terms of increasing union density to a given outlay of recruitment effort by the unions. Hence a given change in union density indicates more militancy at high than at low levels of density. It is difficult to reconcile this proposition with the fact that the large unions have not in the post-war period shown any tendency to grow more slowly than average (if anything they have grown faster), even when account is taken of growth by amalgamation. Moreover, the militancy-ΔT relationship may, as we noted in Section II, be upset by the discontinuous changes in union membership and density which are likely to accompany the granting of recognition or the extension of the closed shop. Hines's alternative explanation, which in his disaggregated study [8] seems to be preferred, is that in the post-war period a leader–follower relationship has operated across different bargaining units, with the result that a given increase in unionisation concentrated in the leading sector becomes associated with a higher rate of increase in the aggregate wage index. For this second explanation to be valid a connection would have to be shown between the emergence of a leader–follower relationship after the second world war and the increase in the level of unionisation post-war as compared with pre-war. If the argument is that unions in follower sectors have been able to emulate the wage increases achieved in the leading sector because they have reached higher levels of density than before the war, this merely strengthens the case for formulating the militancy hypothesis in terms of both T and ΔT. In any case the choice of the 'general unions' sector comprising transport and communications, gas, water and electricity and a number of other heterogeneous industries, for the role of leading sector appears bizarre.

The explanation Hines offers for the increase in the intercept of the regression line for the post-war period is that the post-war rise in the level of union density reflected the organisation of previously unorganised workers. Wage rates in these sectors were pushed up and there was a once for all increase in the general level of wage rates. This explanation would be consistent with an upward shift in the ΔW–ΔT relationship of a temporary nature only. Once the level of unionisation stabilised again after the organisation of previously unorganised workers, any alleged impact which this might have on the constant term of the regression would be expected to disappear. In order to obtain a permanent shift of the regression line it would have to be shown that a permanent increase in the level of unionisation would permanently raise ΔW, not W.

The hypothesis that the coefficient on ΔT has undergone a permanent increase since the war is not borne out when the post-war period of observation is extended up to 1969. In Table 4 we present estimates of two variants of the unionisation hypothesis first

Table 4

Equation estimated	a	b	c	$\bar{R}^2$	DW	Period
(1) $\Delta W_t = a + b\,\Delta T_t$						
	5·557	2·568		0·412	1·850*	1949–69
	(0·364)	(0·663)				
	6·092	4·051		0·607	2·197*	1949–59
	(0·594)	(0·999)				
	5·579	0·791		0·047	2·363*	1960–69
		(0·658)				
(2) $\Delta W_t = a + b\,\Delta T_t + cT_t$						
	1·384	2·546	0·096	0·382	1·883*	1949–69
	(15·274)	(0·685)	(0·353)			
	15·843	4·229	−0·220	0·561	2·208*	1949–59
	(42·812)	(1·315)	(0·997)			
	30·844	1·318	−0·598	−0·058	2·307*	1960–69
	(56·211)	(1·362)	(1·330)			

In each equation the labour force used to calculate T and ΔT was defined as U.K. total working population minus employers, self-employed and armed forces.

* Indicates that the test showed no autocorrelation at the 1 per cent probability level.

for the whole period 1949–69 and then for each of the sub-periods 1949–59 and 1960–69. For the whole period the coefficient on ΔT was not significantly different from that estimated by Hines for the inter-war period (see Table 2), though it is significantly higher than our estimate. When we consider each of the sub-periods separately not only is the coefficient on ΔT significantly reduced for the most recent period but it also becomes completely insignificant.[12] This result holds for both variants of the unionisation hypothesis. Furthermore, the result most favourable to Hines (equation 1, period 1949–59) is achieved only with a very large constant term, and we have already seen that his rationalisation of the increase in the con-

[12] The insignificance of the militancy variable for the 1960s receives support from one of Hines's own estimates [9]. In a wage equation fitted to annual data for the 'policy on' periods, most of which occurred during the 1960s, the 't' statistic on the coefficient of ΔT is 1·11. It should also be noted that when ΔW is computed by the first central difference method and annual average data used the coefficient on ΔT becomes significantly greater than zero in the sub-period 1960–69 but is still lower than in the sub-period 1949–59.

stant term since the inter-war period is consistent with only a temporary upward shift of the regression line. In short, neither of the unionisation variables appears to have been doing much work in explaining ΔW. Before this conclusion can be accepted, however, the explanatory power of the unionisation variables must be re-examined in the context of a full wage determination equation. It is to this question that the next section is addressed.

IV   A reconsideration of the explanatory power of Hines's hypothesis

In his 1964 paper Hines reports on the estimation of a three-equation sub-system of the economy in which ΔW, ΔP and ΔT are simultaneously determined. The model is fitted to data for the whole period from 1921 to 1961 excluding the war years. The wage equation tested is:

$$\Delta W_t = a_0 + a_1 \Delta T_t + a_2 T_t + a_3 \Delta P_t + a_4 \Delta P_{t-1} + a_5 U_t$$

Both Ordinary Least Squares and Two Stage Least Squares methods of estimation result in firm coefficients on the unionisation variables.[13]

Thomas and Stoney [18] have shown that considered as a stochastic difference equation system, the Hines model is dynamically explosive. Godfrey [5] has argued that this property makes it difficult to interpret Hines's original estimates and suggests that the model may be mis-specified. Our present concern is with the comparative explanatory power of the unionisation variables in the wage equation above.

A number of problems relating to data and definitions of variables immediately arise. First, the adjustments described in the previous section to the data used to compute T and ΔT have been maintained in what follows. The labour force statistics used are for the U.K. and exclude the employers, self-employed and armed forces, but include the unemployed. For the inter-war period figures for total insured employees (employed plus unemployed) are used. Second, whereas Hines used the G.D.P. price deflator to compute ΔP for the

---

[13] The similar estimates which Hines reports in his 1971 paper derived from quarterly data for the post-war period alone can be discounted. The observations on T and ΔT are derived by linear interpolation from the semi-annual observations used by Lipsey and Parkin [14]. But these observations were themselves obtained by linear interpolation from the annual observations. Hines, therefore, has inadvertently produced a series with only one true observation in four!

years 1921–58 supplemented by the retail price index for 1959–61, we have used the retail price index throughout on the grounds that this is more appropriate in a model of wage determination. Third, in Hines's model unemployment is entered linearly. There seems to be little justification for this. If the true relationship between ΔW and U is non-linear, then even though a linear approximation may be tolerable within the inter-war and post-war periods separately, it will not be appropriate for the two sub-periods together. Consequently we have entered the unemployment variable in its reciprocal form. Further, we did not place a lag on unemployment, as Hines did implicitly. Fourth, Hines's wage series consists of end-December figures for an index of hourly wage rates. ΔW_t is defined as:

$$\left[\frac{W_t}{W_{t-1}} - 1 \right].100$$

His price series on the other hand consists of annual averages. ΔP_t is defined as:

$$\frac{\frac{1}{2}(P_{t+1} - P_{t-1})}{P_t}.100$$

Two difficulties arise here. On the one hand, the denominators of these two percentage rates of change represent different base lines, the one end-December, the other mid-year. For consistency, ΔW_t should either have been computed from annual averages of monthly figures and defined similarly to ΔP_t, or defined as:

$$\Delta W_t \equiv \frac{(W_t - W_{t-1})}{\frac{1}{2}(W_t + W_{t-1})}.100$$

On the other hand, the use of the first central difference method for calculating only ΔP_t introduces a greater degree of smoothing in this variable than in ΔW_t. To achieve consistency with regard to the base line and to eliminate this differential degree of smoothing we have used a wage series consisting of annual averages of monthly figures for hourly wage rates and have defined ΔW as:

$$\Delta W_t \equiv \frac{\frac{1}{2}(W_{t+1} - W_{t-1})}{W_t}.100$$

For the Two Stage Least Squares estimates reported below a few other minor alterations to Hines's data and definitions have been

Table 5

Equation no.	Estimates of coefficients on						$\bar{R}^2$	DW	Period
	Constant	T_t	ΔT_t	ΔP_t	ΔP_{t-1}	U^{-1}_t			
(1)	-3·634 (1·594)	0·127 (0·053)	0·562 (0·145)	0·078 (0·102)	0·126 (0·081)	-11·043 (11·631)	0·903	2·350*	1924-38
(2)	16·446 (9·858)	-0·332 (0·247)	1·179 (0·406)	0·347 (0·149)	0·080 (0·148)	2·878 (1·607)	0·700	1·220†	1949-69
(3)	-0·813 (2·433)	0·032 (0·060)	0·398 (0·189)	0·299 (0·127)	0·111 (0·096)	5·389 (1·037)	0·900	1·061	1924-38 1949-69
(4)	-0·565 (0·835)		0·554 (0·180)	0·168 (0·130)		15·405 (10·660)	0·825	1·583*	1924-38
(5)	3·142 (0·789)		1·289 (0·398)	0·300 (0·129)		1·912 (1·382)	0·701	1·260†	1949-69
(6)	0·422 (0·273)		0·388 (0·180)	0·392 (0·105)		5·723 (1·010)	0·899	1·110†	1924-38 1949-69
(7)	-2·319 (2·454)	0·096 (0·083)		0·506 (0·903)		-12·893 (19·924)	0·709	1·268†	1924-38

(8)	17·095 (9·325)	−0·358 (0·227)		0·638 (0·129)	2·090 (1·728)	0·578	0·751	1949–69
(9)	−0·382 (2·362)	0·021 (0·058)		0·554 (0·073)	4·443 (0·919)	0·885	1·044	1924–38 1949–69
(10)	0·249 (1·036)			0·505 (0·092)	4·513 (13·151)	0·701	1·323*	1924–38
(11)	2·464 (0·941)			0·564 (0·124)	1·134 (1·683)	0·543	0·637	1949–69
(12)	0·444 (0·287)			0·560 (0·075)	4·515 (0·884)	0·888	1·066	1924–38 1949–69
(13)	−4·062 (1·443)	0·115 (0·035)	0·642 (0·142)	0·107 (0·101)		0·894	1·935*	1924–38
(14)	9·866 (7·991)	−0·141 (0·191)	1·121 (0·418)	0·417 (0·144)		0·678	0·966†	1949–69
(15)	−1·417 (3·212)	0·070 (0·079)	−0·115 (0·222)	0·826 (0·103)		0·802	0·636	1924–38 1949–69

* Indicates no autocorrelation at the 1 per cent level.   † Indicates that the test was inconclusive.
For other values there was positive autocorrelation. Standard errors are shown in parentheses.

made. For consistency with the definitions of ΔW and ΔP the rate of change of import prices, ΔM, and the rate of change of productivity, ΔX, were calculated by the first central difference method. Our productivity index refers to G.D.P. per man year rather than industrial production per man year. Finally in the union militancy equation the level of real profits, π, was entered with a lag of one year.

We first estimated a number of different specifications of the basic wage determination equation by Ordinary Least Squares, imposing different lags on the price variable and systematically omitting one variable at a time. In general the results were not affected by the length of lag on ΔP, nor by the inclusion of both ΔP_t and $\Delta P_{t-1/2}$ or ΔP_{t-1} as regressors. Our main findings are summarised in Table 5.

The unemployment variable was consistently insignificant in the inter-war period and the post-war period considered separately, but consistently significant for the two sub-periods combined. This latter result is not due to the clustering of the observations on ΔW and U in the two sub-periods, as unemployment exhibited great variability in the inter-war period, albeit around a much higher average level than post-war. T was significant at best only in the inter-war period and even then its coefficient was very small, indicating, for instance, that a change of ten percentage points in the level of union density would be needed to bring about an increase in the rate of change of money wages by one percentage point. Contrary to Hines's results T does not become significant when the data are pooled: see equations (3), (9) and (15). Taken together these findings suggest that U rather than T has acted as the shift variable in the wage equation, which accords with the common sense notion that the persistence of relatively full employment since the war has provided a platform for wage inflation, even though the relationship between U and ΔW has not been close within the post-war period. It is noteworthy that when T is excluded from the equation for the combined periods neither the proportion of explained variance nor the size and significance of the parameter estimates are noticeably affected (equation 6), whereas when U is excluded positive autocorrelation is introduced and the coefficients on ΔT and ΔP are considerably affected (equation 15). It should also be noted that Hines [6] does not succeed in establishing the clear superiority of T over U as a shift variable. On his own results the proportion of variance explained is almost exactly the same whether U or T is used.[14] Moreover the coefficient on ΔT is almost exactly the same when T is replaced by U, whilst the correlation between T and U is very poor.

Our findings also indicate that ΔT is a significant explanatory variable.[15] When ΔT is excluded from the equation (equations 7–12) there is positive autocorrelation in the residuals, whilst the proportion of explained variance is somewhat, though not drastically reduced in each of the sub-periods. Two further points, however, stand out. First, when unemployment is excluded as a regressor, not only is there positive autocorrelation in the equation estimated for the pooled data (equation 15), but also ΔT becomes completely insignificant and has the wrong sign. This and the previous findings relating to unemployment are totally at variance with Hines's assertion that the inclusion in the wage equation of a proxy for excess demand adds nothing to the equation's predictive power. Second, although the coefficient estimates on ΔT show some tendency to rise as between the two sub-periods, they are consistently lower than those obtained by Hines, with values of roughly 0·6, 1·2 and 0·4 for the inter-war, post-war and pooled data respectively compared with 2·0, 3·2 and 2·0 found by Hines.

Since ΔT has exhibited little variability in the post-war period the conclusion appears inevitable that although it has had a significant independent influence on ΔW its importance has been greatly overrated. In Figure 1 the relative unimportance of ΔT is vividly illustrated by comparing the ΔW predicted from the actual values of ΔT alone with both the actual ΔW and the ΔW predicted from the actual values of all the independent variables in equation (5) of Table 5.[16]

These conclusions are further borne out by the results of the Two Stage Least Squares estimates reported in Table 6. T is insignificant; U^{-1} is significant; and the coefficient on ΔT is significant but again much lower than that found by Hines, (0·4409 compared with

---

[14] For the period 1923–38 and 1949–61, for $\Delta W = a + b \ \Delta T + cT$ $\bar{R}^2 = 0·804$ while for $\Delta W = a + b \Delta T + cU \ \bar{R}^2 = 0·786$.

[15] ΔT was consistently insignificant in the sub-period 1949–61 (not shown in Table 5) when included together with ΔP_t and U^{-1}. There are, however, too few observations in relation to the number of parameters to be estimated for much weight to be attached to this result.

[16] The ΔW predicted from this equation for 1970 was 10·38 compared with an actual ΔW of 11·03. ΔT registered an increase of 3·27 percentage points in this year and accounted for just under half of the predicted increase in wages.

Figure 1

Points marked **x** are the ΔW_t predicted from the equation
$\Delta W_t = 3.1423 + 1.2893\,\Delta T_t + 0.2998\,\Delta P_t + 1.9121 U_t^{-1}$

The shaded area ▨ represents the independent influence of ΔT_t on ΔW_t

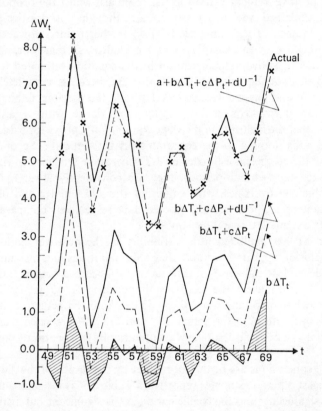

1·5945). The coefficients on the two price variables are surprisingly low and neither is significant separately. They are, however, jointly significant. Thus, even if it is accepted that ΔT is a faithful indicator of union militancy it certainly cannot be maintained in the light of the findings reported in this section that ΔW can be predicted almost entirely from unionisation variables. There are, moreover, considerable grounds for doubting that ΔT does reflect what it is supposed to reflect as we shall show in the next section.

Table 6 Two Stage Least Square estimates for the combined periods 1925–38 and 1950–69

(1) $\Delta W_t = -1\cdot930 + 0\cdot060 T_t + 0\cdot441\ \Delta T_t + 0\cdot123\ \Delta P_t$
    $\quad\quad\quad\ (2\cdot758)\ \ (0\cdot069)\quad\ (0\cdot185)\quad\quad\ (0\cdot167)$
    $\quad\quad\ + 0\cdot232\ \Delta P_{t-1/2} + 5\cdot582 U^{-1}_t$
    $\quad\quad\quad\ (0\cdot162)\quad\quad\quad\ (0\cdot964)$
    $\quad\quad\quad\quad \bar{R}^2 = 0\cdot930 \quad\quad\quad DW = 1\cdot000$

(2) $\Delta P_t = -0\cdot185 - 0\cdot021\ \Delta X_t + 0\cdot236\ \Delta M_{t-1/2} + 0\cdot677\ \Delta W_t$
    $\quad\quad\quad\ (0\cdot280)\ \ (0\cdot115)\quad\quad\ (0\cdot031)\quad\quad\quad\ (0\cdot069)$
    $\quad\quad\quad\quad \bar{R}^2 = 0\cdot936 \quad\quad\quad DW = 1\cdot586^*$

(3) $\Delta T_t = 10\cdot626 - 0\cdot258 T_{t-1} + 0\cdot403\ \Delta P_{t-1/2} - 0\cdot0004\pi_{t-1}$
    $\quad\quad\quad\ (1\cdot624)\ \ (0\cdot039)\quad\quad\ (0\cdot059)\quad\quad\quad\ (0\cdot0003)$
    $\quad\quad\quad\quad \bar{R}^2 = 0\cdot724 \quad\quad\quad DW = 1\cdot192\dagger$

* Indicates that the test showed no autocorrelation at the 1 per cent level.
† Indicates that the test was inconclusive.
For other values the test showed positive autocorrelation.
Standard errors are in parentheses.

V The measurement of union militancy

The variable ΔT is subject to a number of influences which make it a most imperfect measure of union militancy. On the one hand changes in ΔT may occur quite independently of variations in union militancy; on the other hand, ΔT may fail to pick up the possible influence of union militancy on wage rates because the effect of union militancy on ΔT is offset by the effects of the other factors which influence ΔT. In this section we investigate two such other influences on ΔT, the institution of the closed shop and changes in the structure of employment.

McCarthy [15] defines the closed shop as 'a situation in which employees come to realise that a particular job is only to be obtained and retained if they become and remain members of one of a speci-fied number of trade unions'. It is clear that an increase or decrease in the numbers employed in establishments where a closed shop already operates may automatically raise or lower total union membership and, given the total labour force, union density, without necessarily indicating any change in union militancy. If changes in union density are to be taken as reflecting changes in the strength of union militancy, then we must be able to separate out those changes in T which are solely the result of changes in the proportion of the total labour force employed in what we may call 'the closed shop sector' from those changes which are the result of changes in the density of trade union organisation outside the closed shop sector. This can be done if we define

$$T = \lambda_c . 100 + (1 - \lambda_c)\left[\frac{T^* - L_c}{L - L_c}\right]$$

where $\lambda_c = L_c/L$, the proportion between the number of workers in closed shops, L_c, and the total labour force L;

T = aggregate union density;

T^* = the total number of workers belonging to trade unions.

At the same time any extension of the jurisdictional boundaries of the closed shop area of the economy arising from successful union demands for the establishment of a closed shop, will again automatically increase total union membership and, given the labour force, union density. In this case λ_c will rise, not because of any reallocation of the labour force as in the previous case, but because the closed shop boundaries have been enlarged so as to embrace a larger proportion of the labour force given its existing allocation. It might be argued that such an extension of the closed shop could be regarded as a specific manifestation of union militancy. But even if we grant this, changes in aggregate union density measured simply as the ratio of total trade union membership to the labour force, will still remain an imperfect indicator of union militancy. Suppose a union is aiming at 100 per cent unionisation of the relevant labour force, and to this end sustains a constant degree of militancy year after year with regularly repeated demands for a closed shop. We may expect that union's density series will show relatively small increases for the years preceding its final victory on the closed shop issue, followed by a large jump in the year of victory itself, followed by zero changes thereafter. In such a case the impact of the eventual establishment of a closed shop on the union's membership and density will be out of all proportion to the degree of militancy displayed during that year.

There are, then, two distinct types of closed shop impact to be investigated: the static impact arising from changes in the proportion of the labour force employed within given jurisdictional boundaries covered by closed shop arrangements; and the dynamic impact arising from any extensions of these jurisdictional boundaries. Unfortunately it is extremely difficult to estimate either type of impact with any precision, mainly because there are many trades in which the closed shop operates in some establishments but not in others, and the available data simply do not allow accurate estimates of closed shop coverage to be made. We have, however, been able to provide an illustrative estimate of the static effect of the closed shop on aggregate union membership and density.

The most accurate and comprehensive account of the extent of the closed shop in Britain is given by McCarthy [15], whose findings have been closely followed here. According to McCarthy the closed shop is overwhelmingly an institution found among manual workers. The following sections of the labour force were singled out from the total area affected by the closed shop as described by McCarthy and constitute what may be called the 'central closed shop sector'. They each satisfy the following criteria of selection:

(a) they relate to manual workers only;
(b) they each cover a relatively large number of workers;
(c) they all fall into McCarthy's categories of trades which are either 'comprehensively closed' or 'mainly closed'.

Collectively these sections covered nearly 80 per cent of the total number of workers estimated by McCarthy to have been subject to the closed shop at the beginning of the 1960s. The remainder consist of Co-operative workers and other non-manual groups, or of sections which are individually relatively small, or of sections which are widely dispersed throughout the 'mainly open' trades.

Industrial/Occupation area (manual workers only)	Numbers estimated to be subject to the closed shop in 1961
1. Coal mining	605,500
2. Oil refining	23,100
3. Sea transport	56,100
4. Docks	68,000
5. Railway workshops	65,000
6. Road passenger transport	100,000
7. Engineering and electrical goods (including vehicles except railway vehicles)	1,200,000
8. Shipbuilding and ship repair	157,900

9. Iron and steel manufacture	210,000
10. Textiles	110,000
11. Newspapers, periodicals and general printing	194,300
12. Construction craftsmen	100,000
Total	2,889,900

The total numbers of manual workers in each of these areas were estimated for 1948 and 1961. The numbers affected by the closed shop in each area in 1948 were then calculated on the assumption that the proportion between the number of workers subject to the closed shop and the total number of manual workers in each area was the same in 1948 as in 1961. This assumption is a very crude approximation to the assumption that jurisdictional boundaries of the closed shop in the 'central closed shop sector' remained unchanged throughout the period 1948–61. On this basis the labour force in the 'central closed shop sector' rose from 2,815,600 in 1948, to 2,889,900 in 1961, which, however, as a proportion of total employees constituted a fall from 13·6 to 12·5 per cent. This relative decline is partly due to the fact that the 'central closed shop sector' contains a number of declining industries (notably coal mining, shipbuilding and textiles) whose falling shares of total employment more than offset the rising shares of the expanding industries contained within this same sector (notably engineering and printing). Chiefly, however, the decline can be attributed to a fall in the number of manual workers as a proportion of total employees within each industry.

The relative decline of the 'central closed shop sector' automatically reduced aggregate union density below what it would otherwise have been. Thus aggregate density in 1948, calculated according to the formula given above, was 45·16 per cent. Assuming an unchanged union density outside the 'central closed shop sector' in 1961, the redistribution of the labour force away from the 'central closed shop sector' would have produced an aggregate union density of 44·46 per cent. Superficially this decline of 0·70 of a percentage point appears negligible. If the decline had occurred at an even pace throughout the period, aggregate density would have fallen by just over 0·05 of a percentage point each year, other things being equal. When, however, it is remembered that Hines's militancy variable ΔT had a range of only $-0·92$ to $+0·85$ with a mean value of $-0·19$[17] the static impact

---

[17] These figures relate to ΔT calculated on the basis of the labour force defined as U.K. total working population minus employers, self-employed and armed forces.

of the closed shop appears somewhat less than negligible. If we define ΔT_c as the change in union density arising solely as a result of the static impact of the closed shop, and ignore the possibility that extensions of the jurisdictional boundaries of the closed shop might also affect aggregate density figures, then the appropriate specification of the militancy variable for Hines's hypothesis would be $\Delta T_m = \Delta T - \Delta T_c$, where ΔT is the unadjusted change in union density as used by Hines. When account is taken of the likelihood that ΔT_c varies from year to year, there is no reason to suppose that ΔT_m and ΔT will be closely correlated. If they are not, then the adoption of this more refined measure of union militancy ought to affect the simple correlation found by Hines between union militancy and the rate of change of money wage rates. If the Hines hypothesis is correct the explanatory power of union militancy should be improved.

Unfortunately the approximations involved in estimating a series for ΔT_c are too rough to enable such a refined measure of union militancy to be constructed, especially in view of the small orders of magnitude involved. However, the static impact of the closed shop is merely a particular instance of the more general case involving the redistribution of the labour force amongst industries with different degrees of union organisation. Since union densities differ in different industries it is entirely possible for aggregate density to change without any change in density levels within each industry if there are shifts in the structure of employment. As Hines [8] himself notes:

$$T_t = \sum_{i=1}^{n} \frac{Li}{L} \cdot \frac{T_i^*}{L_t}$$

where L_t/L denotes the ith industry's share of the total labour force and T_i^* denotes the number of trade union members in the ith industry. It follows that:

$$\Delta T_t = \sum_{i=1}^{n} \frac{L_i}{L} \Delta\left(\frac{T_i^*}{L_i}\right)t + \sum_{i=1}^{n} \frac{T_i^*}{L_i} \Delta\left(\frac{L_i}{L}\right)t$$
$$+ \sum_{i=1}^{n} \Delta\left(\frac{L_i}{L}\right)t \, \Delta\left(\frac{T_i^*}{L_i}\right)t$$

The measure of union militancy appropriate to Hines's hypothesis is one which abstracts from changes in the distribution of the labour force. Setting

$$\Delta\left(\frac{L_i}{L}\right)t = 0 \quad \text{for all } i$$

the expression reduces to:

$$\Delta T_t = \sum_{i=1}^{n} \frac{L_i}{L} \Delta \left[\frac{T_i^*}{L_i} \right] t = \Delta T_{mt}$$

For convenience we shall refer to ΔT_m as a 'pure militancy index', since it measures the change in aggregate union density arising solely from changes in union density within each industry, such changes being weighted by the (constant) share of the labour force in each industry. Similarly setting

$$\Delta \left[\frac{T_i^*}{L_i} \right] = 0 \quad \text{for all } i$$

we may define

$$\Delta T_{et} = \sum_{i=1}^{n} \frac{T_i^*}{L_i} \Delta \left[\frac{L_i}{L} \right] t$$

which measures the change in aggregate union density arising solely from changes in the structure of employment when union densities in individual industries are held constant.

Series for ΔT_m and ΔT_e were calculated for the inter-war period and post-war period (up to 1961). Corresponding to this division of the year to year changes in union density into two components is a similar division of the annual *level* of union density. At any given time the prevailing level of union density is the resultant of two forces: on the one hand the changes in union density within each industry, on the other the changes in the distribution of the labour force amongst industries with differing density levels, which have occurred over all previous time since the beginning of trade unionism. We cannot, of course, estimate the effects of these forces. We can, however, take the density existing at any arbitrary point in time and then calculate (a) what the level of union density would have been had the distribution of the labour force remained the same as it was in the base period; and (b) what the level of union density would have been given the labour force reallocation which actually occurred but holding density within each industry constant. Denoting these two forces as T_m and T_e respectively we have:

$$T_0 = T_{m_0} + T_{e_0}$$

where T_0 is the actual level of density in the base period.

$$T_t = T_{m_t} + T_{e_t}$$

$$T_{m_t} = T_{m_0} + \sum_{i=1}^{t} \Delta T_{m_i}$$

$$T_{e_t} = T_{e_0} + \sum_{i=1}^{t} \Delta T_{e_i}$$

$$\therefore T_{e_t} = T_0 - T_{m_0} + \sum_{i=1}^{t} \Delta T_{e_i}$$

The equation: $\Delta W_t = a_0 + a_1 \Delta T_t + a_2 T_t$ may now be written as:

$$\Delta W_t = a_0 + a_1 \Delta T_{m_t} + a_2 \Delta T_{e_t} + a_3 T_{m_t} + a_4 T_{e_t}$$

$$= a_0 + a_1 \Delta T_{m_t} + a_2 \Delta T_{e_t} + a_3 \left[T_{m_0} + \sum_{i=1}^{t} \Delta T_{m_i} \right]$$

$$+ a_4 \left[T_0 - T_{m_0} + \sum_{i=1}^{t} \Delta T_{e_i} \right]$$

which estimates as

$$\Delta W_t = b_0 + b_1 \Delta T_{m_t} + b_2 \Delta T_{e_t} + b_3 T_{m_t}^* + b_4 T_{e_t}^*$$

where $b_0 = a_0 + (a_3 - a_4) T_{m_0} + a_4 T_0$

$\qquad b_i = a_i \quad i = 1, \ldots, 4$

$$T_{m_t}^* = \sum_{i=1}^{t} \Delta T_{m_i}$$

and

$$T_{e_t}^* = \sum_{i=1}^{t} \Delta T_{e_i}$$

With this more refined definition of the union militancy variables we retested the basic unionisation hypothesis, regressing ΔW first on ΔT_m and T_m and then on all four unionisation variables ΔT_m, ΔT_e, T_m and T_e. The results are shown in Table 7. The performance of the militancy variables alone is poor. Though both are significant in the inter-war period, neither is significant in the post-war period and T_m has the wrong sign. For the two sub-periods combined the $\bar{R}^2$ is well below that obtained by Hines (0·52 compared with 0·91) and

Table 7

Equation no.	Constant	Estimates of coefficients on				$\bar{R}^2$	DW	Period
		T_m	ΔT_m	T_c	ΔT_c			
(1)	1·218	0·153	0·723			0·881	1·461*	1924–38
	(0·262)	(0·040)	(0·083)					
(2)	5·063	−0·184	1·335			−0·027	1·127†	1949–61
		(1·297)	(1·071)					
(3)	4·371	0·520	0·630			0·519	0·411	1924–38
	(0·531)	(0·109)	(0·283)					1949–61
(4)	0·697	0·227	0·552	−0·470	0·970	0·937	2·079*	1924–38
	(0·534)	(0·038)	(0·088)	(0·243)	(0·973)			
(5)	3·827	−1·442	2·429	1·467	2·453	0·008	1·120†	1949–61
	(1·574)	(1·592)	(1·347)	(1·495)	(3·644)			
(6)	4·952	0·112	1·132	1·482	3·538	0·753	1·513*	1924–38
	(0·412)	(0·122)	(0·237)	(0·383)	(1·666)			1949–61

* Indicates that the test showed no autocorrelation at the 1 per cent level.
† Indicates that the test was inconclusive.
For other values the test showed positive autocorrelation.
Standard errors are shown in parentheses.

there is positive autocorrelation in the residuals. The inclusion of the two structural variables T_e and ΔT_e makes no difference to these results for the two sub-periods, when both are insignificant, but for the combined data both become significant and the autocorrelation found in the previous case disappears.

These results are consistent with the following interpretations. First, although there may be some justification for using the unadjusted ΔT series as an indicator of union militancy in the inter-war period, the same is not true of the post-war period. Inspection of the series for ΔT, ΔT_m and ΔT_e reveals that in the inter-war period ΔT exhibited considerable variability with a range of $-3·06$ to $2·95$ and that its movement is dominated by the movement of ΔT_m. The values of ΔT_e are small by comparison and except in one year, always negative, which reflects the sharp decline of the relatively densely unionised industries such as mining and textiles during this period. In the post-war period, however, not only is the variability of ΔT slight, but also its movement is by no means dominated by the movement of the 'pure militancy index' ΔT_m. Between 1955–6, 1956–7, 1959–60 and 1960–1 the two series moved in opposite directions and six out of thirteen years the indices had opposite signs (ΔT negative, ΔT_m positive and vice versa). Thus in the inter-war period the unadjusted index of union militancy is relatively less distorted by changes in the structure of employment. Moreover, it is not, perhaps, surprising that the union militancy variables perform relatively well in the inter-war period. The 1920s and 30s were years of immense flux in the fortunes of trade unionism. The decline in unionisation which began in the years immediately after the collapse of the boom which followed the first world war was turned into a rout with the defeat of the General Strike which persisted through the years of deep depression. The tide was turned with the beginning of the slow economic recovery about 1933 and in the following years unionisation made rapid advances until by the end of the decade the unions' pre-collapse strength had almost been restored. It is altogether more plausible to regard a continuous sequence of negative values for ΔT followed by a continuous sequence of positive values as reflecting a deterioration or improvement in union bargaining strength. There is considerable evidence that periods of *major* expansion or contraction of union activity can affect the course of money wages (see [17]).

Second, the significance of the 'structural' variables in the combined data may reflect the contrasts in the experience of structural change between the two sub-periods. In both sub-periods the trend in the industrial pattern of employment was running against trade unionism. The unions' traditional bases in industries such as mining, textiles and steel, were undergoing secular decline, whilst the sectors whose share of total employment was expanding were on the whole the least well organised. However, in the inter-war period this adverse trend was especially marked as the best organised sectors were more than normally hit by heavy unemployment. This is reflected in the fact that ΔT_e was negative in all but one of the inter-war years. If there had been no change in the union density within each industry the changes in the structure of employment which occurred would have produced a decline of 4·26 percentage points in aggregate union density. In these conditions wages in the densely unionised declining sectors were under exceptional downward pressure. By contrast in the post-war period (up to 1961) although the decline of the high density sectors continued, it did so at a pace which was more gentle overall and also more uneven, occasionally becoming temporarily retarded and even reversed. Thus ΔT_e for the post-war years exhibits fluctuations around a very slightly downward trend. With no change in industry density levels changes in the structure of employment between 1949 and 1961 would have produced a fall in aggregate union density of only 1·29 percentage points. These conditions provided a permissive environment for wages in the declining sectors to keep pace with the general upward movement. If this interpretation is correct then the differential impact of structural change in the two periods would account for some part of the association between the unadjusted unionisation variables and ΔW via the association between ΔW and our structural variables ΔT_e and T_e.

These interpretations are consistent with the results obtained when the 'pure militancy' and 'structural' variables are included with U^{-1} and ΔP_t as regressors (see Table 8). Thus ΔT_m continues to be insignificant for the post-war period (equations 2 and 5). ΔT_e is not significant in the presence of U^{-1} for the combined data (equation 6). The differential impact of structural change in the two sub-periods referred to above reflects the contrasting unemployment experiences of the inter-war and post-war periods. It is also worth noting that the low values of the coefficient on ΔT unadjusted, reported in Section IV, are reflected with ΔT_m.

The Two Stage Least Squares estimates of the Hines three equation sub-system were repeated using the 'pure militancy' variables, T_m and

Table 8

Equation no.	Constant	ΔT_m	ΔT_e	ΔP_t	U^{-1}	$\bar{R}^2$	DW	Period
			Estimates of coefficients on					
(1)	−0·364	0·508		0·211	11·194	0·809	1·259	1924–38
	(0·856)	(0·182)		(0·128)	(10·772)			
(2)	1·099	0·870		0·386	4·245	0·626	1·139	1949–61
	(1·471)	(0·606)		(0·150)	(2·684)			
(3)	0·057	0·434		0·295	6·412	0·925	1·817*	1924–38
	(0·252)	(0·151)		(0·090)	(0·920)			1949–61
(4)	−0·550	0·506	2·477	0·192	20·075	0·838	1·453	1924–38
	(0·796)	(0·168)	(1·442)	(0·119)	(11·192)			
(5)	0·335	0·162	−3·807	0·604	3·730	0·711	1·730*	1949–61
	(1·355)	(0·650)	(1·999)	(0·174)	(2·377)			
(6)	−0·005	0·420	−0·341	0·307	6·410	0·922	1·847*	1924–38
	(0·322)	(0·161)	(1·064)	(0·091)	(0·938)			1949–61

* Indicates no autocorrelation at the 1 per cent level.
† Indicates that the test was inconclusive.
For other values the test showed positive autocorrelation.
Standard errors are shown in parentheses.

ΔT_m, instead of the unadjusted unionisation variables, T and ΔT. The results are reported in Table 9. In the wage equation the level of unionisation T_m is insignificant; U^{-1} is significant; and the coefficient on ΔT_m is significant but again substantially lower than that found by Hines. As before the price variables are not significant separately but they are jointly significant.

What the findings of this section show is that there are considerable grounds for doubting that Hines's unionisation variables provide in general adequate indicators of union militancy. Moreover, when these variables are adjusted to take account of structural changes in the labour force, just one of the factors which may affect the recorded level and changes in the level of union membership independently of the degree of union militancy, their explanatory power, far from improving, in some respects actually deteriorates.

Table 9   Two Stage Least Squares Estimates for the combined periods 1925–38 and 1950–61

---

(1) $\Delta W_t = 0\cdot558 + 0\cdot081T_t^m + 0\cdot474\ \Delta T_t^m + 0\cdot055\ \Delta P_t$
 (0·360) (0·054)   (0·132)   (0·127)
 $+\ 0\cdot200\ \Delta P_{t-1/2} + 6\cdot368U^{-1}$
 (0·118)   (0·792)
 $\bar{R}^2 = 0\cdot963$ DW = 1·670*

(2) $\Delta P_t = -0\cdot232 + 0\cdot063\ \Delta X_t + 0\cdot239\ \Delta M_{t-1/2} + 0\cdot682\Delta W_t$
 (0·318) (0·148)   (0·363)   (0·082)
 $\bar{R}^2 = 0\cdot930$ DW = 1·668*

(3) $\Delta T_m = 10\cdot054 - 0\cdot40T_{t-1}^m + 0\cdot355\ \Delta P_{t-1/2} - 0\cdot0004\pi_{t-1}$
 (2·074) (0·050)   (0·079)   (0·0005)
 $\bar{R}^2 = 0\cdot6108$ DW = 1·2312†

---

* Indicates that the test showed no autocorrelation at the 1 per cent level.
† Indicates that the test was inconclusive.
Standard errors are shown in parentheses.

VI   Conclusions

We have shown that the leading empirical case in support of the union-strength interpretation of post-war inflation is extremely unsatisfactory. It is theoretically weak, being based on no more than *ad hoc* rationalisations of empirical associations, which are in many cases individually dubious and together imply a specification of the wage rate/militancy relationship different from that actually tested by Hines. The Hines case is empirically weak on several grounds. The data used to measure changes in union density were badly selected, and, in particular, the use of an improved labour force series has been shown to make a substantial difference to Hines's regression estimates for the inter-war period. Further, Hines's postulation of a permanent increase in the coefficient on ΔT in the post-war period is unfounded, the simple association between ΔW and ΔT having disappeared altogether during the 1960s. In addition a retesting of Hines's complete wage determination equation on the basis of improved data and consistent definitions of variables reveals that the explanatory power of the militancy variables is considerably less than Hines claims, and also that the level of unemployment cannot be ignored in comparisons of wage movements between the inter-war and post-war periods. Finally doubt has been cast on the use of ΔT to represent union militancy at all. In particular such factors as the closed shop and the process of labour force reallocation have been shown to have an effect on aggregate union density, which, in the post-war period at least, has been large by comparison with the actually recorded changes in union density. Moreover, when the ΔT series is adjusted so as to abstract from the aggregation effects of labour force redistribution, the explanatory power of the union militancy variables is substantially weakened. Some plausible interpretations of the observed association between ΔT unadjusted and ΔW have been suggested.

We have not set out to refute all possible variants of the cost-push via union strength thesis. In particular the inference cannot be drawn from our study that 'unions do not matter'. A large part of our case against Hines has been that his proposed index of union militancy is seriously deficient. It remains entirely possible that some more satisfactory index may be devised which will succeed in explaining more than a minor part of the movements in money wage rates, and which is theoretically well grounded. What can, however, be asserted on the basis of the results presented here is that Hines's version of the union strength thesis is unacceptable.

Data sources

Hourly rates of wages:
British Labour Statistics: Historical Abstract 1886–1968; Department of Employment Gazette, H.M.S.O. (For period 1924–38, June of each year figures used.)
Labour force figures:
British Labour Statistics: Historical Abstract 1886–1968; Monthly Digest of Statistics, H.M.S.O.
Trade union membership:
British Labour Statistics: Historical Abstract 1886–1968; Department of Employment Gazette, H.M.S.O.

Unemployment (total register):
  British Labour Statistics: Historical Abstract 1886–1968; *Monthly Digest of Statistics*, H.M.S.O.
Retail prices (all items):
  British Labour Statistics: Historical Abstract 1886–1968; H.M.S.O.
  The British Economy: Key Statistics 1900–70. H.M.S.O. (For period 1924–38, June of each year figures used.)
Imports average values:
  The British Economy: Key Statistics 1900–70. H.M.S.O.
Output per man (G.D.P.):
  The British Economy: Key Statistics 1900–70. H.M.S.O.
Profits (companies):
  The British Economy: Key Statistics 1900–70. H.M.S.O.
Price deflator:
  R. G. Lipsey and M. D. Steuer in *Economica* 1961; O.E.C.D. Main Economic Indicators.

References

[1] Bain, G. S., 'Trade union growth and recognition', Research Paper no. 6, Royal Commission on Trade Unions and Employers' Associations, London (1964).
[2] Burton, J., *Wage Inflation*, Studies in Economics, London, Macmillan (1972).
[3] Dicks-Mireaux, L., A. and Dow, J. C. R., 'The determinants of wage inflation: United Kingdom 1946–56', *Journal of the Royal Statistical Society*, Series A (1959).
[4] Eckstein, O. and Wilson, T. A., 'The determinants of money wages in American industry', *Quarterly Journal of Economics*, Vol. 76 (1962), pp. 379–414.
[5] Godfrey, L., 'The Phillips curve: incomes policy and trade union effects', in *The Current Inflation*, eds. H. G. Johnson and A. R. Nobay, Macmillan (1971).
[6] Hines, A. G., 'Trade unions and wage inflation in the United Kingdom, 1893–1961', *Review of Economic Studies* (1964).
[7] Hines, A. G., 'Unemployment and the rate of change of money wage rates in the United Kingdom 1862–1963: a re-appraisal', *Review of Economics and Statistics* (1968).
[8] Hines, A. G., 'Wage inflation in the United Kingdom 1948–1962 a disaggregated study', *Economic Journal* (1969).
[9] Hines, A. G., 'The determinants of the rate of change of money wage rates and the effectiveness of incomes policy' in *The Current Inflation*, eds. Johnson and Nobay (1971).
[10] Hobsbawm, E. J. E., *Labouring Men: studies in the history of labour*, Weidenfeld and Nicolson (1964).
[11] Klein, L. R. and Ball, J. R., 'Some econometrics of the determination of the absolute level of wages and prices', *Economic Journal* (1959).
[12] Lipsey, R. G., 'The relation between unemployment and the rate of change of money wage rates in the United Kingdom 1862–1957', *Economica* (1960).
[13] Lipsey, R. G., *An introduction to Positive Economics*, 2nd Ed. Weidenfeld and Nicolson (1963).
[14] Lipsey, R. G. and Parkin, J. M., 'Incomes policy: a re-appraisal', *Economica* (1970).
[15] McCarthy, W. E. J., *The Closed Shop in Britain*, Blackwell (1964).
[16] Phillips, A. W., 'The relation between unemployment and the rate of change of money wage rates in the United Kingdom', *Economica* (1958).
[17] Phelps-Brown, E. H., 'The long-term movement of real wages', *The Theory of Wage Determination*, ed. J. T. Dunlop, Macmillan (1966).
[18] Thomas, R. L. and Stoney, P. J., 'A note on the Dynamic Properties of the Hines Inflation Model', *Review of Economic Studies* (1970).

Table 10

Year	ΔW_t	T_t	ΔP_t	$\Delta P_{t-1/2}$	U_t	ΔT_{m_t}	T_{m_t}	ΔT_{e_t}	T_{e_t}	ΔX_t	π_t	$\Delta M_{t-1/2}$
1924	1·18	48·98	0·89	0·28	10·33	0·95	0·95	0·43	−0·43	3·79	876·4	1·97
1925	0·58	47·73	−0·29	0·0	11·28	−0·80	0·15	−0·33	−0·76	0·74	830·6	−0·65
1926	−0·73	44·67	−2·68	−0·56	12·56	−2·46	−2·31	−0·07	−0·83	0·75	758·0	−4·67
1927	−1·18	41·74	−0·92	−2·23	9·72	−2·51	−4·82	−0·47	−1·30	1·45	891·7	−4·29
1928	−0·89	40·45	−0·91	−3·25	10·82	−0·92	−5·74	−0·15	−1·45	0·0	924·1	−0·72
1929	−0·45	40·17	−3·44	−0·60	10·43	−0·13	−5·87	−0·27	−1·72	−0·72	984·2	−4·35
1930	−0·15	39·03	−4·87	−3·89	16·00	−0·92	−6·79	−0·08	−1·80	−0·71	973·2	−12·70
1931	−1·65	36·20	−4·14	−6·13	21·25	−2·82	−9·61	−0·18	−1·98	−1·47	919·0	−16·98
1932	−2·17	34·69	−3·17	−4·05	22·05	−1·32	−10·93	−0·22	−2·20	−1·47	840·1	−10·87
1933	−0·47	34·09	−1·47	−1·75	19·93	0·31	−10·62	−0·27	−2·47	1·47	977·2	3·49
1934	0·47	35·42	1·45	0·35	16·74	0·72	−9·92	−0·07	−2·54	2·86	1139·3	2·33
1935	1·71	37·27	2·14	1·39	15·51	2·06	−7·86	−0·07	−2·61	2·08	1288·6	4·44
1936	3·03	39·70	4·17	2·38	13·11	2·88	−4·98	−0·21	−2·82	2·74	1445·0	6·38
1937	3·51	42·65	3·62	4·30	10·83	3·41	−1·57	−0·22	−3·04	0·66	1500·0	5·88
1938	1·84	43·53	1·29	1·56	12·88	−0·06	−1·63	0·04	−3·00	−1·35	1394·0	0·94
1949	2·52	44·84	3·39	3·85	1·63	−0·37	−0·37	0·28	0·28	0·0	1843·0	7·09
1950	5·27	44·03	6·56	3·86	1·63	−0·87	−1·24	0·10	0·38	3·25	2054·3	9·38
1951	8·01	44·88	8·96	7·94	1·32	0·72	−0·52	0·06	0·44	1·90	2203·2	15·91
1952	6·13	45·17	5·48	7·95	2·16	−0·02	−0·54	0·14	0·58	0·0	1822·7	2·24
1953	4·40	44·25	2·00	3·35	1·78	−0·34	−0·88	−0·19	0·39	1·27	1887·5	−6·49
1954	5·50	43·83	3·29	2·49	1·46	−0·30	−1·18	−0·20	0·19	3·05	2045·0	2·04
1955	7·20	44·04	4·88	4·43	1·21	−0·25	−1·43	0·08	0·27	2·38	2250·3	2·25
1956	6·30	43·94	4·12	4·33	1·30	0·25	−1·18	−0·15	0·12	1·16	2160·0	2·20
1957	4·36	44·03	3·28	3·77	1·55	0·16	−1·02	−0·03	0·09	1·70	2191·4	−0·48
1958	3·18	43·17	1·78	2·73	2·25	−0·70	−1·72	0·01	0·10	2·25	2078·6	3·45
1959	3·47	42·46	0·83	0·87	2·28	0·46	−1·26	−0·38	−0·28	3·26	2252·9	1·54
1960	5·23	42·63	2·19	1·23	1·73	0·41	−0·85	−0·27	−0·55	2·11	2499·0	0·51
1961	5·28	42·64	3·71	3·43	1·63	−0·20	−1·05	−0·06	−0·61	1·04	2360·0	−0·51
1962	4·06	42·07	3·01	3·62	2·13					2·06	2252·8	0·0
1963	4·36	41·90	2·60	2·28	2·62					3·50	2528·0	2·03
1964	5·61	42·15	3·92	3·30	1·75					2·88	2772·5	2·22
1965	6·29	42·24	4·26	4·43	1·50					1·89	2770·1	1·21
1966	5·15	41·88	3·16	3·80	1·61					2·31	2507·8	0·96
1967	5·37	42·33	3·56	3·04	2·52					3·60	2483·1	3·10
1968	5·90		4·98	4·24	2·53					3·45	2626·8	5·88
1969	7·71	43·64	5·78	5·37	2·53					2·10	2497·9	4·87

D. L. Purdy
and G. Zis[1]

Chapter 2 On the concept and measurement of trade union militancy

I

The debate over the desirability or otherwise of incomes policies revolves around the question of whether or not trade unions can and do push money wages up independently of the state of demand in the labour market. This interest in the role of trade unions in the inflationary processes has been further stimulated by the recent experience especially of the U.K., which contradicts the Phillips curve relationship between changes in money wage rates and the level of excess demand as reflected by the level of unemployment. A number of studies of wage inflation have endeavoured to quantify what is variously described as union militancy, aggressiveness or pushfulness in the inflationary process. However, little attention has been paid to elucidating the concept of union militancy or to examining the appropriateness of the various proxies which have been used to represent this latent, unobservable variable. This neglect is symptomatic of the absence of any well developed theory of the microeconomics of union–employer negotiations and of the process of cost-push inflation. The present paper does not aim to fill this glaring gap, but has the more modest objective of providing some comments and guidelines for future research in this area. Its central theme is that the value of further empirical work on the role of unions in wage inflation depends chiefly on the construction of a more adequate supporting theoretical framework than has so far been developed. In Section II certain neglected features of union militancy relevant to explanations of wage inflation are drawn out. In Section III the

[1] We are indebted to all members of the Inflation Workshop, University of Manchester, and would like to express our special appreciation to Professor J. Johnston for his valuable comments on an earlier draft. The responsibility for any remaining errors is ours.

adequacy of the various proxies used to represent union militancy is considered. Section IV consists of our general conclusions.

II

Objections might be raised against the use of terms such as 'militancy', 'aggressiveness', etc. at all, inasmuch as they frequently carry value loaded connotations. For many union members to be regarded as a militant is a mark of honour. For the middle class the militant is an agitator, troublemaker and subversive. Yet it is clear that to identify union militancy as a major cause of inflation in itself implies no value judgements about trade unions or about inflation policy, though it does have positive implications for anti-inflation policy. In what follows the term 'militancy' will be retained, it being understood that this term is being used in a purely descriptive sense.

Militancy is an elusive concept. The shorter Oxford English Dictionary simply defines militant as 'engaged in warfare, warring, combative'. In the present context militancy is clearly a feature of union behaviour relating both to the aims of unions and the methods used to pursue them. But there are few aims or methods which can be judged as militant per se. Double figure wage claims once unheard of are now the norm. Similarly McCarthy [16] describes the endemic strike situation in which 'in effect the strike has become a part of the normal custom and practice of industrial relations in the firm, an endemic feature of factory life, accepted by *both sides* as being largely inevitable'. Thus militancy is a relativistic concept. Whether a piece of behaviour is accurately described as a manifestation of militancy depends very much on the wider context in which the behaviour occurs. This rather obvious point will be important subsequently when the suitability of various proxies for union militancy is considered.

Although we refer to the aims and methods of unions as being militant or not, strictly speaking to apply this description to the union as a whole is often inaccurate. The union is a structured institution which like all institutions comes to develop an existence and set of interests separate from those of its members. The literature on trade unions and industrial relations abounds with references to the conflict of roles between union members and union officials. The official's job centres round compromise and accommodation. For him workers' grievances are problems to be solved. He feels an obligation to uphold agreements reached bilaterally with the employers and comes to regard his negotiating relationship with the other side as something to be valued in its own right. He is consequently reluctant to engage in actions which would jeopardise managerial goodwill. His awareness of the longer run consequences of current actions for the bargaining relationship leads him to act as a restraining influence on his members, whose response to grievances is more spontaneous and volatile. Nor is this role conflict confined to full time union officials. Shop stewards are subject to the same pressures, though their close involvement in the work situation of their members and their greater dependence on their constituents' continued approval for the maintenance of their authority, make them less likely to depart very far, for very long from their members' aspirations. It is significant that less than one manager in four considers shop stewards to be more militant than their members.[2]

The union, in short, is not a homogeneous unit. In addition to the discussion between leaders and rank and file the diversity of interests and objectives among the union's constituent sub-groups is especially pronounced in Britain where unions typically organise across occupational and industrial boundaries. It is this internal heterogeneity together with certain other features of trade unions that makes it difficult to analyse union behaviour on the analogy of a monopoly firm marketing a commodity.[3] For one thing, unions do not fit easily into the paradigm of constrained maximisation. Even if we accept, for the sake of argument that if unions are to be subject to economic analysis they must be conceived to maximise something, it is at least not obvious what that something should be, or how the union's objectives are likely to change in different circumstances. Moreover, except in very rare cases where the union acts as the sole agency through which employers in a particular sector obtain labour and workers obtain employment, unions cannot be said to sell the services of their members directly. Rather they act as the members' representative in fixing the terms on which labour market transactions take place, *if* they take place. The union does not own and dispose of its members' services in the same way that the monopoly firm owns its product. It is the members themselves who sell their services. By contrast, the monopoly firm which engages in bilateral negotiations

---

[2] See McCarthy and Parker [17] pp. 31–2.
[3] For a detailed critique of the conception of the union as a monopoly of labour see A. M. Ross [21].

with another firm, commits itself to undertake certain transactions simultaneously with fixing the terms of such transactions.

Does this make any difference in the context of wage inflation? Does it matter if it is union members who display militant behaviour, through, for example, unofficial action, whilst the leadership seeks to moderate such initiatives, or conversely, if the leadership seeks to head off unofficial action and escape internal criticism by itself taking a militant lead? This is not a question which can be decided *a priori*, anymore than can the analogous question as to whether the existence of rival interest within the firm affects its behaviour. But three comments are in order. First, some analytical accounts of union–employer negotiations have explicitly acknowledged the existence in effect of three distinct parties to the negotiating process—the employers' representatives, the union leaders and the rank and file. The phenomenon of what has been called 'intra-organisational bargaining', the process by which attempts are made to harmonise the aspirations of the rank and file with the exigencies of the *inter*-organisational bargaining that is simultaneously taking place with the employers, has been shown to make a qualitative difference to the outcome of union–employer negotiations.[4] And even if the predictive contents of theories which abstract from internal union heterogeneity were not dissimilar from those which do not so abstract, the explanations of these theories for the observed phenomena of union–employer negotiations would be different. For roughly equivalent predictive performance, the more 'realistic' theory might be preferred. Second, if it *is* the case that non-market institutional forces affect the movement of money wages, then there is at least a presumption that, other things being equal, the pace of wage inflation would be different according as union leaders were actively supporting or restraining shop floor initiatives. Third, in so far as explanations of wage inflation aim to do more than simply answer the question of whether or not non-market factors affect the rate of wage inflation, but also aim at a fuller understanding of the inflationary process, the conditions in which union members and/or leaders become militant need to be investigated. Trade union militancy is hardly random or idiosyncratic behaviour. It arises in response to specific structural situations. Casual observation suggests that the role conflict described above would be relevant to such an investigation.

[4] See Walton and McKensie [24].

It has been argued that militancy is a feature of union behaviour. But what is at stake is the independent *influence* that unions exercise on wage movements. Now it is clear that there is a conceptual distinction between militant behaviour and union influence.[5] Militancy *may* be the means by which unions seek to exercise influence. But militancy is only one possible means, and the means by which influence or power is exercised constitute only one of the possible dimensions along which power may be measured. Harsanyi [8] has listed seven such dimensions. Roughly these can be divided into three categories: the sources of power, the means of power and the results of power. The source of power covers both the base of power (sets of resources—e.g. economic assets, constitutional prerogatives, popular prestige—which one party may use to influence the other's behaviour) and the opportunity costs for both sides which are associated with any particular bargaining conjuncture. The means of power relate to the set of actions by which one party utilises his resources to influence the other's behaviour. The results of power comprise the set of actions which one side can get the other to perform by using his means of power, and the net increase in the probability of one's opponent actually performing some specific action X owing to the use of means of power against him.

Of these three main ways in which power can be identified and measured, it would in the context of wage inflation be begging the question to attempt to measure union influence by its results. Since there is no way of knowing what would have been achieved without trade unions, it is precisely whether any results, and if so, what, are produced by union influence that is at issue. We may then consider either the source or the means of power. The chief difficulty with using the source of power is that these dimensions constitute only a *potential* source of actual influence. The unions' resources are, as it were, only the arguments of a production function showing the terms on which the union may transform different amounts of its resources into given results. The union is free to use or not to use these resources. The actual incurrence of the opportunity costs of bargaining situation is similarly discretionary. The sources of power, therefore, provide us only with measures of power in what Harsanyi calls a schedule sense. This conforms to the commonsense notion of power as an ability to

[5] In what follows the term influence is used to refer to the ability of trade unions to achieve results, particularly regarding money wage rates, for their members beyond what could have been achieved in the absence of trade unions.

achieve results which the wielder of power is free to use or not. We can only specify the values of the various dimensions of power at any given time if we know how much of his resources an agent is prepared to sacrifice in order to achieve a given end, i.e. the agent's utility function. Specifying these values gives us what Harsanyi calls power in a point sense which corresponds to the commonsense notion of power as actually exerted influence.

All that we ever observe is actually exerted influence, though of course we may be able to make inferences from our observations about power in the schedule sense. It is probably for this reason that attention has been focussed on union militancy as the means of power. Assuming that we can successfully identify and measure observable correlates of the militancy concept and that we have established some theoretical link between the sources of power and the putative results of power (the power schedule) then, other things being equal, variations in the proxies for union militancy will correspond to variations in the degree to which a given potential union influence is actually being exerted.

This situation is illustrated in diagram I below. The right-hand upper quadrant contains a possible power schedule relating the rate at which money wages can be raised by the union, $\dot{w}$, to one of the sources of its power, the opportunity cost to the employer of resisting

Figure 1

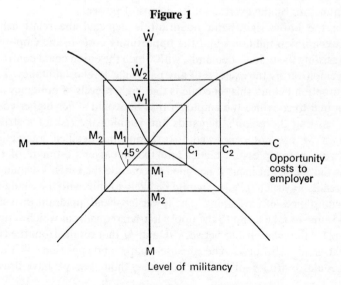

Level of militancy

the union's demands, when the other sources of union power are held constant. The schedule can be thought of as depicting the possible outcomes of bargaining given the various elements of the bargaining situation at a particular point in time. If the parameters of the bargaining situation alter the power schedule will shift. Thus, for example, if the union's resources (funds, membership, legal rights, number of skilled negotiators, etc.) were to diminish, or if the degree of employer resistance to the union's demands were to increase, thus raising the possible cost to the union of holding out for any given demand and running the risk of precipitating a conflict, the schedule would move down and to the right, indicating that for any given cost that the union could inflict or threaten to inflict on the employer to support its demands, a lower wage increase would be achieved.

This construction fudges a number of difficult problems in bargaining theory, notably the fact that the opportunity cost to the employer is not objectively given but depends on his perception of the situation, how seriously he takes the union's demands and so on. It must, however, be stressed that the construction is not intended to provide a theory of bargaining, but is a heuristic device designed to illustrate the implications of distinguishing between militancy and power. In effect the whole complex process of bargaining is collapsed and hidden from view behind the power schedule which simply displays the potential results which the union can achieve in a given bargaining conjuncture by the exercise of its means of power.

In the lower right-hand quadrant is depicted the relationship between union militancy and the opportunity costs to the employer of resisting the union's demands, with which the union could confront the employer by the exercise of any particular level of militancy. The assumption behind this schedule is that higher levels of militancy are required to convince the employer that he would suffer higher costs by resisting the union's demands and running the risk of a strike. Again we are not concerned to examine the detailed interaction between union pressure tactics and the employer's estimate of the loss that he might incur if he failed to concede the union's demands. In reality any such schedule would be likely to shift with the changing circumstances of bargaining. The lower left-hand quadrant provides a 45° line to take us up to the upper left-hand quadrant which simply displays the relationship between W and M that results from the two right-hand schedules. The precise shape and position of these schedules is irrelevant for our purposes, though as we have drawn them they imply diminishing returns to militancy, which seems reasonable enough.

Given the relationship between $\dot{W}$ and C, in order to achieve the result denoted by $\dot{W}_1$ the union must exert the level of militancy denoted by M_1 inflicting a possible cost of C_1 on the employer. In order to achieve the higher rate of wage increase $\dot{W}_2$ the union must step up its efforts to M_2. The move from M_1 to M_2 can be seen to correspond precisely to an increase in actually exerted union influence.

As so often the key assumption in the above description of the union's situation, is contained in the ceteris paribus proviso. Other things may not remain equal. In particular it is quite possible that the index of union militancy may register an upsurge at the same time as the sources of union power are being eroded, for example, through adverse legislation. Indeed these two events may be connected as cause and effect. Similarly a union may find its sources of power enhanced whilst its militancy level remains constant or declines. In terms of our diagram such changes in the sources of union power would be represented by shifts of the power schedule down and to the right and up and to the left in the two cases considered respectively. Clearly to attribute *all* variations in results achieved to variations in union militancy would, to continue the production function analogy, be like attributing all changes in output to variations in capacity utilisation at the same time as capacity and/or techniques of production were changing.

It might be objected that the sources of union power change only slowly and in the long run so that variations in the level of militancy dominate the extent to which union influence is actually exerted in the short run. This may well be so but it cannot be assumed *a priori*. Certainly at the micro level it seems plausible to suppose that the opportunity costs for both sides in any given bargaining situation may change quite quickly. Similarly a union which has just expended a large amount of its resources on strike action is less well placed to repeat such action in the near future, e.g. the seamen in 1966 and the post office workers in 1971. At the aggregate level there may be more justification for regarding the sources of union power as parameters of wage negotiations in the short run. Even here, however, the possibility of sudden shifts in the sources of union power cannot be ruled out. Restrictive legislation eventuating in a few salient defeats for unions which become embroiled in legal processes could easily weaken all unions.

It might also be argued that to the extent that shifts in the unions' power schedule occur the correlation between militancy proxies and the rate of wage inflation would be affected, since shifts in the power schedule cause a given level of militancy to be associated with different rates of wage inflation. Random shifts would presumably destroy any association between M and $\dot{W}$, whilst non-random shifts would be reflected in significant differences in coefficient estimates for different observation periods in time series studies, or for different sectors in cross section studies. It is in fact interesting to note that the co-efficient estimates on the various proxies for union militancy which have been devised do seem to be unstable in both time series and cross-section studies,[6] though this is probably due as much to the rough character of the proxies used as to anything else. In general, however, the possibility of shifts in the power schedule gives rise to an identification problem. Without further investigation there is no way of knowing whether a given set of observations on $\dot{W}$ and M is generated by a constant relationship between these variables or by a series of different relationships.

The upshot of this discussion is that union militancy explanations of wage inflation need to be handled with great care. There is first the problem of identifying and measuring the behavioural manifestations of union militancy. Then there is the need to specify precisely what groups are being militant. Finally, there is the problem whether it is legitimate to identify militancy and influence. All of these problems affect the explanatory power of union militancy hypotheses. Most of the recent literature completely ignores the second and third problems. As one recent study notes: '. . . trade unions have been introduced into the wage determination process by the introduction of additional variables, "intruders", as Archibald calls them into empirical equations'.[7] Enough has already been said to show that this procedure is highly unsatisfactory. Since this *is* the procedure which has been followed, however, we turn our attention in the next section to the adequacy of the various proxies which have been used to represent union wage pressure.

III

Four main variants of the method of representing union militancy by proxy in empirical wage determination equations have been tried:

[6] See Ashenfelter, Johnson and Pencavel [1], Hines [10 and 11].
[7] See Ashenfelter, Johnson and Pencavel [1] p. 28.

(a) a subjective index based on a five point rating of union pushfulness (Dow and Dicks-Mireaux [3]); (b) a dummy variable taking the value zero during periods of conscious wage restraint by the unions and one during other periods (Klein and Ball [13]); (c) the rate of change in the proportion of the labour force belonging to trade unions (Hines [10 and 11]; Ashenfelter, Johnson and Pencavel [1]); (d) measures of strike activity. Ashenfelter, Johnson and Pencavel [1] used the number of strikes beginning in any period relative to the number of trade union members. Godfrey [6] used total number of strikes minus those originating in mining and quarrying. J. Taylor [22] used total number of strikes.

Serious objections can be raised against the use of each of these indices. Before considering these in detail it is worth while enumerating the criteria which a good index of union militancy would have to satisfy. First if it is desired to obtain a reasonably precise estimate of the impact of union militancy on money wage movements, it is desirable that the index should be based on objective data as opposed to subjective judgement. Objectivity, of course, is not an absolute quality but a matter of degree. The requirement really, therefore, is for the degree of subjectivity involved in the construction of the index to be minimised. This matter is discussed more fully below.

Second, it is desirable that the index should, as Hines puts it, be 'sensitive to all the considerable annual variation in the degree of independent pressure brought to bear by the unions on the wage bargain'.

Third, the index should as far as possible be unambiguously an index of union militancy and not capable of other interpretations. It should not, for example, be possible to interpret the index as a proxy for employer resistance, the other main force acting on wage negotiations.

Finally and most importantly the index should be justified in terms of a reasonably well formed theory of wage determination. The inclusion of proxies for union militancy in wage determination equations on the grounds of ad hoc rationalisations and assertions can do little to assist our understanding of the process of wage inflation.

It will be shown that each of the indices referred to earlier is defective by one of more of these criteria.

1   The subjective index

The index proposed by Dow and Dicks-Mireaux clearly fails by our objectivity requirement. It could be objected here that indices based on officially collected statistics are also affected by elements of subjectivity. In the first place there is an inevitable intrusion of subjectivity in the determination of the categories of the items to be recorded in official statistics. In British statistics relating to industrial disputes, for example, only actual stoppages of work are recorded and then only those which last at least one day or involve not less than ten workers except in cases where the aggregate number of working days lost exceeds 100. Thus many forms of industrial action short of striking ranging from go-slows and bans on overtime working to less palpable actions such as the withdrawal of co-operation from management, go completely unrecorded, as well as a large number of short, small-scale work stoppages which do not qualify for inclusion in the official records. In the second place, even given the existing categories of items to be recorded, the methods of collecting the data result in the omission of many work stoppages which would qualify for inclusion in the records. This is particularly true in the private sector where management and supervision may have a vested interest in not reporting work stoppages which do not seriously disrupt production schedules. Nevertheless, allowing for the limitations of official statistics there is clearly a large difference of degree between the subjectivity involved in an index of militancy based on strike statistics and that involved in an index based on the author's intuition.

2   Dummy variables

The two-value dummy variable proxy is clearly deficient by our criterion of sensitivity. Unions are on this approach either militant or not in any particular year and variations in the degree of militancy displayed from one year to the next are simply lost. There is also a good deal of subjectivity involved in deciding whether a particular period was one of militancy or moderation. Moreover in Klein and Ball's study the criterion employed in making this decision was whether or not the Labour Party was in power. This gives their dummy a certain ambiguity since it could be interpreted as reflecting changing government policies and attitudes and associated changes in employers' attitudes just as easily as union attitudes.

3   Changes in union density

Hines argues that ΔT is an index of union militancy which simultaneously manifests itself in increased pressure on money wage rates and increased union membership. The relationship between ΔT and

ΔW is not strictly one of causation since ΔT is only a proxy variable. Nevertheless Hines adduces a number of arguments to account for the observed association of ΔT and ΔW.[8] These arguments in no way add up to a theory of the role of unions in the wage determination process. Nowhere does Hines spell out the objectives of the union and the relative priorities which it attaches to conflicting objectives. Nor, even if we accept Hines's arguments showing that ΔT is an index of changes in union bargaining strength, is it shown that there are no other ways of enhancing the unions' power. The justification for using ΔT as the proxy variable remains, therefore, problematical.

The chief merit of ΔT as a militancy index is that it satisfies our objectivity criterion.

Hines also claims that ΔT satisfies the sensitivity requirement. This is a dubious claim at any rate for most of the post-war period when the observed variation at ΔT has been slight. It may be objected that a minor degree of variability in a proxy variable in itself does not affect the ability of that variable to represent changes in some other variable which cannot be directly observed, provided that a stable relation exists between the proxy and the variable that it stands for. Moreover, Hines argues that the relationship between union militancy M and ΔT has changed since the inter-war period from that indicated by line i in the diagram below to that indicated by line p, owing to the large rise in the *level* of unionisation between the inter- and post-war periods, so that at the higher level of unionisation prevailing since the war a given value of ΔT indicates more militancy than formerly. Thus ΔT is just as good an index whether the relationship between M and ΔT is that denoted by line p or that denoted by the steeper line i. However, it has been shown[9] that small but detectable changes in union density can and are regularly brought about by factors completely unconnected with union militancy such as changes in the numbers of workers employed in closed shops, changes in the industrial structure of the labour force, and changes in employer attitudes and policies towards union recognition. The relationships between ΔT and M shown by lines i and p in the diagram, are, therefore, *ceteris paribus* relationships. In effect we can write $\Delta T = f(M/x)$ where x is a vector of other influences on ΔT whose effect in any

---

[8] For a full critique of these arguments and of Hines's wage inflation studies in general see Purdy and Zis [19].
[9] See Purdy and Zis [19].

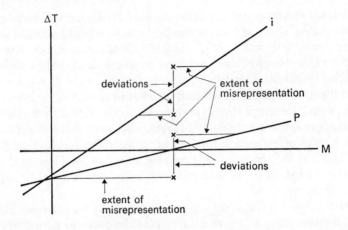

particular year is expected to be small, and may be represented on the diagram by deviations of the actually observed ΔT above or below lines i and p. Now it is clear that if the relationship between M and ΔT were that shown by line i, a given deviation of the actually observed ΔT from the value associated with a given level of militancy as a result of changes in any of the elements of x, would result in a less serious misrepresentation of the actual level of militancy than if the relationship were that shown by line p.

It is significant in this connection that both Hines [10] and Purdy and Zis [19] for the U.K. and Ashenfelter, Johnson and Pencavel [1] for the U.S. found that the explanatory power of ΔT was greatest in the inter-war period when in both countries the observed fluctuations in ΔT were greatest. It seems highly probable, therefore, that ΔT is a sensitive indicator of changes in the strength of the pushing factor only for the inter-war period when the actually observed movement of ΔT was large enough for it to be safely concluded that changes in M and not changes in the elements of x were the dominant factors causing the movement. Yet it is precisely for the post-war period that the influence of union militancy on the movement of money wages has been stressed. Whatever the truth about this question the use of ΔT as a proxy for union militancy in the post-war period is highly unsatisfactory.

Finally, the lack of theoretical amplification of the role of unions in the wage determination process leads to ambiguity in the interpretation of ΔT. An alternative rationalisation of the observed association between $\dot{W}$ and ΔT might be cast in terms of the operation of a security motive. Each pay claim submitted by a union can potentially lead to a strike and hence to a (temporary) loss of earnings by the workers involved. By joining the appropriate union immediately before and during pay negotiations workers may minimise their financial loss by securing entitlement to strike benefit in the event that negotiations actually do break down. During pay negotiations, therefore, an increase in the rate of change of unionisation over and above that which would otherwise have been forthcoming would occur, not as a result of active union recruitment but of the actions of marginal union members who wished to increase their personal security. The aggregate rate of change of unionisation would on this hypothesis depend on the proportion of workers with pay claims pending during any given period and on the probability with which marginal union members in any given bargaining unit expected their negotiations to terminate in a strike. A positive association between $\dot{W}$ and ΔT might be expected for two reasons. First, given the underlying rate of wage settlement the more frequently wage claims are submitted and settled the greater the proportion of workers who face the risk of becoming involved in a strike and who receive wage increases in any given period. Hence an increase in ΔT will accompany a rise in the aggregate rate of change of money wages $\dot{W}$, since the latter is measured as $\dot{W} = \sum_i \dot{W}_i(n_i/N)$ where $\dot{W}_i$ is the rate of increase in money wages in the ith bargaining unit, n_i is the number of workers in the ith bargaining unit and N is the total number of workers. It might also be that the security motive for joining unions is stronger or weaker according as current pay claims lie above or below the range of normal experience. Other things being equal workers would regard a strike as more probable in the case of 'high' claims than in the case of 'low' claims. If the level of claims and settlements were positively related there would be another reason to expect a positive association between $\dot{W}$ and ΔT. Such an interpretation would certainly be consistent with the experience of the last three years in the U.K. when both the frequency and level of claims and settlements, the level of pay—related strike activity and ΔT have all risen sharply. It is also interesting to note that there is a high correlation between ΔT and strike activity measured by official statistics of strike frequency over the whole period 1950–70. According to our calculations the correlation coefficient between ΔT and the total number of strikes in all industries, both variables being measured on an annual basis, was

0·68, whilst when strikes originating in mining and quarrying were excluded from the total the correlation rose to 0·79. Both these estimates were easily significant at the 1 per cent level.

On this alternative account, then, ΔT is an index not so much of union militancy as of variations in the incidence and strength of one of the motives for joining unions. Moreover, if, as we have argued, the strength of the security motive depends on the probability with which workers on the margin of joining the union expected a strike to occur, ΔT could also be regarded as an index of variations in employer resistance inasmuch as the expected probability of a strike would depend on the degree of resistance to union claims which employers are currently displaying.

The Hines militancy index is thus seen to be deficient on grounds of theoretical weakness, insufficient sensitivity and ambiguity.

4   Strike activity

The subjectivity involved in strike statistics has already been noted above. Although it was argued there that despite their limitations strike statistics still afforded a better basis for an index of union militancy than an arbitrary rating of union wage pressure, the limitations are still substantial and could make statistics of strike activity very misleading. For example, the studies which have used strike statistics to represent union militancy have concentrated exclusively on strike frequency (with, incidentally, little explanation as to why this dimension of strike activity should be singled out). But, as we argued earlier, official strike frequency statistics may omit many small strikes, while the records of all aspects of strike activity exclude even large scale and prolonged forms of industrial action short of striking (overtime bans, working to rule, etc.) which may be just as indicative of union militancy as actual withdrawals of labour. Some commentators have noted the increasing use of such 'cut price' forms of organised industrial action as a response to an economic situation in which workers are more reluctant to sacrifice earnings through striking because of mortgage, H.P. commitments, etc. (See Flanders [5].) It should also be noted that Godfrey [6] and Taylor [22] use strike frequency figures on a quarterly and semi-annual basis respectively. But Goodman [7] points out that strikes display a distinct seasonal pattern with a high incidence in the first quarter rising to a peak in March or April, falling to lower levels in July and

August, reaching a secondary peak in September–October and then falling markedly in December. It is, therefore, necessary to correct strike statistics for seasonal variations.

It could in any case be argued that strike frequency figures provide a poor index of union militancy. It takes two to make a fight, so that strike frequency may just as well be taken as an index of employers' resistance. Again strikes occur over many other issues besides 'straight' demand for wage increases. McCarthy's [15] analysis of the Ministry of Labour's classification of strikes by the (principal) reasons given for striking reveals that in the period 1945–57 only 9·2 per cent of strikes were classified as being concerned with straight-forward wage increase demands. Thirty-six per cent concerned other wage questions (primarily disputes over the operation of payment systems) and 48 per cent involved what Knowles [14] termed 'frictional causes' a category corresponding to the Ministry's two categories covering 'disputes over the employment of particular classes of persons' and 'disputes over other working arrangements, rules and discipline'. Nor have these proportions been stable. 'Frictional causes' rose from 22 per cent of the total in 1911–25 to 39 per cent in 1927–47 to 48 per cent in 1948–57. Since the mid-50's this secular trend has been reversed and claims for wage increases have been responsible for steadily rising proportion from 16·6 per cent in 1960 to 55·4 per cent in 1970.

Variations in strike frequency therefore represent far more than simple fluctuations in a number of homogeneous occurrences. It might seem to make more sense to base a militancy index only on disputes arising from claims for wage increases. However, it must be remembered that the classification of strikes by principal causes is not an objectively compiled list of strike causes but rather a list of the principal reasons given for striking. Many strikes involve multiple issues, the relative importance of which in the minds of the protagonists may change in the course of the dispute. The most frequently mentioned reason for striking may also be more or less relevant to the real cause of the dispute. Thus the recent upsurge in the proportion of wage increase strikes certainly tells us something about the form of recent industrial conflict but may well be misleading, except in a purely qualitative sense, as an indicator of the recent movement of union militancy. It is quite possible and indeed to be expected in the prevailing environment of inflationary expectations, that some of the strikes which have assumed the wage form in recent years would have taken a different form a decade earlier.

As noted above strike activity has several dimensions and it is at least not obvious that strike frequency is the only or even the most appropriate dimension for measuring union militancy. For instance does a large number of short and small-scale strikes indicate more or less militancy than a smaller number of longer and larger scale strikes? On the other hand the use of the number of working days lost or the number of workers involved in strikes would not by itself improve the measure of union militancy. Days lost and numbers involved are both subject to wide random fluctuations. A token one day national engineering strike will result in a loss of approximately three million working days. Every year a tiny number of large scale and lengthy disputes dominates the figures for days lost and numbers involved. The 1971 Ford and Post Office strikes between them caused a loss of eight million working days out of a total for the year of 13·5 million. The recent miner's strike caused a loss of 12 million working days.

Another relevant dimension of strike activity is the extent to which it is concentrated or diffused amongst industries. It is well known that some industries and within those industries some firms are far more strike prone than others. From the point of view of measuring union militancy it could be argued that less significance attaches to an increase in strike activity in a sector in which the strike is already a normal occurrence than to an increase in a sector where strikes are relatively rare.

It may be possible to take account of some of these objections to the use of the crude strike frequency figures by developing a compound index along the lines suggested by Evans and Galambos [4]. Strike frequency, S_t, numbers involved, N_t, and working days lost, W_t, could be incorporated into such an index by comparing their values in any period with either their values in a convenient base period or with their average or median values over the whole period. In the latter two cases, it seems sensible to express the resultant figures as a proportion of an index of employment, E_t. Finally the dispersion of strike activity amongst industries could be built into the index by calculating the proportion of strikes occurring outside the five most consistently strike prone industries, d_t. Ideally each of these four components should be weighted but since there is no obvious way of allocating weights a simple arithmetic or geometric average would have to suffice. Symbolically the index would be:

$$M_t = \frac{100}{4}(s_t + n_t + w_t + d_t)$$

where $s_t = \dfrac{S_t}{S_o}$

$n_t = \dfrac{N_t}{N_o} \bigg/ \dfrac{E_t}{E_o}$

$w_t = \dfrac{W_t}{W_o} \bigg/ \dfrac{E_t}{E_o}$

d_t = proportion of strikes occurring outside the five most consistently strike prone industries

or

$$M_t = 4\sqrt{S_t \cdot N_t \cdot W_t \cdot d_t}\,100$$

One difficulty with such an index would probably be that it would display a positive time trend since two of the elements of which it is composed, s_t and d_t, show a fairly marked upward trend whilst the other two N_t and W_t have certainly tended to rise on average though their movement is dominated by year to year fluctuations. If this is so it would lead one to expect a fairly steady acceleration of wage increases over the 60's instead of the sharp jump at the end of the decade which actually occurred. It would, of course, still be possible to consider deviations of the index around its trend value as an indicator of exceptional (high or low) levels of union militancy. In the context of wage inflation one would then be asking: given a tendency for unions to become more militant anyway, are years of exceptional (high or low) levels of union militancy associated, other things being equal, with exceptional movements of money wages?

Whilst some such multifactor index of union militancy would undoubtedly be preferable to the use of the crude strike frequency figures, its insertion into a wage determination equation would be sterile without further theoretical justification. Moreover, precisely because of its contrived nature movements of the index would require careful interpretation, since they do not carry their meaning on their face.

5   Other possible indices

(a) It may be though that the proportion of workers covered by the wage index who obtain a settlement in a given year, i.e. $\sum_i n_i / N$ where N is the number of workers covered by the wage index, and n_i is the number of workers in the ith bargaining unit receiving a wage increase in a given period, may be taken as an index of union militancy.

It is obvious that the greater is this proportion the faster will be the rate of increase in the wage index other things being equal, since the wage index is given by the formula:

$$\dot{W}_t = \sum_i \dot{W}_{it} \frac{N_i}{N}$$

The greater the number of bargaining units for which $\dot{W}_{it}$ is positive the greater will be $\dot{W}_t$, ceteris paribus. The proportion of workers in such bargaining units tells us nothing about union militancy or about the process of wage determination.

(b) The average length of time elapsing between successive claims or settlements. The same argument applies as above. If wage claims/settlements are speeded up this will raise the numbers receiving an increase in any given period but in itself tells us nothing.

(c) The average size of wage claims. On the conceptual level this seems more promising. There is a substantial problem of relativity though. A claim representing a 10 per cent increase in the wage bill is large in relation to the normal run of claims in the 1950's but small in relation to recent claims. It might, therefore, be interpreted as reflecting less militancy today than it would have done a decade ago. It would probably be possible to overcome this problem by comparing the average size of claims at the time t with a weighted average of claims in preceding periods. The main problem with this approach lies in eliciting the necessary data. Sometimes unions simply claim a 'substantial increase' and an actual figure is not brought into the negotiations for some time. There is also great difficulty in identifying the precise size of particular claims when different rates of pay for different groups of workers are involved or when a pay claim comes in the form of a package or when wage earnings consist of several different components which are differentially affected by a national claim. Quite apart from these genuine difficulties the actual impact of a claim on the wage bill is frequently exaggerated or underestimated as part of each side's bargaining tactics.

There is also an *a priori* puzzle in using wage claims in that it is difficult to see how there could be any straightforward relationship between claims and settlements, since if there were and the unions came to realize it, as presumably they eventually would, the unions would simply pitch their claims at such a level as would yield the maximum increase in wages compatible with their other objectives. Assuming that union objectives and the weights assigned to conflicting objectives change only relatively slowly, we would expect to find both claims and settlements stabilising in a sort of steady state development.

More plausibly one might postulate a relationship between unions' initial claims and what the unions' initially expect to receive based on their knowledge of past and current claims and settlements. If the actual settlement were then to deviate from the expected, at any rate by more than a certain margin of tolerance, presumably because of unexpected employer resistance, the union would then be assumed to modify its future expectations and adjust its next claim accordingly. Thus again it is seen that the use of a proxy variable for union militancy cannot escape the problem of how to handle employers resistance, which has been completely ignored in all the studies considering the impact of trade union militancy on money wage movements. Further progress with union wage claims as the proxy would depend, apart from empirical difficulties, on the elaboration of a complete model of wage bargaining displaying union and employer objectives, the process of claims and offers and the accompanying adjustment of expectations.

IV Conclusions

We have argued that the studies attempting to explain wage inflation in terms of union militancy suffer from a serious weakness in that they ignore the distinction between militancy and power or influence, quite apart from the appropriateness of the proxies used to measure union militancy. The identification of these two concepts is one expression of the lack of an adequate theoretical framework for analysing trade union behaviour. Another expression is the fact that all studies have ignored the role of employers' resistance despite their initial postulate that wage bargaining corresponds to the case of bilateral monopoly. The conception of the union as the analogue of the monopoly firm was criticised on the grounds that it ignored the crucial distinction between the union and its members. The ability of some unions to restrict the supply of labour is not a sufficient reason for applying this model to all unions. We conclude, therefore, that an adequate framework for analysing the role of unions in wage inflation would need to incorporate the distinctions between the union and its members and between militancy and power and to recognise explicitly the role of employer resistance.

We have also argued that quite apart from the absence of a satisfactory theoretical framework the various proxies for union militancy which have been used in empirical studies of wage inflation are deficient for a number of reasons. Ultimately, of course, their inadequacy stems from the theoretical shortcomings of these studies. For instance, we have shown that the association between $\dot{W}$ and ΔT discovered by Hines can be rationalised by postulating the existence of a security motive amongst workers on the margin of union membership. According to this alternative hypothesis the observation of a positive relationship between $\dot{W}$ and ΔT would tell us nothing about the relationship between union militancy and wage inflation. Similarly both ΔT and statistics of strike activity could plausibly be rationalised as indices of employers' militancy rather than of union militancy. Doubtless the measure of union militancy could be refined, perhaps along the lines suggested in section III. Fundamentally, however, this would be a futile exercise without the construction of a more rigorous model of union–employer negotiations.

Enough has already been said to justify extreme scepticism towards any policy recommendations based on the existing studies of union militancy and wage inflation. Two further inconsistencies are worth noting. First, Hines's conclusion that incomes policies provide the best means of minimising the inflationary consequences of union militancy depends crucially on the absence of any association between the proxy for union and militancy and various measures of excess demand. The ΔT index appears to pass this test successfully.[10] If, however, we take strike activity as the proxy variable there exists ample evidence both for the U.S.A. and the U.K. of a positive association between strike frequency and the level of excess demand. (See Rees [20], Knowles [24], Turner, Clack and Roberts [23], Cameron [2] and Pencavel [18].) It may, therefore, be doubted whether union militancy is an independent influence on wage inflation. Second, Godfrey [6] and Taylor [22], both find a significant and positive association between $\dot{W}$ and their strike variables. Johnston and Timbrell [12], on

[10] Though Purdy and Zis [19] are sceptical of the view that changes in union membership are completely unrelated to the level of economic activity.

the other hand, contradicts this result. Again, therefore, it may be doubted whether, as Taylor asserts, 'incomes policy has tended to operate through the suppression of union militancy'.

Our general conclusion is that the existing studies of the role of unions in the inflationary process are of little value in helping to reveal either the causes of inflation or the appropriateness and effectiveness of possible remedies.

References

[1] Ashenfelter, O. C., Johnson G. E. and Pencavel, J. H., 'Trade Unions and the Rate of Change of Money Wage Rates in United States Manufacturing Industry', *Review of Economic Studies* (1972).

[2] Cameron, G. C., 'Post-war Strikes in the North East Shipbuilding and Shiprepairing Industry', *British Journal of Industrial Relations* (1964).

[3] Dicks-Mireaux, L. A., and Dow, C. R., 'The Determinants of Wage Inflation: United Kingdom 1946–56', *Journal of the Royal Statistical Society*, Series A, CXXII (1959).

[4] Evans, E. W., and Galambos, P., 'Work Stoppages in the U.K., 1957–64', *Bulletin of the Oxford University Institute of Economics and Statistics* (1966).

[5] Flanders, A., *Management and Unions*, London, Faber and Faber (1970).

[6] Godfrey, L., 'The Phillips Curve: Incomes Policy and Trade Union Effects' in H. G. Johnson and A. R. Nobay (eds.) *The Current Inflation*, London, Macmillan (1971).

[7] Goodman, J. F. B. 'Strikes in the U.K.: Recent Statistics and Trends', *International Labour Review*, Vol. 95 (1967).

[8] Harsanyi, J., 'The Measurement of Social Power, Opportunity Costs and the Theory of Two-Person Bargaining Games', *Behavioural Science*, Vol. 7 (1962).

[9] Hines, A. G., 'Trade Unions and Wage Inflation in the United Kingdom 1893–1961', *Review of Economic Studies* (1964).

[10] Hines, A. G., 'Wage Inflation in the U.K. 1948–1963', *Economic Journal* (1969).

[11] Hines, A. G., 'The Determination of the Rate of Change of Money Wage Rates and the Effectiveness of Incomes Policy' in H. G. Johnson and A. R. Nobay (eds.) *The Current Inflation*, London, Macmillan (1971).

[12] Johnston, J. and Timbrell, M., 'Empirical Tests of Bargaining Theory of Wage Rate Determination', Ch. 4, below.

[13] Klein, L. R. and Ball, R. J., 'Some Econometrics of the Determination of Absolute Prices and Wages', *Economic Journal* (1959).

[14] Knowles, K. G. J. C., *Strikes: A Study in Industrial Conflict*, Oxford, Blackwell (1952).

[15] McCarthy, W. E. J., 'The Reasons Given for Striking', *Bulletin of the Oxford University Institute of Economics and Statistics* (1959).

[16] McCarthy, W. E. J., 'The Role of Shop Stewards in British Industrial Relations', *Research Paper 1, Royal Commission on Trade Unions and Employers' Associations*, London, H.M.S.O. (1966).

[17] McCarthy, W. E. J. and Parker, S. R., 'Shop Stewards and Workshop Relations', *Research Paper 10, Royal Commission on Trade Unions and Employers' Associations*, London, H.M.S.O. (1968).

[18] Pencavel, J. H., 'An Investigation into Industrial Strike Activity', *Economica* (1970).

[19] Purdy, D. L. and Zis, G., 'Trade Unions and Wage Inflation in the U.K.: A Re-appraisal', Ch. 1 above. First published in M. Parkin (ed.) *Essays in Modern Economics*, London, Longmans (1973).

[20] Rees, A., 'Industrial Conflict and Business Fluctuations' in Kornhauser, A., Dubin, R. and Ross, A. M., *Industrial Conflict*, New York, McGraw-Hill (1954).
[21] Ross, A. M., 'Trade Unions as a Wage Fixing Institution', *American Economic Review* (1947).
[22] Taylor, J., 'Incomes Policy, the Structure of Unemployment and the Phillips Curve: the United Kingdom Experience 1953–70', in M. Parkin and M. T. Sumner (eds.) *Incomes Policy and Inflation*, Manchester, Manchester University Press (1972).
[23] Turner, H. A., Clack, G. and Roberts, G., *Labour Relations in the Motor Industry*, London, Allen and Unwin (1967).
[24] Walton, R. E. and McKensie, R. B., *A Behavioural Theory of Labour Negotiations*, New York, McGraw-Hill (1965).

J. Johnston[1]

Chapter 3 A model of wage determination under bilateral monopoly[2]

This problem has recently been reconsidered by Hieser [5], whose analysis is in the tradition of Hicks [4] and Shackle [7]. His treatment improves on theirs to the extent that he gives an explicit discussion of the main gains and losses of the participants to the wage bargain but, as will be argued below, the analysis of the forces determining the level of that bargain is still obscure and unsatisfactory.

The plan of this paper is as follows. Section I describes some crucial elements of the Hieser approach, which will be retained in the subsequent analysis. Section II develops a model of union–employer decisions and contrasts the main features of that model with those currently available in conventional bargaining theory. Section III summarises our analysis, points out some implications for current discussions of wage inflation and indicates some possible lines for empirical research.

I The Hieser analysis

Hieser postulates a monopolist producer faced by the market demand curve, DD', for his product, as in Figure 1. The technical production function is given and the prime cost curve per unit of output is assumed to be horizontal. The monopolist is assumed to be fully integrated, producing his own raw materials, so that the only prime cost is labour. The *initial* prime cost curve is shown by CC' in Figure 1 and is determined by the opportunity wage, OC, at which 'free' labour would offer itself. With labour being the only prime cost

[1] The evolution of this paper has been substantially influenced by valuable comments from Mr. P. R. Fisk, Sir John Hicks, Professor J. N. Wolfe, Mr. G. D. N. Worswick, my colleagues in the S.S.R.C. Inflation Workshop at the University of Manchester.
[2] Reprinted with permission, from *The Economic Journal* (September 1972).

Figure 1   Revenue and cost conditions facing the monopolist

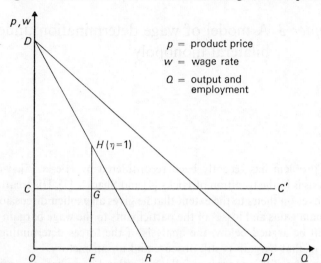

p = product price
w = wage rate
Q = output and employment

a suitable definition of units means that employment and output can both be measured by the same number Q on the horizontal axis in Figure 1.

In addition to the above assumptions Hieser now postulates the existence of a trade union with a closed shop. The union will bargain for a money wage rate in excess of OC and the union's objective is assumed to be to raise the money wage rate (w) until the money wage bill (wQ) is maximised. DR is the marginal revenue curve in Figure 1 and is also the monopolist's demand curve for labour. The elasticities of DD' and DR are defined respectively as

$$\text{elasticity of } DD' = \epsilon = -\frac{dQ}{dp} \cdot \frac{p}{Q}$$

$$\text{elasticity of } DR = \eta = -\frac{dQ}{dw} \cdot \frac{w}{Q}$$

The wage bill is maximised at $\eta = 1$, that is, at the point H in Figure 1, and so the union would desire to push the money wage up from FG to an upper limit of FH. In doing so employment will be continuously reduced but the money wage bill will be increased. Further increases in the money wage above FH would, however, reduce the wage bill.

It can be shown that for any output Q, provided DD' is a straight line,

$$\eta = \tfrac{1}{2}(\epsilon - 1) \tag{1}$$

and the familiar relation between average and marginal revenue gives

$$w = p\left(1 - \frac{1}{\epsilon}\right) \tag{2}$$

or

$$\frac{w}{p} = \frac{\epsilon - 1}{\epsilon}$$

At point H, $\eta = 1$, so $\epsilon = 3$ and at that point $w/p = \tfrac{2}{3}$. Thus the *maximum wage bill* that the union might possibly extract from the employer is *two-thirds of value added*.

So far so good. Hieser's main concern is to analyse the relative bargaining power of the two parties 'in terms of the balancing of gains and losses by both sides in the stances of resistance or concession'. This is done by formulating break-even functions involving the duration of strikes. Thus all bargaining in the absence of strikes is excluded from consideration. The implicit assumption is that any disagreement, however small, leads automatically to a strike. Moreover, there is no formulation in the model of a union claim or the monopolist's response so that the extent of any disagreement does not appear explicitly in the model.

The cost of a strike action to the workers is defined to be

$$L = sQw + Q.U(s, w) \tag{3}$$

where a = duration of strike (in wage periods)
      w = prevailing wage rate
      Q = prevailing employment
    sQw = gross wages lost during the strike, and
  $U(s, w)$ = supplementary function, 'representing the increasing marginal utility of that money loss (sQw)' and thus likely to increase sharply for high values of s.

Net gain per period from a wage increase is defined by

$$G' = Q.\Delta w + w.\Delta Q \quad \text{(ignoring } \Delta w.\Delta Q)$$
$$= Q.\Delta w(1 - \eta)$$

Discounting this stream over time

$$\text{Total gain} = G = Q.\Delta w(1 - \eta)V_m(j) \tag{4}$$

where $V_m(j)$ is the sum of unity over m periods discounted at rate j. Equating (3) and (4) would give a series of break-even points for labour in terms of pairs of s, Δw values at which gain equals loss. The resultant equation is

$$\Delta w = \frac{sw + U(s, w)}{(1 - \eta)V_m(j)} \tag{5}$$

Since $\eta = \frac{1}{2}(\epsilon - 1)$ this can be written as

$$\Delta w = \frac{sw + U(s, w)}{\frac{1}{2}(3 - \epsilon).V_m(j)} \tag{6}$$

Turning now to the second basic element in the Hieser analysis, the loss of profits to the employer as a result of the strike is given by

$$L_1 = \frac{sQw}{\epsilon - 1} + Q.F(s, w) \tag{7}$$

where $F(s, w)$ is the employer's supplementary function, measuring loss of goodwill and financial stress, which again is likely to increase sharply with s. In addition to profits lost during the strike the loss of profits from the wage increase is[3]

$$L_2 = Q.\Delta w.V_n(i) \tag{8}$$

where $V_n(i)$ is the present value of a stream of unit payments over n periods discounted at the rate i.

Hieser then equates L_1 and L_2 to give what he terms the employer's break-even function, namely,

$$\Delta w = \frac{1}{V_n(i)}\left[\frac{sw}{\epsilon - 1} + F(s, w)\right] \tag{9}$$

Hieser's analysis is conducted in terms of these two break-even functions. These functions, however, are simply accounting relations, and while they contain information essential to union and employer decision-makers, no explicit decision strategy for either party is

[3] This again is an approximation derived by dropping a term in $\Delta Q . \Delta w$ as in (4) above.

developed.[4] A proper decision analysis should have at least three features, none of which appears in the Hieser treatment. It should

(i) be probabilistic in character in order to deal with expectations and uncertainty,

(ii) deal explicitly with the *sequential* nature of the bargaining process, in which a wage claim is formulated by the union, a counter-offer made by the employer, negotiations take place with the possibility of breakdowns, strikes, revised offers and so forth, and

(iii) allow for the possibility of bluffing and second guessing by either party.

An attempt is made to develop such a decision analysis in Section II.

II   A decision model

The process starts with the submission of a union claim for a wage increase of amount Δw^c. In the circumstances of the Hieser problem the maximum increase that the union should actually achieve is indicated by GH in Figure 1. The claim should probably be greater than this but for the moment we will not discuss how the size of the claim should be decided by the union. We will discuss first of all the optimal reaction by the employer to the claim.

In deciding how to respond to the claim the employer must consider possible values for three different variables, which we will label Δw_0, Δw_1 and Δw_2. Δw_0 constitutes the initial wage offer with which he opens negotiations with the union. Δw_1, which is greater than Δw_0, is the upper limit to his negotiating range and is defined to be the level at which he will 'stick' and allow a strike to take place, if union agreement cannot be secured at that level. Δw_2 is the wage increase that he expects to have to pay in order to settle a strike, should one actually occur. In principle it may be greater than, equal to, or less than Δw_1. At this pre-negotiation stage Δw_1 is the crucial number and the employer's problem is defined to be that of choosing its *optimal* value, denoted by Δw_1^*. The optimal value in turn is defined as the value which minimises the employer's *expected* costs.

Let us call Δw_1 the final pre-strike offer and consider values over the range 0 to Δw^c. The employer's first step in the determination of Δw_1^* is probably the truncation of this range at one or both ends. At the top end he may 'discount' some part of the claim in the sense that he will feel reasonably certain that an offer in the range Δw^{rc} to Δw^c

---

[4] A more detailed exposition and critique of the Hieser analysis is given in J. Johnston [6].

will be accepted by the union without a strike. Δw^{rc} is thus defined to be the employer's estimate of the 'real claim' and the extent to which it is less than the nominal claim is a measure of the discounting applied by the employer to that claim. For final offers below Δw^{rc} the employer estimates that there is a real probability of a strike and it is plausible to assert that this strike probability must be inversely related to the size of the offer. For a sufficiently low final offer, denoted by Δw^m, he will judge a strike to be practically a certainty. These assumptions are shown in Figure 2, where the strike probability, $\pi(\Delta w_1)$, declines monotonically from unity at a final offer of Δw^m to zero at a final offer of Δw^{rc}. Under the assumptions of the Hieser problem there is no general inflation and Δw^m may well be close to zero. The greater is the rate of general inflation the higher will Δw^m be in general, and it is also likely to be influenced by the level of recent settlements.

The subsequent algebraic analysis will be considerably simplified if we approximate the strike function of Figure 2 by the linear approximation

$$\pi = 1 - \beta.\Delta w_1 \tag{10}$$

where Δw_1 denotes the final pre-strike offer and

$$\beta = 1/\Delta w^{rc}$$

This approximation takes on the value zero when the offer equals the real claim and the value unity when the offer is zero. Thus it is only valid when Δw^m is close to zero. If this is not the case it is simplest to redefine all wage change variables as measured from Δw^m as origin

Figure 2   Employer's subjective estimate of the strike probability associated with a given wage offer

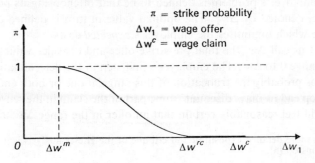

rather than from zero. With this proviso we continue to use equation (10). It must finally be emphasised that Figure 2 and its approximation in (10) represent the employer's subjective estimate of strike probabilities formed prior to the commencement of negotiations.

The situation facing the employer may now be pictured as follows.

$$\text{Final pre-strike offer, } \Delta w_1 \nearrow \begin{array}{l} \text{Accepted with} \\ \text{probability } (1 - \pi) \end{array} \longrightarrow \text{Settlement cost}$$

$$\searrow \begin{array}{l} \text{Rejected with} \\ \text{probability } \pi \end{array} \longrightarrow \begin{array}{l} \text{Strike cost } plus \\ \text{Settlement cost} \end{array}$$

If the offer Δw_1 is accepted without a strike the only cost to the employer is the loss of profits due to the wage increase. This is given by (8) as[5]

$$L_2 = Q \cdot V_n(i) \cdot \Delta w_1$$

If, however, the employer does not succeed in getting Δw_1 accepted then, by definition, a strike ensues. Suppose this strike is settled after s_2 periods by a wage increase of Δw_2. The strike cost from (7) is

$$L_1 = \frac{s_2 Q w}{\epsilon - 1} + Q \cdot F(s_2, w)$$

and the settlement cost is now

$$L_2 = Q \cdot V_n(i) \cdot \Delta w_2$$

Thus the expected cost as seen by the employer, *before any negotiations have taken place*, is

$$E(C) = (1 - \pi)[Q \cdot V_n(i) \cdot \Delta w_1]$$

$$+ \pi \left[\frac{s_2 Q w}{\epsilon - 1} + Q \cdot F(s_2, w) + Q \cdot V_n(i) \cdot \Delta w_2 \right]$$

which, on using (10) becomes

$$E(C) = \alpha_3 \beta (\Delta w_1)^2 + (1 - \beta \cdot \Delta w_1)[\alpha_1 s_2 + \alpha_2 F(s_2) + \alpha_3 \cdot \Delta w_2] \quad (11)$$

---

[5] This assumes that the union negotiators always succeed in pushing the employer to the top of his negotiating range, which is the most cautious or 'conservative' assumption that the employer can make. If this does not always happen then $(1 - \pi)$ has to be re-interpreted as the probability of a settlement without a strike at some level *less than or equal to* Δw_1. The monetary outcomes for the employer would then on average be somewhat more favourable than implied by our subsequent analysis.

where

$$\alpha_1 = \frac{Qw}{\epsilon - 1}, \qquad \alpha_2 = Q, \qquad \alpha_3 = Q.V_n(i)$$

and we have made the supplementary function, $F(s, w)$, depend only on strike length and not on the current wage rate as well.

The evaluation of this expected cost function requires first of all an examination of any possible relationship between the duration of a strike and the wage increase that settles it. Since the publication of the first edition of Sir John Hicks' *Theory of Wages* it has been customary to postulate a negative sloping relationship between these two variables, which we have approximated by a linear relation in Figure 3, namely,

$$s = \delta(\Delta w^{rc} - \Delta w) = \delta\left(\frac{1}{\beta} - \Delta w\right) \tag{12}$$

This gives a strike of zero duration if the offer equals the real claim and a strike of duration $s_0 = \delta.\Delta w^{rc}$ if a zero offer is made. The single parameter, δ, may thus be taken as an expression of the union's propensity to endure a strike for it determines the maximum length of strike, given the real claim, and also indicates the reduction in length of strike associated with a unit increase in the wage offer. Again it must be emphasised that Figure 3 represents the *employer's* subjective estimate of the $s(\Delta w)$ function at the time when he frames his initial negotiating range. Strictly speaking, things cannot be as precise as this diagram implies. For any offer, Δw, the employer will have some subjective probability distribution of the strike length required to secure acceptance of that offer. The diagram, and the

Figure 3   Employer's subjective estimate of the length of strike required to secure acceptance of a given wage offer

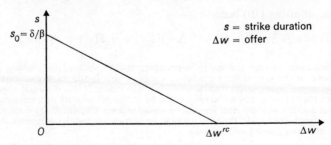

corresponding $s(\Delta w)$ function defined in (12) above, have to be interpreted as the *expected* strike length thought to be required for the acceptance of the offer.

The $s(\Delta w)$ function depends on both financial and psychological factors. First there is the financial ability of the union and its members to sustain a strike, which depends on the size of reserves, savings and borrowing power in relation to the cost per period of the strike. Second there is the intensity of the union's strength of will or determination to carry out the strike, and there is a presumption that this will be related to the extent to which their expectations have been disappointed or their sense of 'justice' outraged. For any individual worker these two factors would determine his 'acceptance' wage at a given moment of time, that is, the minimum wage at which he would currently be prepared to return to work. As time passes his acceptance wage would be expected to decline because of the run down of his savings, increasing difficulties with contractual payments and possibly diminishing will to carry on the strike. Since workers have different savings, different financial obligations, different degrees of militancy or dissatisfaction and so forth, one can then postulate that there exists a distribution of acceptance wages over the members of a union at a particular time and, moreover, that the distribution will shift to the left as time passes. If a proposed settlement is put to the ballot it will secure a majority if the offer exceeds the median of the distribution of acceptance wages. Since this distribution shifts leftwards with time the median acceptance wage must eventually fall below any given offer and the smaller the offer the greater is the length of strike required to secure union acquiescence. Thus the $s(\Delta w)$ function is downward sloping, which agrees with Hicks' 'resistance curve'.[6] The break-even function for labour shown in (6) above also lies in the s, Δw plane and has a positive slope, which corresponds to Shackle's 'inducement curve'.[7] Shackle's criticisms of the negative slope of Hicks' curve would seem misplaced. The truth would appear to be that both curves are valid and correct. They measure different things and both have a place in a complete theory as we shall see below.

In view of (12) the expected cost, $E(C)$, is a function of both Δw_1 and Δw_2. Thus in deriving the optimal Δw_1^* the possible post-strike

---

[6] See J. R. Hicks [4].
[7] See G. L. S. Shackle [7], p. 302, and also pp. 299–305 for his comments on the Hicks construction.

offer must be considered as well. The solution is to consider the second-stage first of all and to derive the Δw_2^* and the associated s_2^* which constitute an expected minimum-cost settlement to the strike. Then letting

$$\alpha_4 = \alpha_1 s_2^* + \alpha_2 F(s_2^*) + \alpha_3 \Delta w_2^* \qquad (13)$$

it is seen that α_4 is some given constant, which on substitution in (11) gives

$$E(C) = \alpha_3 \beta (\Delta w_1)^2 + \alpha_4 (1 - \beta . \Delta w_1) \qquad (14)$$

which can now be minimised with respect to Δw_1, thus yielding the optimal pre-strike offer.

Once a strike has actually begun the costs to the employer will be $L_1 + L_2$ where

$$L_1 = \alpha_1 s + \alpha_2 F(s) \quad \text{and} \quad L_2 = \alpha_3 . \Delta w_2$$

The cost-minimising strike length can then be determined from

$$\frac{dL_1}{ds} = -\frac{dL_2}{ds}$$

Assuming that the supplementary function can be represented by $F(s) = bs^2$, so that supplementary costs increase ever more rapidly with the duration of the strike, this last condition gives

$$s_2^* = \frac{\alpha_3 - \alpha_1 \delta}{2\alpha_2 b \delta} \qquad (15)$$

The corresponding cost-minimising wage increase can then be determined from relation (12) as

$$\Delta w_2^* = \frac{1}{\beta} - \frac{s_2^*}{\delta}$$

$$= \Delta w^{rc} - \frac{\alpha_3 - \alpha_1 \delta}{2\alpha_2 b \delta_2} \qquad (16)$$

The significance of these results can be illustrated with reference to Figure 4.

The L_1 curve shows the cost of the strike to the employer. The L_2 line shows the cost of various possible settlements at various lengths

Figure 4 Factors influencing the cost-minimising strike length

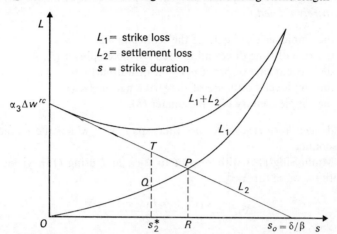

of strike and is simply proportional to the union resistance curve. The 'optimal' strike length s_2^* occurs where the slope of the L_1 function is numerically equal to that of the L_2 function, that is, where the marginal strike cost is just offset by the marginal reduction in the settlement cost. If both L_1 and L_2 were linear, the optimal strike length would be either zero or the maximum possible, $s_0 = \delta/\beta$, that is, the optimal strike-settling offer would be either the real claim, Δw^{rc}, or else zero, depending on whether the slope of the L_2 line was numerically smaller or greater than that of the L_1 line. With L_2 linear and L_1 convex from below it is still theoretically possible that the minimum value of $L_1 + L_2$ occurs at one of the boundary points. It is probable, however, that the minimum occurs at an interior point so that we would expect

$$s_2^* < \delta/\beta$$

and

$$\Delta w_2^* < \Delta w^{rc}$$

Rewriting (16) in terms of the original parameters gives

$$\Delta w_2^* = \Delta w^{rc} - \frac{V_n(i) - w\delta/(\epsilon - 1)}{2b\delta^2} \tag{17}$$

This gives the following qualitative conditions on the optimal strike-settling offer. The optimal Δw_2^* in response to a claim Δw^c will be *positively related to*

the employer's estimate of the real claim (Δw^{rc}),
the rate of time discounting used by the employer (i),
the current rate of profit per unit of output ($w/(\epsilon - 1)$),
the employer's estimate of the strike parameter (δ),
the supplementary cost parameter (b),

and *negatively related* to the time span over which the employer discounts.

Minimising (14) with respect to Δw_1, and using (13), yields the optimal value for Δw_1 as

$$\Delta w_1^* = \frac{\alpha_1 s_2^* + \alpha_2 F(s_2^*) + \alpha_3 \Delta w_2^*}{2\alpha_3}$$

$$= \tfrac{1}{2}\Delta w_2^*\left(\frac{L_1^*}{L_2^*} + 1\right) \tag{18}$$

where L_1^* and L_2^* are shown by the points Q and T in Figure 4 and are the strike costs and settlement costs corresponding to the optimal s_2^*, Δw_2^* values derived above. If the optimal strike length, s_2^*, had turned out to be equal to the distance OR in Figure 4 then $L_1^* = L_2^* = PR$ and from (18) $\Delta w_1^* = \Delta w_2^*$. This clearly is a special case. When L_1^* and L_2^* are equal we have a point on Hieser's 'break-even' function for the employer and then the optimal strike-settling offer, Δw_2^*, would turn out to be identical with the optimal final pre-strike offer, Δw_1^*. For the case illustrated in Figure 4, L_1^* is less than L_2^* and the optimal pre-strike offer will be less than the optimal strike-settling offer. This will be true for all s_2^* which lie to the left of the point R in Figure 4, while for points to the right of R the optimal strike-settling offer would be less than the optimal pre-strike offer.

Finally we note, in view of (18), that the same qualitative conclusions can be drawn about Δw_1^* as were listed above for Δw_2^*. These qualitative conclusions will also not be upset by the removal of the linearity assumptions that were made for the $\pi(\Delta w)$ and $s(\Delta w)$ functions. The essential requirement is that these functions should decrease monotonically.

We will now attempt a brief sketch of how the bargaining sequence between the union and employer might proceed, and, in the process, say something about the strategy that might influence union decisions.

(i) The union formulates a claim Δw^c. The actual size of the claim is not a very important factor in our analysis because the employer will almost certainly 'discount' it to arrive at an assessment of the 'real claim', Δw^{rc}, which is his estimate of the wage offer needed to reduce the strike probability to negligible proportions. Marginal increments to the claim may have zero effect on Δw^{rc} and thus on the employer's response. The union must thus attempt to fix the claim at a level which will push Δw^{rc} as high as possible. The employer's estimate of Δw^{rc} is likely to be especially influenced by evidence of union militancy and by the level of other settlements. The union is assumed to employ economists who are as skilful as those on the other side. Thus they conjecture that the employer will use some cost-minimising strategy on the lines sketched above. In particular they realise that, in addition to Δw^{rc}, the employer's response depends vitally upon his assessment of the shape of the strike probability, $\pi(\Delta w)$, and strike duration, $s(\Delta w)$, functions. Thus it is again in the union's interest that current and recent indications of militancy, strength and solidarity should be as convincing as possible. In a partial equilibrium analysis, such as that of Hieser, the more success the union enjoys in pushing up the wage rate the greater is the reduction in the level of employment of the union's members, since the demand function for the product is assumed unchanged. In a more realistic macro context, however, a union will observe other unions currently making and settling claims, so that it will reasonably expect a general expansion of monetary demand to offset, at least partially, any adverse effects of the success of its own wage claims on the employment of its members. In so far as the level of employment enters the union utility function, it must exercise a moderating influence on their push for higher wage rates.

(ii) Faced with the claim, the employer applies as best he can the cost-minimising calculus outlined above. The result is an estimated optimal value, Δw_1^*, which is the *upper* limit to his negotiating range. It is difficult to say anything very precise about the *lower* limit to that range, Δw_0, which constitutes the employer's initial offer to the union. If it is set too low skilful union negotiators will quickly push the employer upwards; if it is set too high there is very little room left for negotiation before the employer is up against his sticking point at Δw_1^* and a deadlock is imminent. The implication of the negotiating range is that a serious strike threat at a level short of Δw_1^* can force the employer to revise his offer upwards closer to Δw_1^*. It is also possible that during the course of the negotiations the employer revises his estimates of the $\pi(\Delta w)$ and $s(\Delta w)$ functions on the basis of his latest assessment of union attitudes. Thus he may revise his estimate of Δw_1^* before the negotiations have reached agreement or broken down. This is a possible additional source of revised offers but in practice it would be impossible to distinguish between revisions due to recalculations and revisions which were part of the initial negotiating plan.

(iii) If the union has pushed the employer to his sticking point it should only go on strike if the *expected net gain* from the strike is at least as great as the certain gain which is currently available to them without a strike. These factors may be elucidated by reference to Figure 5. Substitution of the pre-strike offer, Δw_1^*, in equation (4) gives the gain currently available to the union, denoted by G_1^*. The union is assumed to have conjectured the nature, but not necessarily the actual results, of the employer's decision-making process. Thus it expects a revised offer of about Δw^e after a strike length of about s^e. Let this expectation be pictured by the E space in Figure 5, where there is a non-zero subjective probability attached by the union to each point in the E space. For each point in that space there is a gain to the union depending on the size of the wage increase. There is also a cost depending on the length of strike and this relationship is shown by the L curve of equation (3). The difference gives the net gain for each point. Applying the associated probabilities the expected net gain implied by the E region can be estimated.

Figure 5   Factors influencing the union decision to strike

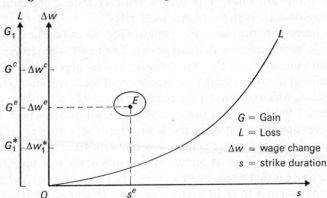

(iv) Once the strike is under way the employer updates all his assessments of the relative parameters and estimates the s_2^*, Δw_2^* combination, which he thinks is the cost-minimising strike settlement. In so far as he has changed his assessments of the various parameters, the new estimates of s_2^* and Δw_2^* will differ from those that he had employed in (ii) above in working out his negotiating range. Thus at some time close to s_2^* the employer should reopen negotiations at a level a little below Δw_2^*. The time and level at which he re-opens negotiations can be represented by a point in Figure 5 and as negotiations proceed this point would trace out an arrow in Figure 5 rather like a blip on a radar screen. The arrow will be horizontal if the employer does not raise his offer during the new negotiations and, more generally, will point in the NE direction as he moves up his new negotiating range.

(v) If the arrow falls in the E space the union has correctly estimated the employer's response and the chances of agreement will be high. However, the E space is that estimated by the union at the beginning of the strike, and they may have acquired additional information during the course of the strike which leads them to revise their estimate of the position of the E space.

(vi) If the arrow depicting the revised negotiations appears to the left of the E space then a lot depends on whether it lies above or below Δw^e. In the former case union expectations turn out to be incorrect in the nicest possible way, namely, more money than they expected sooner than they expected. Thus agreement is very likely. In the latter case there is a benefit and a loss, namely, an earlier offer but a smaller offer. Everything then depends on how the second round of negotiations affects the union's expectations. There is some net gain, positive or negative, associated with the revised offer and the union will now have to decide whether to settle for this or continue the strike in the expectation of an incremental net gain.

(vii) If the employer's revised offer has not appeared by s^e the union knows that its expectations have been incorrect. It must seek additional information in order to up-date its expectations and may well approach the employer to re-open negotiations. As before, a settlement will occur when an employer arrow appears either inside the current union E space or outside and to the left of the E space, and the union revision of its expectations about the E space does not lead them to expect a positive net gain from a further extension of the strike. The settlement point would also have to lie on or above the $s(\Delta w)$ curve; otherwise the terms of the settlement would be unlikely to command majority support from the union members.

The model of this section differs in a number of crucial respects from conventional bargaining and strike models such as those surveyed in Coddington [2] and presented in particular by Ashenfelter and Johnson [1] and Cross [3]. The Ashenfelter and Johnson model assumes that a strike is inevitable if the employer does not concede the full claim, so there is no role in their model for our $\pi(\Delta w)$ function nor any explicit role for negotiation to secure acceptance of an offer less than the claim. Moreover there is no treatment of, nor indeed on their assumptions, any reason for revised offers in their model. More conventional bargaining models of the Cross–Coddington type generally give a symmetrical role to the two parties to the bargain; they also assume the existence of a concession rate for each party and generally postulate some mechanism for the adjustment of each party's expectations as he finds discrepancies between the observed and expected concession rates. The concession rate assumption in a wage bargaining context implies that the union merely has to let time pass to secure ever higher offers from the employer. This seems unrealistic and carries the implication that post-strike settlements are always greater than the first stage offer, which is demonstrably untrue in practice. Our analysis assumes that at each stage the employer makes the best (that is, cost-minimising) offer. The result is a pre-strike negotiating range, which may be modified as new information is obtained, and likewise a post-strike negotiating range which may also be modified. The reasoning behind the $s(\Delta w)$ function does, however, imply the existence of a concession (or resistance) function for the members of the union, so in this sense there is an asymmetry in our model between the two sides. Both sides are assumed to be 'maximisers': the employer is minimising costs and the differential calculus applies for he can consider offers anywhere in a postulated range of values: the union, however, has a *discrete* problem in that it has to compare the gain currently available with the expected gain thought to be attainable in the future. We have felt it implausible to make any mechanistic assumptions about how the expectations of either party are revised. Rather we have put the emphasis on delineating those parameters, estimates of which are essential for optimal decision-making at each stage. Finally, our analysis makes a sharp distinction between the pre- and post-strike stages, for the probability and cost considerations are radically different at each stage; many bargaining models do not make this crucial distinction.

III Conclusions

The two contributions of the Hieser analysis are the explicit derivation of the upper limit for the wage share and the elucidation of the various costs and benefits to employer and union. The outcome of the bargaining process in his analysis, however, remains obscure. By the use of probabilistic considerations and the development of an expected cost function for the employer it is shown that there is, in general, a unique cost-minimising pre-strike final offer and, if this fails, a unique cost-minimising strike settlement offer. The levels of these offers and the connection between them are seen to depend on a few basic parameters of the relevant cost and probability functions.

It might be thought that an implication of the above analysis is that at each negotiation the union should extract as much as possible from the employer without ever putting a strike threat into effect. Thus the union should make claims, get some fraction of the claim each time and proceed towards its ultimate goal without incurring the losses and hardships of strikes. This, however, is a false conclusion. The employer's estimates of the $\pi(\Delta w)$ and $s(\Delta w)$ functions will not remain unchanged over time. They are affected by all his experience and knowledge, including that gained from past negotiations and strikes as well as from the current situation. Downward revisions by the employer of his estimate of the union's strike parameter, δ, automatically reduce his optimal offer and could, in fact, reduce it to zero. The actual occurrence of strikes is thus an essential condition for the continuing rise of the money wage bill in this model. As time passes and the power of the union to sustain a strike is built up again one would expect subsequent claims, which in turn would be partially successful, and the union would over time approach the maximum possible share for wage income.

The assumptions of the Hieser problem are essentially static—no change in technology, no change in the monopolist's demand function and no general inflation or deflation. In a general inflation a proportionate marking up of all prices and wage rates will keep real wage rates approximately constant. Any bargaining for money increases beyond that level will put us back in the framework of the Hieser problem and will be influenced by the specific factors already analysed and specified in equations (17) and (18), namely, the time span over which the employer discounts, the rate of discounting he uses, the rate of profit per unit of output, the union strike parameter and the employer's supplementary cost parameter. Variations in general economic conditions as reflected, say, in the general un-employment rate, might be expected to have some marginal influence on these specific variables, but it is only through such mediation that they will affect the settlements reached. Thus, in sectors of the economy where the institutional arrangements correspond approxi-mately to the Hieser assumptions, rational economic calculation on the part of the employers can lead to wage increases in response to union demands even though there has been no change, or even an adverse change, in the level of excess demand that a conventional Phillips curve analysis regards as an essential pre-requisite for a wage increase. Thus the analysis of this paper has theoretical implications for wage settlements which are different from those of the con-ventional Phillips curve analysis. The empirical testing of these theoretical implications would depend on finding direct measures or proxies for the set of explanatory variables listed above. If that could be done a comparison could then be made between the explanatory power of this type of theory and that of a conventional Phillips curve analysis.

References

[1] Ashenfelter, O. and Johnson, G., 'Bargaining Theory, Trade Unions and Industrial Strike Activity', *American Economic Review* (March 1969), pp. 35–49.
[2] Coddington, A., *Theories of the Bargaining Process*, London, Allen and Unwin (1968).
[3] Cross, J. G., 'A Theory of the Bargaining Process', *American Economic Review* (March 1965), pp. 67–94.
[4] Hicks, J. R., *The Theory of Wages*, London, Macmillan, second edition (1963).
[5] Hieser, R. O., 'Wage Determination with Bilateral Monopoly in the Labour Market: A Theoretical Treatment', *Economic Record* (March 1970), pp. 55–72.
[6] Johnston, J., 'Wage Determination with Bilateral Monopoly in the Labour Market', Chapter 5 in *Uses of Economics*, ed. G. D. N. Worswick, Oxford, Blackwell (1971).
[7] Shackle, G. L. S., 'The Nature of the Bargaining Process', Chapter 19 in *The Theory of Wage Determination*, ed. J. Dunlop, London, Macmillan (1964).

J. Johnston
and M. Timbrell

Chapter 4 Empirical tests of a bargaining theory of wage rate determination[1]

Introduction

Ever since the publication of the celebrated article by Phillips [6], empirical studies of wage rate determination have relied heavily upon the unemployment rate (u), the vacancy rate (v), or some combination of the two as an explanatory variable. The rationalisation for this approach was provided by Lipsey [5] in terms of a competitive theory of price formation applied to labour markets in which the variable ($v - u$) proxies the level of excess demand. In given institutional arrangements, as indicated by Hansen [2], the vacancy rate is likely to be related to the unemployment rate, and so ($v - u$) reduces to a function of u only, thus justifying the use of u for countries or periods with no satisfactory vacancy statistics. The economic experience of the United Kingdom in recent years suggests two main conclusions, firstly that the relationship existing between the vacancy and un- employment rates has changed substantially since 1967, and secondly that conventional Phillips curves have failed to explain the wage inflation of the past few years, in which very substantial wage increases have been associated with ever *higher* levels of unemploy- ment. This positive association between wage change and unemploy- ment level does not necessarily refute the Phillips curve, which postulates a negative relation. It could be that the effect of expected inflation on wage determination has more than offset the negative influence of rising unemployment levels, and that previous studies have failed to capture the inflation effect adequately. Taylor [8] has also argued that registered unemployment is an inadequate proxy for

[1] The research underlying this paper was financed by the S.S.R.C. Inflation Project at the University of Manchester. We are indebted to David Laidler and David Purdy for helpful comments on an earlier draft. This chapter is an expanded version of an article published in The Manchester School of Economic and Social Studies in June 1973. We are indebted to the Editor for permission to reprint.

excess demand and that when it is supplemented by an estimate of labour hoarding the Phillips curve is rehabilitated.

A second difficulty with previous studies is the confusion about the variable to be explained. Some concentrate on *rates*, others on *earnings*, and there is little discussion of which should be used or whether the same set of explanatory variables should be employed irrespective of the choice of dependent variable. It would seem that there is a hierarchy of *three* variables: at the bottom is *rates*, which are usually *nationally agreed minimum* levels typically resulting from a bargaining process between unions and employers; next comes *earnings net of overtime*, a variable given special emphasis by Taylor [8]. National minimum rates provide a skeleton which is usually filled out by local bargaining and competition between firms and industries within various regions, giving wages for a normal working week which can exceed the national minima by various margins. Finally there is *earnings inclusive of overtime*. All three variables may further be defined in weekly or hourly terms.

It would seem that different variables may play a crucial explanatory role at various levels of this wage hierarchy. Support for this view is found in Taylor [8] where his amended unemployment variable fails, as does registered unemployment, in explaining movements in *weekly wage rates*, but performs significantly better than registered unemployment in explaining movements in *hourly earnings net of overtime* (Taylor [8], Tables 1–4). This is to be expected in view of the fact that 'labour hoarding appears on the shop floor, within the factory, and will therefore have a direct personal impact on the wage bargaining mechanism, unlike the registered and hidden unemployed' (Taylor [8], p. 4). The focus of this paper is on the first level of the wage heirarchy. The dependent variable is taken as the percentage change in the weekly wage rate for all manual workers in all industries and services, and an attempt is made to see what explanation of this variable is provided by concepts derived from a bargaining theory of wage determination.

A bargaining theory

Johnston [4] studies wage rate determination under bilateral monopoly. The union makes a claim for a wage increase of amount Δw^c. The employer's response is assumed to be determined by the principle of minimising his *expected* costs. This involves the employer in estimating the likelihood of a strike for any given wage offer on his part in response to the claim, and also in estimating the probable length of strike should one occur. A crucial element in the outcome is the employer's assessment of the 'real claim', Δw^{rc}. This is defined to be the size of offer for which the strike probability is effectively zero. The main conclusions of the theoretical analysis are that the size of the wage settlement, Δw^*, will be *positively related* to:

the employer's estimate of the real claim (Δw^{rc});
the rate of time discounting used by the employer (i);
the current rate of profit per unit of output or per man ($w/(\epsilon - 1)$), where w is the current wage rate and ϵ the elasticity of demand for the product;
the employer's estimate of the strike parameter (δ);
the supplementary cost parameter (b);

and *negatively related* to the time span over which the employer discounts. The strike parameter, δ, expresses the union's propensity to endure a strike, for in the model it determines the maximum length of strike given the real claim and a zero offer from the employer, and also indicates the reduction in length of strike associated with a unit increase in the wage offer. The supplementary cost parameter indicates subjective costs imposed by the strike on the employer. These are in addition to the direct costs such as lost profits, and include such things as possible loss of goodwill and future sales, liquidity problems, etc. These supplementary costs are assumed to rise quadratically with strike length and b indicates the degree of curvature of the supplementary cost function. The theoretical analysis relates to a simple bilateral monopoly case, where the employer faces a static demand curve for his product and there is no general inflation or deflation. The statistical implementation of the theory at the level of all manufacturing involves the usual aggregation problems. We have no special solution to propose for these. The use of a simple macroequation implicitly assumes that the major bargaining groups in the economy are influenced by the factors outlined above and that the relative importance of the groups in determining the movement of the wage index over the sample period has not changed substantially. The existence of a general inflation will have an important effect in determining the estimate of the real claim, Δw^{rc}, and we will discuss that point in detail below.

The first explanatory variable to be discussed, however, does not appear in the list given above. It is the proportion of workers covered

82   J. Johnston and M. Timbrell

by the index actually receiving an increase in a unit time period, denoted by n/N where n is the number receiving an increase and N the total number covered by the index. Inspection of the statistics shows that this proportion varies substantially from month to month, quarter to quarter, and even from year to year. Our analysis is based on yearly data and so we must decide how this variable should be treated. On an annual basis, and *a fortiori* on any shorter basis, this statistic is always less than unity, so that even if some groups of workers achieve more than one increase in a year a greater number do not manage an increase in rates every year. Since bargaining theory is concerned with the factors determining the level at which a claim is settled, and since the current level of settlements is a matter of public concern this is the variable that we wish to explain. It is not, however, given by a conventional wage rate index. For example, if half the labour force receives a 10 per cent increase in the current year and the other half nothing because they had no current claim, then the wage index rises by 5 per cent, although the current rate of settlement is 10 per cent. It would seem that all one needs to do is to

Table 1   The corrected wage index with a settlement rate of 3 per cent per annum

Year	Percentage increase for groups				Wage index (w)	$\frac{n}{N} \times 100$	Corrected index $= w \times \frac{N}{n}$
	I	II	III	IV			
(1)	(2)	(3)	(4)	(5)	(6)	(7)	(8)
1	3	0	0	0	0·75	25	3·0
2	3	6	0	0	2·25	50	4·5
3	3	0	9	0	3·00	50	6·0
4	3	6	0	12	5·25	75	7·0
5	3	0	0	0	0·75	25	3·0
6	3	6	9	0	4·50	75	6·0
7	3	0	0	0	0·75	25	3·0
8	3	6	0	12	5·25	75	7·0
9	3	0	9	0	3·00	50	6·0
10	3	6	0	0	2·25	50	4·5
11	3	0	0	0	0·75	25	3·0
12	3	6	9	12	7·50	100	7·5

'correct' the index by multiplying by the reciprocal of the proportion receiving an increase, but this is incorrect, as the following example shows.

Suppose there are four equal-sized groups in the labour force and under existing institutional arrangements one group has a wage rate adjustment every year, one every two years, another every three and the last group every four years. Suppose, further, that the underlying rate of settlement is 3 per cent per annum. Then to the nearest whole number the percentage increases *since the last settlement* will be 3, 6, 9 and 12 for the four groups. Table 1 shows a possible disposition of the settlements over time and the effect of correcting the wage index in the manner suggested above. By assumption the wage mechanism underlying Table 1 is producing a *steady* increase of 3 per cent per annum for all groups. Yet the wage index, recorded in column (6) shows substantial variation around this figure, from a low of 0.75 per cent to a high of 7·5 per cent. Its average value of the 12 years is, of course, 3 per cent but this value is actually shown by the index in only 2 of those 12 years. The corrected index is, in fact, worse. It does record 3 per cent in 4 years out of 12, but in all other years it *overstates* the underlying settlement rate. However, if we regress w on (n/N) the result is

$$\hat{w} = -1.58 + 8.8\left(\frac{n}{N}\right) \quad \text{with } R^2 = 0.98$$

and if we substitute the average value of (n/N), namely 25/48, in this regression the result is a regression value of 3 per cent. To summarise, even in the hypothetical case of a constant settlement rate both a conventional and a corrected wage index will show substantial variations due to the presence of systematic and/or random variations in the proportion (n/N) receiving settlements in any year. One way to deal with this 'noise' is to introduce (n/N) as an explanatory variable in a regression where the uncorrected wage index is the dependent variable. (n/N) is not a perfect regressor, since it deals only with the sizes of the various groups and ignores the length of time since each group last had an increase. For instance in years 2 and 3 in Table 1, n/N has the same value (0·5) and the wage index has two different values, so n/N will explain most, but not all, of the institutional variation.

It is possible that accelerating price inflation will put pressure on institutional arrangements, causing a reduction in the average interval between wage settlements and thus a rise in the average values of n/N. If true, this does not mean that n/N should not be used as an explanatory variable in the wage rate equation, but rather that a second equation should be added to the model in which an attempt is made to explain movements in n/N in terms of changes in the rate of inflation. The nature of the variation in n/N is discussed later in the paper.

Among the bargaining variables we expect the employer's estimate of the real claim, Δw^{rc}, to play a crucial role. Our basic hypothesis about the unions is that they are essentially concerned with the growth of net real earnings. Like other sections of society they are growth conscious and conditioned to expect rising real standards. In an age of inflation they clearly understand the distinction between money and real income, and in an era of substantial movements in Government fiscal policy it would be unrealistic to expect them to be insensitive to changes in certain major taxes. We have not felt it plausible or realistic to postulate any specific collective utility function to be maximised by the unions. All we assert is that adverse movements in taxes and/or prices will lead to wage demands pitched at a higher level and pursued with greater force and vigour than would otherwise have been the case.

As an illustration of the range of movement in certain taxes we have calculated the annual position of a hypothetical male worker from October 1949 to October 1971. He is postulated to receive a wage equal to the average earnings of all industrial adult male workers and to be married with two children, one under the age of eleven and one between eleven and sixteen. All compulsory deductions, such as income tax, national insurance and graduated pension contributions and all tax allowances for wife and family were calculated for each year and a retention ratio calculated, which is net weekly earnings expressed as a percentage of gross weekly earnings. Gross weekly pay rose from £7·13 in 1949 to £30·93 in 1971 and net pay from £6·89 to £25·70. The retention ratio, which was 96·6 per cent in 1949, had fallen to 83·1 per cent in 1971. Year to year movements in the retention ratio are shown in Table 2.

The very substantial reduction in the retention ratio over the period did not take place at an even rate. Throughout most of the fifties the ratio was roughly constant at 96 per cent. Even by 1964 it was still over 91 per cent. The next six years, however, saw a decline of nine percentage points in the ratio. Put another way, the percentage of the

Table 2   Ratio of net to gross pay (λ) for an 'average' worker, 1949–71

1949	1950	1951	1952	1953	1954	1955	1956
96·6	96·3	96·4	96·8	96·9	96·4	96·8	96·4

1957	1958	1959	1960	1961	1962	1963	1964
96·3	95·2	94·9	94·1	92·2	91·9	92·7	91·4

1965	1966	1967	1968	1969	1970	1971	
89·7	89·0	88·4	86·5	85·1	82·4	83·1	

average wage taken in compulsory deductions quintupled over the whole period and doubled between 1964 and 1971.

This is only the picture for a hypothetical average worker. For lower paid workers the variations could be even greater as they move in and out of tax, depending on the balance of wage increases and changes in allowances and tax rates.

Detailed calculations of tax and price effects for workers at various positions on the income scale are given in Jackson et al. [3], which appeared when this study was substantially completed. For example they estimate the rate of growth of net real earnings at different levels of manual worker earnings, for married men with two children under eleven years of age, as shown in Table 3. Since a single price index has been used as the deflator for all groups these rates of change show the relative effects of taxes, insurance contributions and other deductions. The lowest decile showed the largest rate of increase, but all the other rates lie within the interval of approximately 1·1 per cent to 1·5 per cent per annum. Further calculations by Jackson and

Table 3   Rates of growth of net real earnings at different levels of manual worker earnings (married men with two children under 11 years old)*

Compound increase %	Lowest decile	Lower quartile	Median	Upper quartile	Highest decile
1960–1970	2·04	1·51	1·23	1·09	1·17

* Reproduced from Jackson et al [3] Table 7 page 78. With permission.

his colleagues show very small variations in the rate of growth of real net income (at the average income level) for various family sizes.

Ignoring these variations about the average level, the question remains whether the facts described in Table 2 would be expected to have an impact on the size of a union claim and an employer's reaction to that claim. Suppose, for example, that we had a year in which there was no change in the price level and no change in wages but an increase in direct taxation on workers' income. If the workers were indifferent between the Government spending a pound 'on their behalf' and having it in their wage packet to spend as they please, they would not feel worse off as a consequence of the taxation increase and would not therefore be pressing for any consequential wage increase. If, however, a pound of personal expenditure, or savings, gives greater satisfaction than a pound in taxation, the reduction in take-home pay would be expected to trigger off a wage claim in order to make up the loss of utility.

For any given system of deductions, allowances and tax rates, it is in principle possible for any worker to calculate his current average and marginal retention ratios and to estimate the change in gross pay that he would need in order to achieve any target increase in net pay. Under a tax system where different bands of income are taxed at ever higher rates, average and marginal retention ratios both decline as income rises. *Thus the higher the level of income the greater is the percentage rise in gross pay required to achieve any given percentage in net pay.* Apart from surtax, the British system had tax bands at the lower end of the taxable income scale until 1970/71, when the standard rate was applied to any taxable income. However, even if individual workers were sufficiently knowledgeable and concerned to carry out this type of calculation in advance of the formulation and pursuit of a new wage claim, the implications for the union negotiators cannot be very precise because of the spread of earnings and retention ratios among their members. There is, in addition, the very formidable problem of *forecasting* the system of taxes, deductions and allowances that will be in force when the new pay rates come into effect. Appendix A in Jackson *et al* [3] lists the changes in income tax rates and allowances and also in national insurance contributions over the last two decades. In the great majority of years there was a change of some kind, sometimes major, sometimes minor. There were, for example, twelve increases of various kinds in the system of

National Insurance contributions between 1960 and 1972, and in the field of income tax the first two reduced rates were increased substantially in 1963/4 and the third reduced rate abolished, the standard rate was increased in 1965/6, the first reduced rate again increased in 1969/70 with the second reduced rate abolished and finally the sole surviving reduced rate eliminated in 1970/1. The forecasting difficulties are further exacerbated by the often lengthy time between the formulation of a wage claim and the resultant settlement coming into effect.

We have thus assumed that unions are unlikely to be able to forecast future changes in the retention ratio at all precisely. The best they can do, therefore, is to react to changes in the recent past and attempt to compensate for unfavourable movements in the retention ratio. We have thus defined the following explanatory variable for use in the wage equation, namely,

$$\dot{\lambda}_t^c = \frac{1}{3} \sum_{j=1}^{3} \dot{\lambda}_{t-j}$$

where $\dot{\lambda}_t = (\lambda_t - \lambda_{t-1})/\lambda_{t-1}$

Since λ_t denotes the retention ratio in year t, $\dot{\lambda}_t$ measures the percentage change in the retention ratio from year $t - 1$ to year t. $\dot{\lambda}_t^c$ thus denotes the average percentage change over the three years prior to t. There is no compelling reason for the choice of three years as the base of this average. It postulates essentially that unions react with a lag to fairly short-term trends in the retention ratio. We expect that adverse movements in this variable will increase the size of union claims and the strength and vigour with which they are pursued, and that these two factors will in turn influence the employer's estimate of Δw^{rc} and the strike parameter δ.

An alternative variable, that we have employed in our regressions, which focuses more directly on the growth of net real income, is a 'catch-up' variable. The net wage defined above is deflated by the retail price index to give a series for the net real wage. The extent to which annual percentage changes in this variable fall short of some postulated constant such as 2 or 3 per cent is the basis of a catch-up variable. Several variants have been tried, namely,

$$C_{1t} = - \sum_{j=1}^{3} (X_{t-j} - 2\%)$$

where X_{t-j} = percentage change in net real wage from year $t - j - 1$ to year $t - j$,

C_{2t} is defined in the same way as C_{1t} except that any positive values of $(X_{t-j} - 2\%)$ are omitted from the summation.

C_{3t} is again similar to C_{1t} but positive deviations are given only half the weight of negative deviations.

Thus C_{1t} is a perfectly symmetrical catch-up variable in that an increase in net real wages above the target level in any year can offset *pari passu* any shortfall in other years. C_{2t} is asymmetrical and assumes that any improvement above the target level is treated by the unions as a windfall gain and does not moderate their drive to make good deficiencies in other years, while C_{3t} is a compromise between the other two measures. The 2 per cent target is again an arbitrary figure so alternative measures have been derived by recalculating C_2 and C_3 on a 3 per cent target and labelling them C_4 and C_5 respectively. Recalculating C_1 on a 3 per cent basis will have no effect on the coefficient attaching to C_1 in a regression equation, but only on the intercept term.

Figure 1 shows the movements in net real wage for an average man and the consequent values of the various catch-up variables. The two outstanding features of section (a) of Figure 1 are the very large swings from year to year and the generally lower figures recorded in the middle and late sixties. Negative changes occurred in 1951, 1958, 1961, 1966 and 1968, but, while these were offset by large gains in several years in the fifties and early sixties, since 1964 only one year has shown a gain of more than 2 per cent. From the definition of the catch-up variables values *above* the horizontal axis in (b) indicate a *cumulative deficiency* below a 2 per cent growth rate. As section (b) of the figure shows all three curves are solidly above the horizontal axis since 1966. If the symmetrical catch-up variable, C_1 were defined in relation to a 3 per cent growth rate the horizontal axis would be shifted down to minus 3 per cent on the vertical scale and we would then see that the curve was solidly above the horizontal axis since 1962. Figure 1 thus tells a similar story to the retention rates in Table 2.

The theoretical bargaining model contained no general inflationary component, but it is clear that expectations about the general rate of inflation must have an impact on the employer's estimate of the real claim, Δw^{rc}, and possibly also on the strike parameter, δ. If unions

Figure 1   Performance of a hypothetical average worker: (a) Per cent change in net real wages; and (b) Catch-up variables on an assumed two per cent target

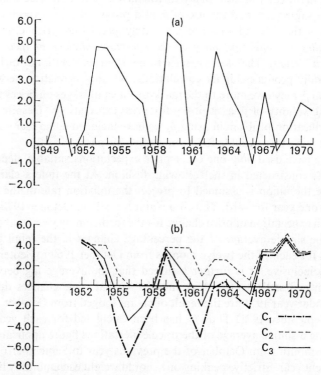

are concerned with the real wage rate, then the higher they expect the rate of inflation to be the greater will be their wage claims and the vigour with which they are pursued, thus leading a rational employer to increase his estimates of Δw^{rc} and δ.

The crucial questions then concern the form of the price expectations variable and nature of its relationship to Δw^{rc} and δ. Many empirical studies have simply used $\dot{p}_t$, the actual current percentage change, as the price expectations variable. This implicitly assumes that *many months earlier* when the wage claims were formulated and the bargaining took place, which resulted in the current wage change $\dot{w}_t$, *the unions were forecasting price changes with an average error of zero*. Whatever strength this assumption may have, the use of $\dot{p}$

becomes progressively more invalid the longer the unit time period of the analysis. For example, some of the wage changes that take place in the early months of a year will have an effect on price changes in the same year, and the use of $\dot{p}_t$ as a proxy for price expectations implies that the unions are accurately predicting price changes, *including the effect on them of the uncertain outcome of their own current actions.* The use of $\dot{p}_t$ rather than some expectational variable generally produces higher correlations, but the correlation between $\dot{w}_t$ and $\dot{p}_t$ may owe more to the mark-up effect of wages on prices than to the validity of $\dot{p}_t$ as a proxy for price expectations. Despite this identification problem in using $\dot{p}_t$ we have included some regressions employing this variable for comparative purposes.

We have used only one other price expectations variable, denoted by $\dot{p}_t^e$, constructed in the following fashion. At the time a claim is made the union is assumed to project the inflation rate of the past year one year forward. Thus if a claim is made in October 1970, the union expectation of price change for the forthcoming year is taken to be the simple average of the percentage changes in the retail price level for each of the twelve months from October 1969 to September 1970 inclusive. It is further assumed that the average lag between claim and settlement is three months so that wage changes during calendar year 1971 are the result of claims lodged from October 1970 to September 1971. Thus $\dot{p}_t^e$ has been calculated for each year by taking a simple average of the price expectations figure applicable to each month from October of the previous year to September of the current year. Strictly speaking one should weight each monthly figure by the number of workers affected by the claims lodged in that month, but these data are not readily available and in view of the admitted crudity of our expectations assumption it did not seem worthwhile to attempt this modification.

Since the role of $\dot{p}^e$ in a bargaining model is as a crucial determinant of the size of the 'real claim' and the vigour with which it is prosecuted, it is not clear that it must enter the wage equation in a simple linear fashion. Certainly a plot of *nominal* wage claims against price changes for recent years would give a highly nonlinear relationship, and while some discounting will inevitably be applied to nominal claims it would not be implausible to expect the prices determinant of the real claim to be an increasing non-linear function of recent rates of price change. Thus in some regressions we have replaced $\dot{p}^e$ by $(\dot{p}^e)^2$ to allow for this possibility.

The basic wage equation which we are attempting to fit to the data is of the form

$$\dot{w} = f\left(\frac{n}{N}, \dot{p}^e, \dot{\lambda}^c \text{ or } C, \pi, i, \delta\right) \tag{1}$$

where n/N, $\dot{p}^e$, $\dot{\lambda}^c$ and C have already been discussed.

The price expectations variable and some form of retentions or catch-up variable are essentially determinants of Δw^{rc} and δ, which are unobservable. We have still left δ explicitly in the equation as we will report the results of some attempts to proxy it with data on strike activity in the regressions of the next section. Of the remaining variables π represents rate of profit per unit of output and i is some measure of the rate of discounting used by employers. Of the two remaining variables of the bargaining theory model, we have omitted the time span over which the employer discounts, as we have no direct measures of this variable, and we have not, as yet, experimented with proxies for the supplementary cost parameter. For the individual firm it reflects the seriousness of the strike as strike length increases. For an aggregative analysis over time it would be plausible to expect strikes to be potentially more serious at some times than others, depending on the pressure of market demand, the level of orders in relation to stocks, etc. and it might be possible to proxy the cost parameter by some such variable.

Empirical results

The regressions reported in this paper are all based on annual data. We have also studied the results of fitting given relationships to two different sample periods, firstly because other studies have indicated instability or structural change within periods and secondly because some of our variables such as the retention ratio have come into prominence in the sixties and one could not expect to pick up their effect from the negligible variation displayed in the fifties. The sample periods employed are denoted by:

$$A = 1959\text{--}71$$
$$B = 1952\text{--}71$$

Table 4 gives the results of regressions run on annual data for the period 1959 to 1971. In each case the dependent variable is the annual percentage change in weekly wage rates for all manual workers in all

Table 4 Regressions for 1959–71

Regression	Const.	n/N	$\dot{p}$	$(\dot{p}^e)^2$	$\dot{p}^e$	C_1	C_4	C_5	λ^c	R^2	d
A.1	0·074	2·72 (0·78)	0·758* (3·95)			0·430* (2·36)				0·731*	1·04
A.2	-3·900	3·72 (1·09)	0·848* (4·66)				1·105* (2·68)			0·758*	1·50
A.3	-1·235	3·20 (0·94)	0·780* (4·26)					0·668* (2·61)		0·753*	1·14
A.4	0·524	-0·48 (2·17)	0·440 (2·21)						-3·18 (3·25)	0·800*	1·
A.5	-0·038	2·43 (0·57)			1·04* (2·79)	0·271 (1·15)				0·606*	1·97
A.6	-0·910	2·79 (0·65)			1·05* (2·94)		0·432 (1·30)			0·620*	2·10
A.7	0·492	0·06 (0·02)			0·383 (0·82)				-3·44* (2·27)	0·714*	2·13
A.8	1·05	2·72 (0·80)		0·158* (4·06)		0·213 (1·11)				0·741*	2·67
A.9	1·09	0·70 (0·22)		0·100 (1·53)					-2·25 (1·35)	0·755*	2·53

Figures in parentheses are 't' values and an asterisk denotes a coefficient which is significantly different from zero at the 5 per cent level.

industries and services. Each regression has three explanatory variables apart from a constant term, namely, the proportion of workers receiving a wage increase (n/N), a price variable ($\dot{p}$, $\dot{p}^e$ or $(\dot{p}^e)^2$) and a catch-up or tax variable. The parentheses below coefficients give 't' values and asterisks indicate coefficients which are significantly different from zero at the 5 per cent level. In view of the small number of observations and the crudity of an annual analysis too much attention should not be paid to significance levels. Nonetheless, some fairly strong patterns appear from the regressions.

The intercept term is, in general, quite small, being about one per cent or less in absolute value in 7 of the 9 regressions. The coefficient of n/N is positive, as expected, in 8 cases out of 9. Though it is nowhere statistically significant, it obviously plays a useful role in explaining some of the variance in $\dot{w}$. The coefficients on the price variables are everywhere positive, in accord with expectation. The use of $\dot{p}$ is open to the feed-back/simultaneity problem mentioned in the previous section and moving from $\dot{p}$ to $\dot{p}^e$ tends on average to reduce correlation coefficients, though it does lead to more acceptable Durbin-Watson statistics. When $\dot{p}^e$ is entered in a linear fashion its coefficient is statistically significant in two of the three regressions and in these cases has a value which is not significantly different from unity. The use of $(\dot{p}^e)^2$ instead of $\dot{p}^e$ in the last two regressions gives a noticeable improvement in R^2, thus lending support to the hypothesis of a non-linear effect. The 'catch-up' variables have positive signs in every case as expected and the retentions variable has a negative sign in every case, again as expected. C_1 is a symmetric catch-up variable based on a desired 2 per cent per annum growth in net real earnings per capita, C_4 a non-symmetric variable similar to the definition of C_2 given earlier but based on 3 per cent growth rather than 2 per cent, and C_5 is a partially symmetric variable also based on 3 per cent. Similar results were also obtained with regressions involving C_2 and C_3. The retentions (taxation) variable comes out strongly in regressions A.4 and A.7. The explanation contributed by a variable is the product of its coefficient and the variation in the variable over the sample period. Figures 2a and 2b show the contributions of the explanatory variables in the regressions A.5, A.6, A.7 and A.9. Building up from the horizontal axis the contribution of the constant term (denoted by a) has been merged with that of n/N and the joint result is shown by the first solid line. The vertical distance between this and the next solid line shows the contribution

Figure 2a   Contribution of explanatory variables

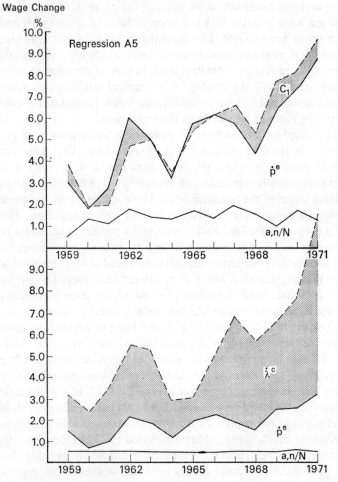

of the price expectations variable (or its square), while the shaded area indicates the contribution of the catch-up or retentions variable. The resultant regression values for $\dot{w}$ are shown by the dotted line. The unexplained residuals are not shown but, as seen in Table 4, regressions A.7 and A.9 have the best fits of the four. The main impression from the figures is that the retention variable has been of greater quantitative importance than the catch-up variable. The latter, of course, is influenced by the former but the calculation of the cumulative extent by which real disposable income has varied from

Figure 2b Contribution of explanatory variables

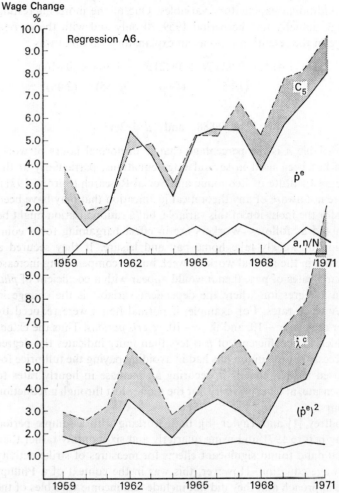

some target growth path is a fairly sophisticated operation compared with that of knowing whether taxes have taken a greater bite out of gross wages, and so there is no inherent contradiction in the tax variable registering a greater impact on wage rate changes. Thus it would appear that taxation changes and price expectations have played an important role in wage negotiations in the sixties, as hypothesised in the discussion of the Δw^{rc} and δ variables in the previous section.

In spite of the smallness of the sample, some regressions were run with additional explanatory variables. One of the more interesting (though actually for the period 1959-70 only and with the *current* change in the retention ratio as an explanatory variable) was

$$\dot{w} = 1{\cdot}412 + 2{\cdot}92n/N + 0{\cdot}221\dot{p}^e - 1{\cdot}36\lambda + 0{\cdot}816h$$
$$\quad\quad\quad (1{\cdot}65) \quad\quad (1{\cdot}06) \quad\quad (5{\cdot}65)^* \quad (2{\cdot}48)^*$$

with

$$R^2 = 0{\cdot}888 \quad \text{and} \quad d = 2{\cdot}67$$

The variable h is the percentage change in normal hours of work, which has been used in several wage equations, particularly at the National Institute of Economic and Social Research (Surrey, 1971). We are not aware of any theoretical justification that may have been given for the inclusion of this variable, but a rationalisation might be attempted as follows. Workers are in effect bargaining for a combination of weekly take home pay and leisure. If they secured a reduction in the normal working week but no compensating increase in hourly rates of pay, then h would appear with a coefficient of *plus one* in a regression where the dependent variable is the change in *weekly* wage rates. For example, if normal hours were reduced by 10 per cent, $h = -10$, and $\dot{w} = -10$, *ceteris paribus*. Thus the extent to which the coefficients of h is less than unity indicates the degree of success that the union has had in avoiding paying the full price for increased leisure, that is in securing an increase in hourly rates to compensate, at least partially, for the money lost through a reduction in hours.

Godfrey [1] and Taylor [8], both working with a sample period ending before 1971 and using quarterly and six-monthly rather than annual data, found significant effects for measures of strike activity in a wage equation. However, this was in the context of a Phillips curve approach and they did not include real income variables of the type discussed above. The sign to be expected on *a priori* grounds on some measure of strike activity would seem ambiguous in a bargaining type model. On the one hand, if employers interpret an increase in the number of strikes recently as an upsurge in union militancy and raise their estimate of the δ parameter upwards, this would lead to higher offers and settlements than would otherwise have obtained, and we would expect a positive sign on the strikes variable. On the other hand, δ is concerned with the *probability* of a strike for any given offer, and this probability need not increase just because there have actually been more strikes recently. Indeed a recent increase in strikes may *reduce* the probability of future strikes through depletion of union funds, increased indebtedness of union members and perhaps decreased willingness to endure another strike. The theoretical analysis also examined the relation between the optimal post-strike offer by the employer and the optimal pre-strike offer, and showed that the former might be greater or less than the latter depending on the balance between the loss of profits inflicted by the strike and the present value of the loss associated with any given wage increase: Johnston [4], Figure 4 and pp. 846–7. Thus, on these grounds also, a strikes variable has no clearly unambiguous sign in a bargaining model.

The actual effect of including S_t, the total number of strikes (beginning) in year t, in some of the regressions in Table 4 is shown in the following results:

$$\dot{w}_t = -2 \cdot 420 + 1 \cdot 37 n/N + 1 \cdot 065 \dot{p}^e + 0 \cdot 203 C_1 + 1 \cdot 183 S_t \quad \text{(A.5a)}$$
$$(0 \cdot 31) \qquad (2 \cdot 83)^* \qquad (0 \cdot 82) \qquad (0 \cdot 95)$$

with

$$R^2 = 0 \cdot 647^* \quad \text{and} \quad d = 2 \cdot 17$$

$$\dot{w}_t = -2 \cdot 22 - 0 \cdot 60 n/N + 0 \cdot 40 \dot{p}^e - 3 \cdot 26 \lambda^c + 1 \cdot 268 S_t \quad \text{(A.7a)}$$
$$(0 \cdot 18) \qquad (0 \cdot 91) \qquad (2 \cdot 23)^* \quad (1 \cdot 30)$$

with

$$R^2 = 0 \cdot 763^* \quad \text{and} \quad d = 2 \cdot 25$$

and

$$\dot{w}_t = -0 \cdot 891 + 1 \cdot 91 n/N + 0 \cdot 158 (\dot{p}^e)^2 + 0 \cdot 61 C_1 + 0 \cdot 98 S_t \quad \text{(A.8a)}$$
$$(0 \cdot 54) \qquad (4 \cdot 06)^* \qquad (0 \cdot 81) \qquad (0 \cdot 98)$$

with

$$R^2 = 0 \cdot 769^* \quad \text{and} \quad d = 2 \cdot 83$$

These regressions may be compared directly with A.5, A.7 and A.8 in Table 4. The strikes variable in each case has a positive sign but none of the coefficients is significant. The R^2 all rise somewhat, but the increase is nowhere significant. The coefficients on the price expectations variable are almost unchanged and the coefficients on the tax and real income variables very slightly reduced in absolute terms. At this level of aggregation, therefore, and for this short time period it has not been possible to discern any significant statistical effect for strikes, over and above the effects of the real income/tax variable. The same result emerges if one redefines the strikes variable, as many investigators do, to exclude stoppages in coal mining, because of the change from very many localised pit disputes to broader regional and national disputes in that industry between the fifties and sixties. If, however, one omitted the taxation/real income variable from the analysis then the strikes variable would show up strongly, since the incidence of strikes, including those directly concerned with wage questions, increased sharply in the late sixties and early seventies. In our view the *primary* cause of the wage inflation was the cumulative retardation in the growth of net, real wages, as evidenced in Figure 1. This led to ever larger *money claims* in an attempt to make *real gains*. The resultant struggles involved a substantial increase in strike activity, but the two variables moved so closely together over this period that the primary variable gets most of the statistical mileage.

The deterioration in the retention ratio and in the growth of net, real income was basically a phenomenon of the middle and late sixties. It is of interest, therefore, to see whether the effects of these variables on wage bargaining still shows through when the sample period is extended backwards in time. The results for a smaller set of regressions for the period 1952–71 are shown in Table 5. These have been numbered to correspond with similar regressions in Table 4. The catch-up and retentions variables still have the expected signs but the impression is much less strong. The first three regressions in the table have reduced to simple correlations between current wage and price changes with a large unexplained residual displaying positive autocorrelation. Regression B.7 is perhaps the best, with the price expectations variable coming out strongly and the retention variable bordering on significance, though again it must be noted that there is an unsatisfactorily low Durbin-Watson statistic.

Figures 3, 4 and 5 illustrate the effects of extending the sample period backwards a year at a time. Figure 3 refers to regression 1 of Table 4 with explanatory variables $\dot{p}$, n/N and C_1. The value of R^2 is steady at 0·73 as we add the years 1958 and 1957, but then falls fairly steadily to 0·56 for the period 1952–71; the coefficient of $\dot{p}$ remains fairly stable throughout, but n/N and C_1 gradually lose significance and correspondingly the intercept term rises and the residuals become highly autocorrelated. Figures 4 and 5 refer to the price expectations variable $\dot{p}^e$, plus the catch-up and retentions

Table 5 Regressions for 1952–71

Regression	Const.	n/N	$\dot{p}$	p^e	C_1	C_4	C_5	λ^c	R^2	d
B.1	1·964	0·82 (0·24)	0·703 (4·05)*		0·101 (0·81)				0·556*	1·00
B.2	1·168	1·01 (0·30)	0·713 (4·21)*			0·241 (0·92)			0·561*	1·04
B.4	2·658	−1·04 (0·31)	0·661 (3·82)*					−0·877 (1·29)	0·581*	1·11
B.7	1·683	0·66 (0·18)		0·605 (3·03)*				−1·49 (2·07)	0·490*	1·27

Figure 3   Coefficients of regression 1 for various sample periods

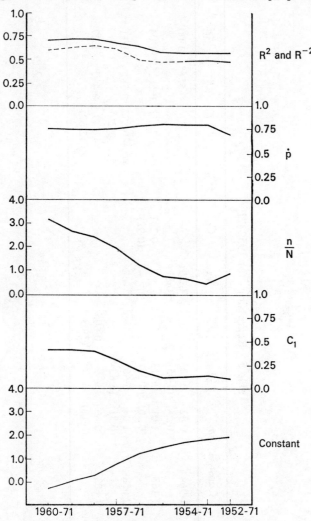

variables respectively. Again there is a fairly steady decline in both
R^2 and $\bar{R}^2$. The price expectations variable holds up well in both
regressions; the coefficient of $\dot{p}^e$ is unity or above in all regressions in
Figure 4 except those for the two longest sample periods. The
retentions and catch-up variables steadily lose significance as the
sample period is extended backwards. Finally, there appears to be a

Figure 4   Coefficients of regression 5 for various sample periods

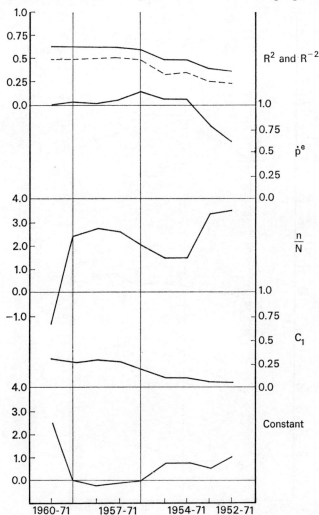

peculiar factor at work in the n/N series. This is endorsed by the regressions for 1960–71 and those for 1959–71. Adding 1959 raises the coefficient for n/N substantially and also reduces the intercept term in both Figures 4 and 5. This is caused by an abnormally low value for n/N in 1959, in which year a number of major groups had no wage increase.

Figure 5   Coefficients of regression 7 for various sample periods

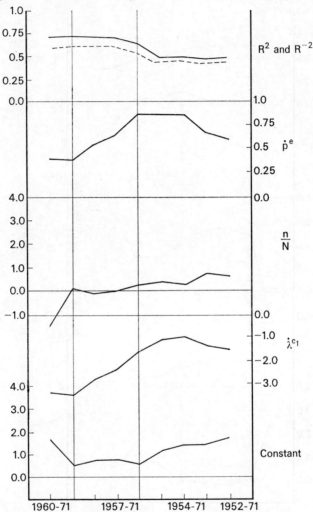

The variation in n/N over the period 1952–71 is shown in Figure 6. If we split the period into 1952–61 and 1962–71 the means are 49·12 and 64·25 respectively and a 't' statistic for the difference would be significant at the 5 per cent level. A linear trend for the whole period gives

$$n/N = 46·41 + 0·98t \quad \text{with } r^2 = 0·96$$
$$(19·18)$$

Although statistically significant the linear trend is a poor representation of the data in that Figure 6 shows substantial fluctuations in both the fifties and the sixties but around a higher mean level in the later period. A linear trend fitted to the sixties is essentially horizontal. The movements of this variable are not significantly correlated with economic variables such as the rate of inflation or the level of excess demand in the labour market, and so we have not included a second structural relation for n/N in the model.

The contrast between the A and B regressions, reinforced by Figures 3 to 5, suggests that the sample period 1952–71 cannot be taken as homogeneous. Any regression fitted to whole period is, therefore, best done with some constraints imposed. We have experimented with a number of sets of constraints and have also experimented with totally asymmetric and partially symmetric versions of the retentions variable, exactly comparable to the corresponding versions of the catch-up variable. Thus:

λ^{c_1} the average of the three previous percentage changes in the retention ratio (previously noted by λ^c);

λ^{c_2} as in λ^{c_1} except that *increases* in the retention ratio are ignored;

λ^{c_3} as in λ^{c_1} except that increases are given half-weight compared with decreases.

Figure 6   Variations in n/N, 1952–71

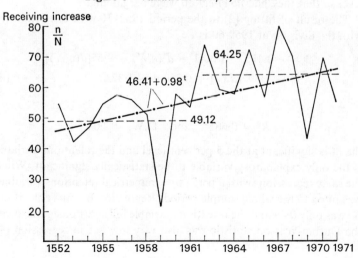

In general the retentions variables perform better than the catch-up variables, with the asymmetric versions performing least well and the partially symmetric performing best.

The choice of constraints can best be explained in relation to the general equation

$$\dot{w} = b_0 + b_{11}(1 - d)(n/N) + b_{12}[d(n/N)] + b_{21}(1 - d)\dot{\lambda}^{c_3}$$
$$+ b_{22}(d\dot{\lambda}^{c_3}) + b_{31}(1 - d)\dot{p}^e + b_{32}(d\dot{p}^e) + b_4 d + \text{residual} \quad (2)$$

where d is a dummy variable taking the value zero for any year in the 'early' period and unity for any year in the 'later' period. For example, if the division of the whole period is made at 1959/60 then $d = 0$ for 1952 through 1959 and $d = 1$ for 1960 through 1971. If (2) is fitted without any prior constraints the result is a separate regression for each sub-period with b_{11}, b_{21} and b_{31} being the coefficients of the explanatory variables in the early period, and b_{12}, b_{22} and b_{32} the corresponding coefficients in the later period. A plausible set of constraints might be

$$b_{31} = b_{32} \quad \text{and} \quad b_{21} = 0 \quad (3)$$

The first ensures that the price expectations variable has the same coefficient throughout the whole period 1952–71, while the second sets the coefficient of the retentions variable at zero in the early period. This amounts to asserting that the 'small' variations in the retentions variable in the early period were below some threshold level so that they had *no effect* on wage bargaining.

The result of fitting (2) to the period 1952–71 with restriction (3) with the division at 1959/60 is

$$\dot{w} = -0{\cdot}417 - 1{\cdot}30(1 - d)(n/N) + 9{\cdot}65[d(n/N)]$$
$$- 1{\cdot}39^*(d\dot{\lambda}^{c_3}) + 0{\cdot}250\dot{p}^e + 1{\cdot}372d \quad (4)$$

with

$$R^2 = 0{\cdot}685^* \quad \text{and} \quad \text{D.W.} = 2{\cdot}04$$

the fit is significant at the 5 per cent level and the retentions variable is the only explanatory variable to be statistically significant. When the same regression (with a perfectly symmetrical retentions variable) was fitted to the whole sample period (Regression B.7 in Table 5) the R^2 was only 0·49 and the retentions variable fell short of significance; the Durbin-Watson statistic was also very low but in regression (4) it is at a much more acceptable value. Varying the break between periods from 1959/60 up to 1962/63 makes no material difference to the results of regression (4).

Forecasts
We have very short sample periods with very few degrees of freedom, and we have used the annual data up to the end of 1971 in our estimation process. It is of interest, nonetheless, to see how the various equations forecast for 1972. We have made two forecasts as follows: (a) using all information that was available at the time the forecast was actually made, namely end September 1972, and (b) using data only on variables up to end-December 1971.

In the (b) forecast the average value of n/N over the previous ten years, 1962–71, was used, whereas in the (a) forecast the actual value of n/N for January to August 1972 was taken and grossed up to a twelve-month basis. The results are shown in Table 6. The numbering of the regressions correspond to Table 4. It is seen that there is not too much difference in any forecasts according to the time at which it was made, since the retention and real income variables are both lagged so that differences can only arise from the values inserted for n/N and the price forecast. There is, however, a substantial difference between the levels of the forecasts from different regressions. The most striking feature being the lower forecasts from regressions A.5 and A.7, which both use $\dot{p}^e$, and the higher forecasts from regressions A.8 and A.9, which both use $(\dot{p}^e)^2$. The actual change in the wage index and the first nine months of 1972 was, in fact, $12\frac{1}{2}$ per cent, so that regression A.9, using the non-linear price effect and the retentions variable, comes closest to the observed change.

Table 6 Forecast percentage change
in the wage index for 1972

Regression	Forecast (a)	Forecast (b)
A.5	10·9	10·6
A.7	8·4	8·2
A.8	15·3	14·0
A.9	12·3	11·4

Comparisons with a Phillips curve approach

As a contrast with the above regressions we have also fitted a number of Phillips-type regressions to the same data, using various definitions of the excess demand variable and both sample periods. We have retained n/N, since the arguments for its inclusion relate to the choice of dependent variable and apply to a Phillips curve approach as well as a bargaining theory approach. We have also retained the same price expectations variable, $\dot{p}^e$, as in the previous analysis. So far as the excess demand variable is concerned, the results are uniformly the same: in every case the variable has the *incorrect a priori* sign. Typical results for the 1959–71 and 1952–71 periods respectively are:

$$\dot{w} = -3{\cdot}19 + 1{\cdot}71n/N + 0{\cdot}60\dot{p}^e + 2{\cdot}699u \qquad (5)$$
$$(0{\cdot}47) \qquad (1{\cdot}39) \qquad (1{\cdot}96)$$

with

$$R^2 = 0{\cdot}684^* \quad \text{and} \quad d = 2{\cdot}09$$

and

$$\dot{w} = 1{\cdot}16 + 2{\cdot}16n/N + 0{\cdot}530\dot{p}^e - 0{\cdot}998(v - u) \qquad (6)$$
$$(0{\cdot}60) \qquad (2{\cdot}49)^* \qquad (1{\cdot}82)$$

with

$$R^2 = 0{\cdot}464^* \quad \text{and} \quad d = 1{\cdot}26$$

where u denotes the unemployment rate and v the vacancy rate. Regression (5), for the sixties, reflects the *positive* association between unemployment and wage change, especially in the latter years of the period and the positive coefficient on the unemployment variable borders on statistical significance. In regression (6) for 1952–71, price was the only significant variable, as it was in the regressions of Table 5: the excess demand variable again has a fairly strong coefficient, but also again has the wrong sign.

The addition of excess demand variables to bargaining type equations might also be justified on the assumption that the greater is the excess demand for labour the greater is union bargaining power and thus the higher the resultant wage increase. The same sign would then be expected on the excess demand variable as in the Phillips curve analysis. The empirical results, however, did not bear out this hypothesis. When $(v - u)$ was added to regression A.5 the coefficient of $\dot{p}_e$ was halved and became insignificant, the coefficient of C_1 became effectively zero and $(v - u)$ came out with the strongest coefficient but perverse sign. Similar results were obtained when u or $(v - u)$ was added to regressions A.7, A.8 and A.9, in each case the coefficients of the price and retentions (or real income) variables were reduced and the excess demand variables had in every case statistically insignificant but perversely signed coefficients.

Thus in every case where the excess demand variables were employed, whether in a conventional Phillips curve approach or as additions to explicit bargaining, the coefficients were of the wrong sign and statistically insignificant. The signs of the coefficients would be consistent with a theory that suggested variations in unemployment as the *consequence* of changes in wage rates, so that increases in money wages, beyond what current shifts in the production function and current market conditions as determined by exogenous Government and world variables would bear, result in lower employment and higher prices.

Conclusions
Experiments with annual data at this level of aggregation are admittedly fairly crude, but certain tentative conclusions do seem possible at this stage.

(i) Movements in the retention ratio (or alternatively in a 'catch-up' variable) have had a significant effect on wage rate movements in recent years.

(ii) Price expectations also have an effect on wage rate bargaining and this effect has been fairly steady and persistent throughout the whole sample period, 1952–71. There is some evidence here for a non-linear effect.

(iii) Variations in the proportion of workers receiving an increase in a given period will also have an effect on the wage rate index, and should be allowed for in the regression. These variations do not appear to be systematically linked to the rate of inflation or any other macro-variable, such as the level of excess demand in the labour market. There does, however, appear to have been a structural shift in the mean level from the fifties to the sixties with fairly substantial fluctuations about the respective mean level in each decade.

(iv) An equation with a non-linear price term and the taxation variable gives a very accurate forecast for the actual change in the wage index in 1972.

(v) It has not been possible to find a conventional Phillips curve for either the short or long sample period, which does not have perverse signs on the excess demand variable. Similarly, the addition of an excess demand variable to the bargaining equations tends to weaken or eliminate the bargaining variables and to give consistently perverse signs on the excess demand variable.

(vi) It has not been possible at this level to make any systematic examination of other specific variables in the bargaining model such as profit rate and the employer's discounting rate. These, together with the above tentative conclusions will be explored in future work on disaggregated data.

References

[1] Godfrey, L. G., 'The Phillips Curve: Incomes Policy and Trade Union Effects', Chapter 6 in H. G. Johnson and A. R. Nobay (eds.), *The General Inflation*, London, Macmillan (1971).

[2] Hansen, B., 'Excess Demand, Unemployment Vacancies and Wages', *Quarterly Journal of Economics* (Feb. 1970).

[3] Jackson, D., Turner, H. A. and Wilkinson, F., 'Do Trade Unions Cause Inflation?' *University of Cambridge Department of Applied Economics, Occasional Paper 36*, Cambridge, Cambridge University Press (1972).

[4] Johnston, J., 'A Model of Wage Determination under Bilateral Monopoly', *Economic Journal* (Sept. 1972).

[5] Lipsey, R. G., 'The Relation between Unemployment and the Rate of Change in Money Wage Rates in the U.K. 1862–1957: A Further Analysis', *Economica* (1960).

[6] Phillips, A. W., 'The Relationship between Unemployment and the Rate of Change of Money Wage Rates in the U.K. 1861–1957', *Economica* (1958).

[7] Surrey, M. J. C., 'The Analysis and Forecasting of the British Economy', *NIESR Occasional Paper XXV*, Cambridge, Cambridge University Press (1971).

[8] Taylor, J., 'Incomes Policy, the Structure of Unemployment and the Phillips Curve: U.K. Experience 1953–70', in M. Parkin and M. Sumner (eds.), *Incomes Policy and Inflation*, Manchester, Manchester University Press (1972).

G. C. Archibald
Robyn Kemmis
and J. W. Perkins

Chapter 5 Excess demand for labour, unemployment and the Phillips curve: a theoretical and empirical study[1]

Introduction

The main object of this paper is to explore the relationship between the rate of change of wages and the structure of unemployment. By 'structure' we mean the cross-section dispersion, or some other measure to be defined. In an earlier paper, one of the present authors (Archibald [2]) proposed the following model, designed to test Lipsey's [17] aggregation hypothesis:[2]

$$\frac{\dot{w}}{w} = a_0 + a_1 U^{-1} + a_2 \sigma^2 + a_3 \frac{\dot{p}}{p} \qquad (0.1)$$

In this equation, σ^2 is the cross-section variance of unemployment measured either on industry or regional data. Fitted to post-war U.K. annual data, and post-war U.S. quarterly data, σ^2 had the predicted positive sign, and was significant. We shall report below our tests of this 'moments model' on the pre-1914 period (annual), the inter-war period, and the post-war period (both quarterly).

We propose, however, an alternative structural model, which is explained in Section I below. This, on the whole, fits about as well as

[1] Work reported here was financed by a grant from the S.S.R.C. which is, of course, not responsible for any opinions expressed. This grant expired in the summer of 1970 when, in addition, all three authors left the University of Essex. Thus no serious revision or updating since that time has been possible, nor has any but the most cursory notice of the latest literature. Data and print-out, etc. are stored at the University of Manchester, under the care of Professor Michael Parkin. One of the authors has had the advantage of close association with Professor F. P. R. Brechling in his work on the U.S. data. His generous assistance is gratefully acknowledged here: it is too comprehensive to acknowledge in detail. For comments, we are much indebted to the editors of the present volume, to Professor John G. Cragg, and to members of the Labour Workshop at the University of Essex. We are also indebted to officials of the D.E.P. (Statistics Division) for making available a substantial amount of unpublished data.
[2] See also Thirlwall [28] and [30]. The 'moments model' has also been ingeniously extended by Thomas and Stoney [31].

the moments model, but offers certain other important advantages. It is well known that, in most reported work on the Phillips curve to date, it is not possible to distinguish between the reaction function, $\dot{w}/w$ on excess demand, and the transformation between excess demand and unemployment.[3] The former is sometimes supposed to be linear, and the latter non-linear, but all that is observed is the relationship (sometimes linear, sometimes not) between $\dot{w}/w$ and U (or U and vacancies, in some combination). In this paper, we shall postulate an explicit functional form for the transformation from excess demand to unemployment. Using the assumption of linear reaction functions, we shall then derive the equations to be fitted.

This procedure permits us to make extensive use of cross-section data, as does the moments model. We require very stringent aggregation assumptions, and we are able to offer some test of these too. This follows from the fact that, given the postulated transformation, we derive a frequency function for cross-section unemployment if one is postulated for excess demand.

A further advantage of the model proposed here is that it enables us to distinguish between variables that alter the transformation from excess demand to unemployment, variables that alter the *slope* of the reaction function, and variables that alter the *intercept* of the reaction function. Thus consider a fitted equation of the form

$$\frac{\dot{w}}{w} = g(U) + h(z) + \epsilon \qquad (0.2)$$

where z is a variable (or vector of variables) such as trade union strength, productivity, or the rate of change of prices. Equations of the form of 0.2 have been widely reported. They do not, however, allow us to make the required distinction with any confidence. If we write $\dot{w}/w = f(x)$, where x is excess demand, the appearance of z in 0.2 may be taken to imply that $f(0) \neq 0$. This is, however, not necessarily the case. We hope that the model proposed here may make it easier to determine the role of these 'intruder' variables in the fitted equations. It also affords a method for testing the hypothesis that the matrix of reaction coefficients is not diagonal, i.e. that there are interrelations between markets that we may take into account.

In Section I we set out the model to be tested. This includes consideration of the role of price expectations (see particularly Phelps

---

[3] But see Thirlwall [29], and Corry and Laidler [7].

[20] and [21], Friedman [8]). Although our main concern in this paper is with the relationship between the 'macro' behaviour of wage rates and the structure of excess demand, the rate of change of prices is such an important determinant of $\dot{w}/w$ that we shall have to give it considerable attention. We shall, however, only briefly discuss the important new generation of dynamic models (see particularly Mortensen in Phelps [22]). Some reasons for this decision are given later. In Sections II, III and IV we report our results for the pre-1914 period, the inter-war period, and the post-war period, respectively. In Section V we report on the cross-section distribution of excess demand, and in VI we offer a brief conclusion. Details of the data employed will be found in the Appendix.

I The model

.1 We now propose a functional form for the transformation between registered unemployment and excess demand. By postulating a density function for excess demand, we also derive a distribution for unemployment which may be tested (see V below).

Let proportional excess demand be defined by

$$x = \frac{D - S}{S} \qquad (I.1)$$

Then we have

$$-1 \leq x < \infty$$

To avoid negative numbers, it is convenient to shift the origin by defining

$$y = x + 1 \quad \text{(whence } y = 0 \text{ when } x = -1, \quad y = 1 \text{ when } x = 0) \quad (I.2)$$

Now, percentage unemployment is defined over the range 0 to 100, and unemployment is a decreasing function of excess demand, whence we might expect the transformation to look something like that in Figure I.1. A two-parameter mapping with a possibly appropriate shape is the simple exponential[4]

$$U = a\,e^{\eta y} \quad (\eta < 0) \qquad (I.3)$$

---

[4] This form rules out the possibility of 'perverse effects' discussed by Corry and Laidler [7]. Thirlwall [28] does not find evidence in favour of the perverse effects. Over a small interval such as ab, a linear approximation may be acceptable; see Parkin [19].

Figure I.1

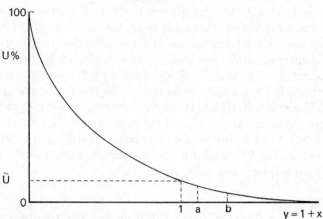

We may take advantage of the limits of range and domain to reduce this to a one-parameter mapping. Thus putting $y = 0$, we must have

$$U = 100 = a \tag{I.4}$$

whence we can replace I.3 with

$$U = 100\, e^{\eta y} \tag{I.5}$$

which we shall use henceforth.

Some properties of I.5 may be noted at once. First, if it holds as an acceptable approximation, vacancy information is redundant (compare Hansen [13]). This is just as well, since vacancy data are unavailable for two of our three periods, and are in any case a matter of some debate.[5] Second, if excess demand is zero, $y = 1$ and $U = \tilde{U}$, whence

$$\eta = \log \frac{\tilde{U}}{100} \tag{I.6}$$

η may thus be interpreted as the 'friction parameter', of interest in its own right. We shall later investigate the stability of η.

---

[5] We must acknowledge that, if there is measurement error in our x–U relationship, then the independent use of vacancies, or of U itself, may give additional information. We shall not explore this possibility here. If the error were such that we could rewrite I.5 as $U = 100\, e^{\eta y + \epsilon}$, ϵ a normally distributed random variable, then the stochastic specification of I.9 below would be simply altered.

.2 We now assume that I.5 holds for each individual labour market. Then we have

$$\log U_i = \log 100 + \eta_i y_i \quad (i = 1, \ldots, n) \tag{I.7}$$

We additionally assume, what is not in fact true,[6] that $\eta = \eta_i = \eta_j$, all i, j. If we postulate a density function for proportional excess demand we obtain from the change of variables I.7 the density function for U_i or $\log U_i$. Our experiments with the distributions are described in V below. We may note here, however, the main result. We might plausibly expect the distribution of proportional excess demand *across* markets, measured for some suitably brief time-interval, to be normal (or as near normal as is possible, given the range of definition of x). If this were the case, the cross-section distribution of unemployment should be log normal. Subject to qualifications discussed below, the cross-section distributions, on a geographical basis, appear to be well described by the log-normal distribution. This encourages confidence in the transformation postulated here, crude approximation though it may seem. Further, it is not easy to imagine a cross-section analogy to Gibrat's Law to account for the observed log-normality of cross-section unemployment, whereas it is at least a plausible hypothesis that cross-section excess demand is normally distributed, whence a logarithmic transformation is the required link.

.3 We now complete the simple model by adding the linear reaction function

$$\frac{\dot{w}_i}{w_i} = \alpha_i x_i \tag{I.8}$$

Using I.2 and I.5, we have

$$\frac{\dot{w}_i}{w_i} = \frac{\alpha_i}{\eta} \log \left(\frac{U_i}{100} \right) - \alpha_i \tag{I.9}$$

[6] We in fact know that this is false. From the Sample Census 1966, *Economic Activity Tables, I*, we can compute, region by region (and for men and women separately) the ratio of registered unemployed to non-registered unemployed. The ratio (for men and women only) varies from 0·58 (West Midlands) to 1·79 (Northern). We may take it that the total of registered and unregistered unemployment reflects excess demand better than the former alone, and we see that the cross-section correspondence varies widely. We are indebted to Mr. E. K. Grant for drawing our attention to these data. The aggregation assumption is further discussed in V below.

We do not have adequate wage data for individual labour markets, and are, in any case, sceptical about our ability to identify 'true' micro-markets, whence we now require to aggregate. There is no alternative to the strong and implausible assumption that $\alpha = \alpha_i = \alpha_j$, all i, j. For weights, we use $\gamma_i = L_i/L$, $\sum \gamma_i = 1$ (where L_i and L denote the labour force in the ith market and the total labour force, respectively).[7] Under these assumptions, aggregating the right-hand side of I.9 gives

$$\frac{\alpha}{\eta} \sum_i \gamma_i \log \left(\frac{U_i}{100}\right) - \alpha$$

whereas aggregating the left-hand side gives

$$\sum \gamma_i \frac{\dot{w}_i}{w_i}$$

The difficulty here is that a weighted index of wage rates is given by

$$w = \sum \gamma_i w_i$$

whence

$$\frac{\dot{w}}{w} = \frac{\sum \gamma_i \dot{w}_i}{\sum \gamma_i w_i}$$

Since we cannot rebuild our wage rate series there is nothing we can do about this. Furthermore, the official weights and our γ_i do not correspond. Hence our basic equation

$$\left(\frac{\dot{w}}{w}\right)_t = a_0 + a_1 \sum_i \gamma_i \log \left(\frac{U_{it}}{100}\right) \qquad (I.10)$$

involves a 'fudge', the seriousness of which cannot be judged.[8]

---

[7] This choice of weights is, of course, arbitrary.

[8] An alternative approach that is tempting but wrong may be worth noting. If we expand I.9 in a Taylor series about mean unemployment, $\bar{U}$, and then sum, we obtain

$$\frac{\dot{w}}{w} = a_0 + a_1 \log \frac{\bar{U}}{100} - \frac{200 a_1}{\bar{U}^2} \sum \gamma_i \left(\frac{\bar{U}}{100} - \frac{U_i}{100}\right)^2 + \dots$$

which is most suggestive. We have the log of macro-U, a variance term reminiscent of the moments model, and higher moments if we wish. The trouble is simply that the Taylor series is not convergent: while $\bar{U}/100$ and $U_i/100$ are both less than unity, their ratio obviously exceeds unity approximately half the time. Thus if the logarithmic transformation is a reasonable approximation, a moments model is better the earlier it is truncated!

For convenience, we shall henceforth write $V = \sum \gamma_i \log (U_i/100)$ and refer to I.10 as the 'addi-log model'. (We shall also write u_i for $U_i/100$.) Since the log of a sum is, of course, not equal to the sum of the logs, $V \neq \log (\overline{U}/100)$, where $\overline{U}$ is 'macro-U' or $\sum \gamma_i U_i$ (although, in fact, the two are closely correlated in our data samples). The signs of the coefficients in I.10 are unambiguous: $a_0 = -\alpha$, negative, and $a_1 = \alpha/\eta$, also negative. An estimate of η, and thus $\overline{U}$, may be obtained directly from an estimate of I.10. We also note that the form of I.10 is such that, for estimating purposes, it is equivalent to restricted least squares, where the restriction is precisely our aggregation assumption that $\alpha_i/\eta_i = \alpha_j/\eta_j$, all i, j. (Thus our aggregation hypothesis is, in principle, potentially testable: the difficulty is, of course, with degrees of freedom.)

.4 Before extending the model to deal with the 'intruders', it may be helpful to consider the relation between the 'addi-log model' and the earlier 'moments model'.[9] The latter, which may be written

$$\frac{\dot{w}}{w} = \beta_0 + \beta_1 \overline{U}^{-1} + \beta_2 \sigma^2_{U_i}$$

was designed to test Lipsey's dispersion hypothesis.[10] (The third moment was also introduced, due to skewness in the distribution of

[9] We should make it clear that we do not regard either statistical regions or industries as labour markets (although the former are probably better approximations than the latter). To quote Archibald [2]: '...available data are usually for geographical or industrial sub-aggregates that need by no means coincide with "true" labour markets...The measure of dispersion used is simply the variance of unemployment computed from whatever data are available, whether geographical or industrial...We thus assume, without test, that although the basis of reporting may not coincide with individual markets, the dispersion computed from available data will serve as a good proxy for the dispersion of excess demand over the true markets.' For recent criticism of the moments model, see Hines [11].

[10] We note an alternative model. If, for the micro-markets, we write

$$\left(\frac{\dot{w}}{w}\right)_i = \alpha_i + \beta_i U_i^{-1},$$

then, aggregating as above

$$\frac{\dot{w}}{w} = \alpha + \beta \sum \gamma_i U_i^{-1}$$

i.e. the independent variable is the reciprocal of the weighted harmonic mean of the U_i. As in the addi-log model, no additional dispersion term is called for. This is doubtless preferable to the moments model, and actually fits better in the inter-war period. We have not persisted with it as an alternative since it does not offer the other advantages of the addi-log model. We are indebted to Mr. M. R. Gray for suggesting it.

116   G. C. Archibald, Robyn Kemmis and J. W. Perkins

U_i. It proved not to be generally important.) It was argued that convexity of individual-market Phillips curves was a sufficient condition for an increase in dispersion, under the condition $d\overline{U} = 0$, to increase $\dot{w}/w$, i.e. for β_2 to be positive. Whether convexity was provided by the reaction function or the x–U mapping, or both, was not specified. In the addi-log model, convexity is explicitly provided by the exponential transformation. The dispersion effect is, of course, still predicted to be positive. We cannot write an analytic relation between V and $\overline{U}$, σ^2, so there is no one-to-one correspondence between the two models. The operation of the dispersion effect in the addi-log model is, however, illustrated in Fig. I.2. Here u is measured from 0 to 1 on the positive horizontal, and its log (V) on the negative vertical axis. A range of values of $\dot{w}/w$ is measured to the left. $\tilde{u}$ maps through $\tilde{V}$ into $\dot{w}/w = 0$. Now for illustration, suppose two markets with equal weights, and a dispersion of unemployment round $\tilde{U}$, indicated by a and b. Logs are indicated by a' and b'. The weighted sum of the logs is not $\tilde{V}$, but the higher value V_1, whence $\dot{w}/w > 0$. Increasing dispersion, illustrated by c and d, obviously leads to a yet higher value of $\dot{w}/w$. In the moments model the shift from ab to cd was captured by σ^2. In the addi-log model it is measured directly:

Figure I.2

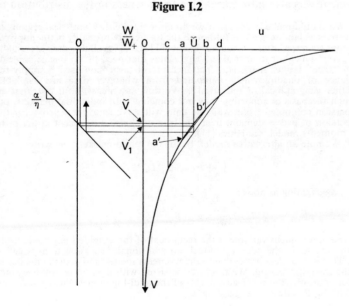

there is no place for an additional dispersion term. In this sense, the addi-log model is a 'tighter' specification than the moments model.

.5 The first 'intruder' we shall discuss is productivity. It has been suggested that, since equilibrium real wages depend on productivity, there is something wrong in the omission of productivity from Phillips' analysis[11] of the rate of change of money wages. This is mistaken. The categories, supply and demand, are supposed to provide an exhaustive taxonomy of the factors determining the price of any economic good. Productivity change alters one of them, perhaps both. It therefore alters excess demand, the independent variable of Phillips' disequilibrium model. It is the appearance of productivity (or its rate of change, or departure from trend, etc.) as an *additional* variable in the fitted linear equation that is inconsistent with theory, *unless* its role is to improve the proxy measure of excess demand.[12] Without a separate specification of the U–x mapping and the reaction function, it is, of course, impossible to interpret the presence of productivity in the fitted equation. We are now in a position to do so.

Taylor [27] and Vanderkamp [33] have argued convincingly that the role of productivity change is to improve the measure of excess demand. It is not necessary to review their analysis, or their empirical results (for U.S. and Canadian data, respectively). The argument is that a fall from the trend level of measured productivity per man is associated with labour hoarding (the phenomenon of counter-cyclical change in measured productivity is well known: see Brechling [1965]). This in turn will mean that the level of excess demand corresponding to the measured level of unemployment will be lower than it otherwise would be. Vice versa, when measured productivity is above trend, we have high utilisation of the employed labour force, and excess demand for labour will be understated by measured unemployment. It follows that our simple U–x mapping is defective. We now consider how ρ (interpreted as the deviation of measured per-man-year or per-man-quarter productivity from trend) may be introduced.

----

[11] See Kuh [16].
[12] It is, of course, true that an *anticipated* change in productivity could lead to an alteration in the wage rate, without any change in measured current excess demand. We have not explored this hypothesis. Expectations are discussed in .7 below.

A very simple functional form is

$$U = 100 \, e^{\eta y + \xi \rho} \tag{I.11}$$

Ignoring aggregation problems, and using I.2 and I.8, we obtain

$$\frac{\dot{w}}{w} = \frac{\alpha}{\eta} V - \alpha \frac{\xi}{\eta} \rho - \alpha \tag{I.12}$$

whence

$$\frac{\partial(\dot{w}/w)}{\partial \rho} = -\alpha \frac{\xi}{\eta} \tag{I.13}$$

The argument is that a positive ρ is associated with a higher excess demand than is measured by $(1/\eta)V$, whence I.13 should be positive, which in turn requires that ξ be positive.

Equation I.12 is, of course, readily estimated (the parameters are exactly identified). As a regression equation, it is of the same form as 0.1 above. Thus our conclusion is that, granted the exponential form of the basic U–x mapping, the presence of productivity as an additional term in a linear wage equation is consistent with the basic Phillips' model: productivity need be regarded neither as a rival explanation nor as an intruder, but as a means of reducing the error of measurement of excess demand.

A more complicated alternative to I.11 is to make η a function of ρ. Thus we might write

$$\eta = \frac{\eta_0}{\eta_1 \rho + \eta_2} \tag{I.14}$$

which leads to

$$\frac{\dot{w}}{w} = \alpha \frac{\eta_2}{\eta_0} V + \alpha \frac{\eta_1}{\eta_0} \rho V - \alpha \tag{I.15}$$

This introduces ρ in multiplicative form. I.15 could be estimated, but we have not in fact attempted to do so.

(A further improvement in the transformation might take account of changes in the participation rate—see Simler and Tella [25] as well as Taylor [27] and Vanderkamp [33]—we have not attempted this.)

.6 Before discussing the role of price changes, and the expectations arguments of Friedman [8] and Phelps [20], [21], we present a method of analysing the effect of other intruders in equation 0.2. We want to

Figure I.3

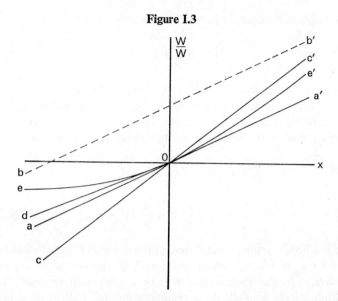

distinguish between a variable that alters the speed of reaction and one which causes $f(0) \neq 0$. We have no theory about the speed of reaction: if, e.g. union pressure causes wages to rise faster, when there is excess demand, than they otherwise would, this is simply an empirical observation. If, however, unions, or the level of profits, or any other z-variable, cause wages to rise *independently of excess demand*,[13] we have some new problems. The distinction is illustrated in Figure I.3, where we draw some possible reaction functions. *aa'* is the simple case assumed so far. *bb'* is displaced so that $f(0) \neq 0$.[14] A z-variable that everywhere operates to speed up the reaction will swing the *aa'* curve clockwise to *cc'*. A z-variable that speeds up wage increases and slows down decreases will produce something like *dc'*. We wish to distinguish between these cases. Let us start with *cc'*.

This requires that α be a function of z, so we write

$$\frac{\dot{w}}{w} = \alpha(z).x \qquad (I.16)$$

---

[13] This phrase deserves emphasis. If excess demand is altered by a shift in the supply curve, whether caused by institutions or otherwise, we have no new problem.
[14] Hansen [13] assumes that this is a standard case. He does not consider the cases *cc'* and *dc'*.

The simplest assumption is that α is linear in z, so that

$$\frac{\dot{w}}{w} = (\alpha_0 + \alpha_1 z)x \qquad (\text{I.17})$$

(where, of course, $\dot{w}/w = 0$ if $x = 0$, whatever the value of z). Let us assume that the effect of z is positive, i.e. $\alpha_1 > 0$ as well as $a_0 > 0$. (If a variable is assumed everywhere to slow down the reaction, we merely put $\alpha_1 < 0$.) Applying our transformation, we obtain

$$\frac{\dot{w}}{w} = (\alpha_0 + \alpha_1 z)\left\{\frac{1}{\eta} V - 1\right\}$$

$$= -\alpha_0 + \frac{\alpha_0}{\eta} V + \frac{\alpha_1}{\eta} zV - \alpha_1 z \qquad (\text{I.18})$$

This is a little startling. It says that, granted our $x: U$ transformation, a variable which influences the *speed of reaction only* appears additively, in the transformed equation, with sign reversed, and multiplicatively as well. As a regression model, I.18 is, of course, overdetermined, but it can be estimated.[15] It is to be compared with the bb' case, $\dot{w}/w = \alpha x + \beta z$.

To deal with the kinked case, cd', it is only necessary to assume that the sign of α_1 depends on that of x—both positive or both negative. A test will, of course, require division of the data according to the sign of x. This model allows us to do this: results are reported in III.7 below. We may, however, note that the linearity assumption, adhered to throughout, is restrictive, and may even be misleading. Thus if the reaction function were of the form of ee' in Figure I.3, bb' would give a better linear approximation than could aa'. To explore this possibility, we require non-linear functional forms that lead to manageable regression equations, and, so far, we have failed to find any. The possibility of non-linearity is, however, an additional reason for doubting if a regression equation of the form 0.2 necessarily establishes a true intruder in the sense of the bb' case.

---

[15] It can also be generalised easily to deal with several variables simultaneously. If there are k variables affecting the speed of reaction, we have

$$\alpha = \alpha_0 + \alpha_1 z_1 + \ldots + \alpha_k z_k$$

and

$$\frac{\dot{w}}{w} = -\alpha_0 + \frac{\alpha_0}{\eta} V + \frac{\alpha_1}{\eta} z_1 V + \ldots + \frac{\alpha_k}{\eta} z_k V - \alpha_1 z_1 - \ldots - \alpha_k z_k.$$

.7 One argument that there is no stable trade-off between unemployment and inflation,[16] since expected inflation will shift the Phillips curve, depends simply upon the uniqueness of real equilibrium. Suppose that there is an equilibrium vector of quantities (inputs as well as outputs) associated with an equilibrium vector of relative prices. Doubling all prices leaves relative prices unaltered, and therefore the vector of equilibrium quantities (the homogeneity postulate). If, instead of the comparative-static experiment of multiplying all prices by θ, we conduct the experiment of having *all* absolute prices rise at a constant rate λ, *expected with certainty*, then no relative price changes or is expected to change, whence the equilibrium vector of quantities is again unchanged. This is a steady-state argument. The reaction function, given certain expectations universally held, should shift by exactly λ. What is predicted for a less certain world, in which transients are also important, and relative prices do change during the inflationary process, is less obvious. Our experiments with price expectations are reported in III and IV below. This part of our investigation is, unfortunately, far from conclusive.[17]

This is a convenient point to remark on the problem of simultaneity between wages and prices, a chronic problem for all single-equation Phillips curves studied. If it is the lagged rather than the contemporaneous rate of change of prices that has the explanatory power we may be somewhat encouraged. For expectations, we use the standard Koyck form $(\dot{p}/p)^e = \lambda(\dot{p}/p) + (1 - \lambda)(\dot{p}/p)^e_{-1}$, and generally obtain significant coefficients on the contemporaneous rate of change. It cannot be argued that the problem of simultaneity has been satisfactorily resolved. Nor, in fact, has the general problem of expectations. As was noted above (.5, fn. 12), an anticipated change in productivity could directly change wages. To this we may add that the same thing can be said about expected change in any other variable affecting excess demand. With the exception of the effect of expected unemployment we have not explored more general expectations hypotheses here.

[16] For discussion, see particularly Phelps [20, 21 and 22], Brechling [5], Friedman [8], and Gordon and Hynes, in Phelps [22].

[17] The 'strong' argument of the text (unique natural rate of equilibrium unemployment; inflation perfectly anticipated) leads to the limiting case in which the Phillips curve pivots around its intercept on the horizontal axis. On weaker assumptions (transients, imperfect learning processes) it may be shifted bodily by expectations. For discussion, see Brechling [6] and Laidler in Johnson and Nobay [14]. (Unfortunately, both time and space constraints prevent us from responding adequately to the papers in the latter.) See also the masterly review by Tobin [32].

.8 In equation I.8 above, we assumed that the rate of wage change in a market depended only on excess demand in the market, but 'We have no choice but to admit that the rate of adjustment in one market may depend on the excess demand in *other* markets . . . *H* [the matrix of reaction coefficients] need not now be a positive diagonal matrix' (Samuelson [24], p. 274). We now seek some device that will incorporate this possibility, yet lead to an equation that may be estimated with available data.

We may, in fact, imagine several cases, but shall not be able to distinguish satisfactorily between all of them. The first is, of course, that the matrix contains certain non-zero off-diagonal elements. The second is that the 'general pressure of excess demand' affects markets that are otherwise in equilibrium. The third, which perhaps captures the idea of a 'spill-over', is that the matrix is asymmetrical in important ways. We cannot investigate the third case,[18] but can suggest at least *a* device for exploring the first and second.

If the speed of reaction in each market depends on excess demand in certain other markets, we have presently no means of knowing what these markets may be, nor of estimating separately their levels of excess demand. We therefore introduce the simplifying hypothesis that the speed of reaction in the ith market depends on x_i and *the average level of excess demand* in all markets, $\bar{x}$. It could, of course, be that $\bar{x}$ is a suitable proxy for the particular x_j, x_k, etc., that are of importance to the ith market: this must depend a good deal on how the distribution of excess demand behaves (see V below). It could alternatively be that it *is* the overall level of excess demand, rather than that in a few particularly related markets, that affects the ith market. The analysis presented above suggests two ways in which $\bar{x}$ might be introduced into the individual market reaction functions, multiplicatively (changing the slope) and additively (changing the intercept). The last would, of course, imply that 'general pressure' could alter wages in the ith market even if that market were in (partial) equilibrium. Let us explore these two cases in turn.

In the multiplicative case we write, as in I.17 above,

$$\frac{\dot{w}}{w_i} = (\alpha_0 + \alpha_1 \bar{x}) x_i \qquad (I.19)$$

----

[18] This is explored in a most important new paper by F. P. R. Brechling, Ch. 7 below [6].

Applying our transformation and aggregation procedure, this gives

$$\frac{\dot{w}}{w} = (\alpha_1 - \alpha_0) - \frac{1}{\eta}(2\alpha_1 - \alpha_0)V + \frac{\alpha_1}{\eta^2}V^2 \qquad (I.20)$$

an equation non-linear in three regression coefficients and three structured parameters. The drawback of I.20 from the point of view of testing is that only the sign of the V^2 coefficient is unambiguous (positive).

In the additive case we write

$$\left(\frac{\dot{w}}{w}\right)_i = \beta_0 x_i + \beta_1 \bar{x} \qquad (I.21)$$

which leads in the same way to

$$\frac{\dot{w}}{w} = -(\beta_0 + \beta_1) + \frac{1}{\eta}(\beta_0 + \beta_1)V \qquad (I.22)$$

Comparison with I.10 above shows that the signs of the coefficients are the same. The conclusion is, therefore, that we cannot distinguish, in regression results with the addi-log model and our aggregation procedure, between the hypotheses of I.8 and I.21. Given our procedures, this is hardly surprising: if V is the independent variable, we do not know whether it operates purely as an aggregation of I.8 (diagonal matrix case), or reflects an additive 'general pressure' effect as well (I.21). We shall, therefore, not discuss this case further (it also unfortunately turns out that we are unable to test I.20 with our data).

.9 We finally consider the role of the rate of change of unemployment as an explanatory variable. Phillips [23] and Lipsey [17] both reported that $\dot{U}$ has explanatory power, and accounted for the famous loops. Arguing that the rate of change of excess demand was an intruder in the reaction function, Lipsey introduced his aggregation hypothesis, and suggested that $\dot{U}$ had been serving as a proxy for dispersion. The moments model was designed to test this hypothesis. It appeared to give satisfactory results (a positive coefficient for σ^2; but see below), but the correlation between $\dot{U}$ and σ^2 was very weak. $\dot{U}$ itself was not significant in the fitted equations.

The subject has now developed considerably. Contributors to the Phelps volume [22] have been concerned to develop the theory of optimising behaviour in disequilibrium and uncertainty, rather than to accept the *ad hoc* reaction functions used here. Mortensen's paper, in particular, provides a most comprehensive and elegant model from which a Phillips curve, with loops, is derived. We do not attempt here to apply this model to the British data for two reasons. The first is that the model is not presently in a form that lends itself conveniently to empirical testing. The second is that we can find very little evidence of important rate of change effects in the British data. This is in sharp contrast to results with U.S. data.[19] The present state of knowledge suggests that level effects have dominated for the U.K., rate of change effects for the U.S. (given the available data). This plainly calls for further enquiry. A brief discussion of the Mortensen model may now be helpful.

Very crudely, the model may be caricatured as suggesting two equilibrium conditions for the labour market rather than one:

$$\text{(i)} \quad N = N^* \tag{I.23}$$

$$\text{(ii)} \quad U = \tilde{U} \tag{I.24}$$

(where N is current employment, N^* desired employment). If the first condition is not satisfied, firms will wish to change their relative wage offers in order to alter the flow supply of labour, $\dot{N}$, to them. The first condition may be satisfied where the second is not. If $N = N^*$, but $U \neq \tilde{U}$, firms will be able, or be required, to alter their relative wage offers (and to change N^*). It may be plausible to suppose that inequality between N and N^*, at least in the direction $N^* > N$, has faster effects than inequality between U and $\tilde{U}$, at least in the direction $U < \tilde{U}$. The effects will not, however, be independent: $N^* > N$ will change wages more rapidly if $U < \tilde{U}$ than if $U > \tilde{U}$.

We might conjecture that, in the post-war world, U has been generally below $\tilde{U}$ in the U.K. but not in the U.S., whereas the former economy has been better stabilised, leading to less inequality, on the average, between N and N^*, than in the latter. This would be consistent with our results, but leaves unexplained the unimportance of rate of change effects for the U.K. in the inter-war period (which is mysterious in certain other respects too: see III below).

---

[19] That rate of change effects appear more important than level effects is well known: see, e.g. Brechling [5]. Preliminary work by Professor Brechling on Mortensen's model, and further tests of the moments model for the U.S., confirm this finding. It should, however, be noted that, in most work on the U.S., the dependent variable is an *earnings* rather than a wage *rate* variable, and we should expect the former to be more sensitive to rate of change effects.

We now introduce a primitive device, consistent with the addi-log model but not capturing the spirit of the Mortensen model, which may be used to 'fish' for a rate of change effect. We simply postulate, *ad hoc*, that

$$\left(\frac{\dot{w}}{w}\right)_i = \alpha(x_i, \dot{x}_i) = \alpha_0 x_i + \alpha_i \dot{x}_i \qquad (I.25)$$

Applying the standard procedure, this yields [20]

$$\frac{\dot{w}}{w} = -\alpha_0 + \frac{\alpha_0}{\eta} V + \frac{\alpha_1}{\eta} V^* \qquad (I.26)$$

where

$$V^* = \sum \gamma_i \frac{\dot{u}_i}{u_i}$$

i.e. the weighted sum of the proportional rates of change.[21] V^* is, not surprisingly, closely correlated with $(1/V)(dV/dt)$. The reason that I.25 is not in the spirit of the Mortensen model is that excess demand itself does not appear in that model: firms optimising over time always adjust their relative wage offer so as to secure the optimal flow supply of labour to them, whence neither x nor $\dot{x}$ is defined.

The Mortensen model also introduces expected unemployment as an explanatory variable. On the supply side, the reason is that an expected increase in unemployment will reduce the probability workers attach to obtaining better offers, and therefore reduce their 'acceptance wage' (see also Holt in Phelps [22]), and vice versa. On the demand side, the reason is that an expected increase in unemployment will deter firms from wishing to increase their relative wage offers (or persuade them to reduce them) in order to attract the desired flow supply of labour. U^e can readily be incorporated in the simple model presented here as a variable affecting the speed of reaction to a given excess demand, i.e. multiplicatively as described in I.6 above; but this treatment will pose obvious econometric difficulties. Our experiments with expected unemployment are described below.

[20] Since

$$\dot{y}_i = \dot{x}_i = \frac{1}{\eta} \frac{\dot{u}_i}{u_i}$$

[21] In the discrete-time case, $\sum \gamma_i \Delta \log u_i$ would be a better approximation. We have not made use of V^* in the regression results reported below.

Table II.1.a   Annual model 1892–1913 O.L.S. first central difference moments and addi-log models

Dependent variable ẇ/w	Const.	U^{-1}	σ^2	ṗ/p	U̇/U	V	$\bar{R}^2$	D.W.
1. Phelps Brown	− 2·50 (2·8)	13·35 (4·0)		0·21 (1·9)			0·606	1·27
2.	− 4·26 (3·6)	16·51 (4·8)	0·28 (2·1)	0·41 (2·9)			0·664	1·70
3.	−2·69 (3·4)	14·18 (4·7)		0·16 (1·6)	0·01 (2·6)		0·698	1·56
4.	−4·00 (3·7)	16·36 (5·3)	0·21 (1·7)	0·32 (2·4)	−0·01 (2·3)		0·728	1·84
5.	−9·05 (3·5)					−3·40 (4·1)	0·426	1·00
6.	−7·08 (2·9)			0·28 (2·4)		−2·65 (3·3)	0·537	1·12
7. Bowley	−2·78 (1·8)	15·81 (2·7)		0·24 (1·2)			0·384	0·97
8.	−6·42 (3·3)	21·95 (3·8)	0·58 (2·6)	0·64 (2·7)			0·525	1·09
9.	−3·00 (2·0)	16·57 (2·9)		0·18 (0·9)	−0·02 (1·6)		0·431	1·04
10.	−6·17 (3·2)	21·80 (3·9)	0·52 (2·3)	0·55 (2·3)	−0·01 (1·2)		0·540	1·03
11.	−10·89 (2·8)					−4·12 (3·2)	0·309	1·04
12.	−8·74 (2·2)			0·31 (1·6)		−3·30 (2·5)	0·360	0·97

Finally, we note that we proceed, except where otherwise noted, as though trade unions did not exist. This may seem a sufficient reason for regarding the model developed above as inappropriate. All we can really say on this point is that the model does seem to be reasonably consistent with a good deal of the evidence but, as we shall see below, leaves many important matters quite unsettled.

II   The period 1890–1914

.1 To test either the moments model or the addi-log model, we must have some disaggregated data. The only available series before the First World War are reported unemployment of union members, and, at that, we can only disaggregate consistently into five major groups. These data were used, perforce, to compute both σ^2 and V. Detail is

Table II.1.b Models as for Table 1a but using a
lag ρ transform

Dependent variable $\dot{w}/w$	Const.	U^{-1}	σ^2	$\dot{p}/p$	$\dot{U}/U$	V	$\bar{R}^2$	ρ
1. Phelps Brown								
2.								
3.								
4.								
5.	−3·35					−2·83	0·264	0·5266
	(2·3)					(2·9)		
6.	−2·96			0·23		−2·31	0·375	0·4860
	(2·0)			(2·0)		(2·4)		
7. Bowley	−1·40	16·20		0·39			0·384	0·5691
	(1·5)	(2·6)		(2·2)				
8.	−2·95	21·03	0·44	0·59			0·479	0·4976
	(2·6)	(3·4)	(2·1)	(3·0)				
9.	−1·63	17·73		0·36	−0·02		0·438	0·5811
	(1·9)	(2·9)		(2·1)	(1·6)			
10.	−2·90	21·94	0·40	0·54	0·01		0·518	0·5313
	(2·8)	(3·6)	(2·0)	(2·9)	(1·5)			
11.	−6·27					−4·61	0·272	0·4924
	(2·5)					(2·9)		
12.	−4·71			0·36		−3·76	0·359	0·5364
	(2·1)			(1·9)		(2·4)		

given in the Appendix. Here we merely note that these are very poor data, and that it is a bit of a miracle that we get any useful results at all.

Results are reported in Table II.1. We note that there is a choice of three wage indices, the official Board of Trade Series, Bowley, and Phelps Brown. The first is the worst (it is unweighted), and results are not reported. The second and third give reasonably consistent results. The data are, of course, annual, and first central differences were (somewhat arbitrarily) used for all rate of change variables. Table II.1.a shows the presence of positive serial correlation in the residuals. The lag-ρ transformation was applied to remove bias in the standard errors,[22] with results reported in Table II.1.b.

[22] This is probably not strictly appropriate, since use of first central differences is introducing a moving average.

Table II.2   Estimates of $\tilde{U}$ from the
addi-log model, 1892–1913

Equation number Table 1b	$\hat{\eta}$	$\tilde{U}$
5	−2·50	8·2
6	−2·49	8·2
11	−2·68	6·7
12	−2·70	6·7

On the whole, the moments model does rather better than the addi-log model, at least in the proportion of the variance explained. Given the data, we do not put much emphasis on this. What seems more important is that the coefficients in both models have the predicted signs: the dispersion effect is discernible even in these data. There is some evidence of loops, although the coefficients of $\dot{U}$ in Table II.1.b are not significant. The rate of change of prices is almost everywhere significant. These results do not, however, appear to be worth dwelling on (nor the result, not reported, that in some equations U seems to do better than U^{-1}).

.2 A method of computing from the moments model the level of unemployment consistent with stable prices, and the reduction in that level consequent upon a reduction in dispersion, is given in Archibald [1]. Here we give, in Table II.2, the estimates of n and $\tilde{U}$ derived from the addi-log model. $\tilde{U}$ appears to be around 7 per cent for this sample of unionised labour. There are no other estimates for the same period with which we may compare it. We shall compare it below with estimated $\tilde{U}$ for our two other periods. It does not, at any rate, appear to be implausible.

III   The inter-war period
.1 For the part of the period that Britain was not on the Gold Standard, the standard Phillips curve augmented by $\dot{p}/p$ fits quite well. (Regression results are presented below. The importance of the Gold Standard is discussed in .2.) We originally expected, however, that the addition of σ^2 (whether calculated from industrial or regional data) would improve the fit. It was a period of considerable structural

change as well as serious unemployment, and cross-section unemployment had a large dispersion (measured unemployment reached 100 per cent in some areas in the worst years). These phenomena are, of course, well known, and have been much discussed in a more or less qualitative way. It seemed reasonable to suppose that our measured variances, which had previously appeared to be significant both before the first war and after the second, would capture the structural change and upheaval of this period, and have good explanatory power. As will be seen in greater detail below, the results are quite otherwise: the variance term is not significant and adds nothing to the explanatory power of the equations. (The variance is quite strongly positively correlated with U. This, however, is usual, and has not prevented us from obtaining 'sensible' results with the moments model elsewhere.) We conclude that the moments model does not capture the effects on $\dot{w}/w$ of the structural maladjustment of the inter-war period. If, however, the cross-section distribution of unemployment is highly skewed (as it was in the period) and even approximately described by the log-normal distribution, then the fact that the variance, in natural numbers, has poor explanatory power is not to be wondered at. (See also fn. 8 above.)

The addi-log model in fact fits about as well as the ordinary Phillips curve. It has, however, the overwhelming advantage of capturing structural effects via the estimate of η, or $\tilde{U}$. We report below some startling estimates of $\tilde{U}$, which, if reliable, provide a quantitative measure of the structural difficulties experienced by the U.K. economy in the inter-war period. The addi-log model also permits us to experiment further with the intruder variables.

.2 The failure of σ^2 in this period was at first sight disappointing: it induced us to take many experiments[23] too tedious to report! We eventually found, however, as can be seen in Table III.1, that the introduction of a dummy variable for the period Britain was on the Gold Standard gave significant results. This in turn led us to divide the whole period into two sub-periods, On and Off the Gold Standard (see Tables III.2 and 3). The results are dramatic. Off the Gold Standard, the models fit rather well, particularly the addi-log model. The period On the Gold Standard looks, econometrically speaking,

[23] Some induced by the thought that an overvalued exchange rate might be expected to alter the structure of the cross-section excess demand associated with a given level of U.

Table III.1 Inter-war results, moments and addi-log models. Total period—1924(2)–1938(3)

III.1.a. O.L.S.

Dependent variable ẇ/w	Const.	U^{-1}	σ^2	ṗ/p	V	V_{-1}	D	G	$\bar{R}^2$	D.W.
1.	−1·12 (2·3)	23·27 (3·3)					1·32 (4·3)	−1·09 (3·2)	0·805	0·59
2.	0·24 (0·2)	11·16 (0·9)	−0·01 (1·1)	0·21 (3·8)			1·19 (3·6)	−1·05 (3·0)	0·806	0·66
3.	−5·22 (6·4)			0·21 (3·8)	−2·91 (6·8)		1·57 (5·1)	−2·06 (7·0)	0·786	0·65
4.	3·33 (3·5)			0·18 (3·3)	−1·95 (4·0)		1·28 (4·3)	−1·32 (3·7)	0·817	0·63
5.	−3·85 (4·0)			0·17 (3·2)	−0·43 (0·5)	−1·82 (2·1)	1·21 (4·2)	−1·51 (4·3)	0·830	0·68

III.1.b. Lag-ρ

Dependent variable ẇ/w	Const.	U^{-1}	σ^2	ṗ/p	V	V_{-1}	D	G	$\bar{R}^2$	ρ
1										
2.										
3.	−0·10 (0·7)				−0·45 (0·7)		1·03 (2·0)	−0·64 (1·7)	0·077	0·9017
4.	−0·10 (0·6)			0·11 (2·4)	−0·41 (0·7)		1·06 (2·2)	−0·47 (1·3)	0·188	0·8644
5.										

Table III.2   Inter-war results, moments and addi-log models on Gold Standard—1925(2)–1931(3)

III.2.a.   O.L.S.

Dependent variable $\dot{w}/w$	Const.	U^{-1}	σ^2	$\dot{p}/p$	V	V_{-1}	$\bar{R}^2$	D.W.
1.	−0·41 (0·4)	0·95 (0·1)		0·18 (2·2)			0·195	0·57
2.	3·73 (1·7)	−34·68 (1·8)	−0·02 (2·1)	0·23 (2·9)			0·300	0·92
3.	−4·11 (2·9)				−1·48 (2·4)		0·153	0·57
4.	−1·75 (0·9)			0·15 (1·7)	−0·60 (0·7)		0·213	0·56
5.	−2·62 (1·2)			0·13 (1·4)	0·10 (0·1)	−1·05 (0·8)	0·199	0·62

III.2.b.   Lag-ρ

Dependent variable $\dot{w}/w$	Const.	U^{-1}	σ^2	$\dot{p}/p$	V	V_{-1}	$\bar{R}^2$	ρ
1.								
2.	−0·85 (0·6)	−15·49 (1·1)	−0·31 (0·5)	0·48 (0·8)			−0·049	0·922
3.	−0·27 (1·2)				−0·08 (0·1)		0·43	0·855
5.								
6.								

Table III.3 Inter-war results, moments and addi-log models off Gold Standard—1924(2)–1925(1) and 1931(4)–1938(3)

III.3.a. O.L.S.

Dependent variable $\dot{w}/w$	Const.	U^{-1}	σ^2	$\dot{p}/p$	V	V_{-1}	D	$\bar{R}^2$	D.W.
1.	−2·47 (6·4)	45·37 (7·9)		0·24 (5·4)			0·86 (4·3)	0·928	1·07
2.	−3·08 (2·8)	50·52 (4·8)	0·005 (0·6)	0·25 (5·2)			0·91 (4·1)	0·928	1·10
3.	−7·72 (8·8)				−4·26 (9·1)		1·22 (4·7)	0·858	0·83
4.	−5·47 (6·9)			0·23 (5·0)	−3·11 (7·5)		0·80 (3·8)	0·922	1·25
5.	−5·53 (7·5)			0·25 (5·6)	−1·26 (1·4)	−1·91 (2·3)	0·73 (3·7)	0·932	0·99

III.3.b. Lag-ρ

Dependent variable $\dot{w}/w$	Const.	U^{-1}	σ^2	$\dot{p}/p$	V	V_{-1}	D	$\bar{R}^2$	ρ
1.	−1·33 (4·4)	47·30 (5·2)		0·22 (3·8)			0·81 (2·7)	0·840	0·4780
2.									
3.	−2·00 (4·9)				−3·71 (5·3)		1·08 (2·3)	0·566	0·7001 $\sigma^2 = ·290$
4.	−3·17 (4·5)			0·23 (4·0)	−2·95 (4·8)		0·80 (2·7)	0·849	0·3851 $\sigma^2 = ·203$
5.									

like the post-world war two wages policy On periods (see Lipsey and Parkin [18]). We appear, in fact, to have discovered the 'econometric consequences of Mr. Churchill' (and to have discovered that they are very similar to the econometric consequences of Sir Stafford Cripps or Mrs. Castle)! This requires some explanation.

It is natural to consult Keynes [15] first. He argued that, by going on to Gold at the chosen figure, the Government had committed itself to forcing money wages down by 10 per cent. He expected, however, that this would be done by conventional measures, using monetary policy to generate the required level of unemployment. If that were all, there is no reason why our models should not fit. We are led to suspect some sort of 'wages policy', or at least governmental interference with the ordinary course of wage bargaining. One might further conjecture that interference of the type postulated might have helped to provoke the General Strike, and its failure, and the subsequent weakness of unions, might have further disrupted normal bargaining relations.[24] We do not know how to develop or test these rudimentary ideas: perhaps explanation is now best left to historians.

It is obviously possible that we might simply be looking at the twenties versus the thirties, or before and after the Great Crash. Since we have too few observations before Britain went back to Gold to permit estimating as a separate sub-period, we have pooled these observations with the Gold Standard Period as well as with the thirties. Comparison so overwhelmingly favours the proposition that these observations belong with the other Gold Standard Off observations (the thirties) that these are the results reported. We in fact also experimented by altering the dates at which we entered or removed the dummy, 'fishing' for the appropriate period. We 'fished' for the General Strike, and experimented with continuous foreign-exchange-rate indices in place of the Gold Standard dummy. None of these experiments generated any results worth reporting.

Whenever a 'normal' price (or wage) adjustment equation is suspended, we expect other consequences (price control: queues or black markets). Thus to test our interpretation of the Gold Standard

---

[24] This does not, of course, explain why 'normality' was apparently restored precisely when the Gold Standard was again abandoned. It is easier to postulate 'special' behaviour by the Government in the Gold Standard Period. We have not attempted any serious explanation of the Gold Standard Period. To do so, we should certainly experiment with variables such as union push-fulness, with which Hines [9] obtained strong results for the inter-war period.

Period, or Lipsey and Parkin's of the wages policy periods, some further predicted consequences should be derived. In this sense, it might be argued that the Lipsey–Parkin study is incomplete (as were, of course, other studies of the effects of wages policy). We cannot claim that we can do much better: we do not have an adequately articulated model of the structure of the economy when the wage-reaction mechanism is suspended. Since the effects of government interference are not uniform, we might expect some structural effect. We endeavoured to test for this by regressing V on U and σ^2 (industrial) separately for the Gold Standard Off and On periods. The results were not significantly different. Thus whatever structural effects there may have been, we have failed to capture them.

.3 We now turn to our main O.L.S. results in more detail. Data are available (for description see the Appendix) for a quarterly model, 1924.II to 1938.III. For the construction of σ^2 or V quarterly, we use regional unemployment figures ($n = 8$) or the industrial classification ($n = 25$).[25] In fact, except for the moments model, it makes so little difference which we use that, in order to economise on space, we report only the industrial results. In all equations, w is the Ministry of Labour Index of Weekly Wage Rates. This index was base-weighted by the proportions of the total wage bill by industry in 1924 until 1934, when the 1934 weights were adopted. We have endeavoured to deal with this change of base by introducing an intercept dummy (D, the 'data dummy' of the tables).

We have a choice of definitions for rate of change variables:

First Central Difference (FCD) $\dfrac{\dot{x}}{x} = \dfrac{x_{+1} - x_{-1}}{2x}$

One Quarter Difference (OQD) $\dfrac{\dot{x}}{x} = \dfrac{x - x_{-1}}{x_{-1}}$

Four Quarter Difference (FQD) $\dfrac{\dot{x}}{x} = \dfrac{x_{+2} - x_{-2}}{\frac{1}{2}(x_{+2} - x_{-2})}$

We have in fact experimented with all three. (The level variables, U, σ^2 and V are measured in the same way in all cases.) It would be

[25] More finely disaggregated cross-section unemployment data are, in fact available after 1927, and were used to investigate the form of the distributions: see V below. That they are not used here is due partly to their not being available in the earlier part of the period and partly to the sheer cost of processing.

impossible to report all results. With the exceptions given below, each of the first two gives results broadly consistent with the FQD results. Each of the first two gives rise, however, to special problems. The series for $\dot{p}/p$ generated by FCD exhibits strong serial correlation, and the residuals from the fitted equations do likewise. Application of the standard ρ-lag transform does not, however, seem appropriate if the autocorrelation is in an independent variable.[26] OQD leads to several difficulties. The most serious for present purposes is that we require seasonal dummies, which are inconvenient when we come to Constrained Non-Linear Least Squares (CNLS). Coefficients on $\dot{p}/p$ (current or lagged) are not significant. Using FQD, we not surprisingly find autocorrelated residuals.

It cannot be pretended that the situation is satisfactory. In a quarterly model results with lags, rate of change variables, etc., must be substantially influenced by the definition chosen. For this reason, we should have chosen to avoid the 'smoothing' introduced by FQD. Our choice was sadly governed by practical considerations.

We fitted the simple Phillips curve, the moments model and the addi-log model for the whole period (Table III.1, where G is an intercept dummy for the Gold Standard period), and for the two sub-periods (Gold Standard On, Off) separately (Tables III.2, .3). Tables III.1.a, .b give results for the four-quarter model, without and with the lag-ρ transform, and similarly for Tables III.2 and III.3.[27] Some less important experiments ($\dot{U}$, etc.) are also reported. It seems reasonable to conclude that the addi-log model fits at least as well as the moments model.

.4 We now take up some of the possibilities suggested in I above. (Note that in what follows we report our results for the Gold Standard Off period exclusively.)

Experiments with $\dot{U}$ and with lagged values of V do not suggest any rate of change effects (although, on the whole, V_{-1} is perhaps more important than V). We have therefore not pursued the suggestion, made in I.9, that V^* (the weighted sum of the proportional rates of change) might be an appropriate variable. To test for 'spill-

[26] The $\dot{p}/p$ series is extraordinarily regular—two high values followed by two low ones. We could calculate the (seasonal) behaviour of the original p series that would give this result under the FCD transform but, since other definitions are available, do not pursue the matter.

[27] To avoid unnecessary clutter, we have omitted from the b-Tables equations which do not add anything of interest to the picture.

over effects' (the matrix of reaction coefficients non-diagonal) we suggested the variable V^2. This is highly correlated with V itself, and the consequence of introducing it into the regression equation is that neither V nor V^2 is individually significant. Thus we are unable to report any definite result on this point. Data for intruder variables (productivity, trade union strength, profits) are generally bad or absent for this period, and we introduce them only in the post-war period.

.5 We therefore now turn to the CNLS estimates. We have two cases to investigate, expected $\dot{p}/p$ additive and current $\dot{p}/p$ multiplicative. For the first, we used the Koyck transform, for the second the form derived in I.18 above. (A third possibility is, of course, expected $\dot{p}/p$ entering multiplicatively; but this leads to an intractable functional form.) Results are reported in Table III.4, where we also report results with expected unemployment. We now want to compare these CNLS results, and to compare them with the preferred O.L.S. equation in which $\dot{p}/p$ is additive. The comparable O.L.S. equations are in Tables III.3.a and .b, equations 4. For the lag-ρ equation, $\hat{\sigma}^2 = 0 \cdot 203$. A first reaction might well be that equation III.4.2, using $(\dot{p}/p)^e$, was to be preferred. We are, however, a little hesitant about such a conclusion. If we write

$$\frac{\dot{w}}{w} = a_0 + a_1 V + a_2 \left(\frac{\dot{p}}{p}\right)^e + a_3 D + u \tag{III.1}$$

where

$$\left(\frac{\dot{p}}{p}\right)^e = \lambda\left(\frac{\dot{p}}{p}\right) + (1 - \lambda)\left(\frac{\dot{p}}{p}\right)^e_{-1}$$

we obtain

$$\frac{\dot{w}}{w} = \lambda a_0 + a_1 V - a_1(1 - \lambda)V_{-1} + \lambda a_2 \frac{\dot{p}}{p} + a_3 D - a_3(1 - \lambda)D_{-1}$$

$$+ (1 - \lambda)\frac{\dot{w}}{w_{-1}} + u - (1 - \lambda)u_{-1} \tag{III.2}$$

The problems in estimating III.2 are well known (see, e.g. Goldberger [12]). If III.2 is appropriate, the O.L.S. regressions, leading to serially correlated residuals, are inappropriate and biased. Vice versa, if we start with the O.L.S. regressions, adding the lagged value of the dependent variable to the right-hand side (the important difference

Table III.4 Constrained non-linear Least Squares (Gold Standard off)

Dependent variable $\dot{w}/w$	Const.	$\dot{p}/p$	V	V^e	$\dot{p}^e/p$	$\dot{p}^v/p$	D	$\hat{\sigma}^2$
1.	$-7{\cdot}347$ (8·0)	$-0{\cdot}303$ (1·1)	$-4{\cdot}048$ (8·2)			$-0{\cdot}167$ (1·1)	$1{\cdot}131$ (4·3)	$0{\cdot}406$
2.	$-0{\cdot}441$ (0·3)		$-0{\cdot}570$ (0·7)		$0{\cdot}467$ (4·1)		$0{\cdot}553$ (1·6)	$0{\cdot}149$
3.	$-4{\cdot}805$ (4·0)	$0{\cdot}229$ (4·2)		$-2{\cdot}780$ (4·4)			$0{\cdot}840$ (3·0)	$0{\cdot}166$

between III.2 and II.1) is bound to improve the fit. Noting that the Koyck transform saves degrees of freedom by imposing a structure on the coefficients of $\dot{p}/p$, $(\dot{p}/p)_{-1}$, etc., we may therefore ask if the imposed lag structure is justified by using O.L.S. with some lagged values of $\dot{p}/p$. We have in fact only used $\dot{p}/p$, $(\dot{p}/p)_{-1}$ and $(\dot{p}/p)_{-2}$, but with a fairly clear result: the coefficient on $(\dot{p}/p)_{-1}$ is not significantly different from zero, although that on $(\dot{p}/p)_{-2}$ is. This suggests that the Koyck structure is inappropriate. Thus, on the evidence of Table III.4, it is hard to be sure whether current $\dot{p}/p$ is appearing as an additive intruder, or as a legitimate expectations variable.

Equations III.4.3 suggests that expected unemployment is very successful; but again, the equation is essentially the O.L.S. equation plus the lagged value of the dependent variable. We notice again that the coefficients on V and V_{-1} in the O.L.S. equation (equation 5 of Table III.3.a) appear to be inconsistent with the Koyck structure. (We in fact use V rather than U in expected unemployment.)

It appears that the evidence is against the hypothesis that $\dot{p}/p$ alters only the slope of the reaction function. In I.6, however, we pointed out that there were two possibilities: a uniform change of slope, or a kink at the origin. Further, if the kinked reaction function is correct, the addition of $\dot{p}/p$ will give a better approximation than a uniform change of slope. Equation 1 of Table III.4 is the uniform-change model. Thus it is still possible that $\dot{p}/p$ operates on the slope, but differently in the two quadrants. We give our results for the 'kinky' case in .7 below.

.6 Let us now consider our estimates of $\tilde{U}$. First, we have some *a priori* information which may be of use. $\tilde{U}$ must obviously lie in the range 0–100. We can, however, narrow the acceptable range further than this. Suppose that, for the post-war period, the level of unemployment, U^*, consistent with price stability has been about $2\frac{1}{2}$ per cent. $\tilde{U}$ (wage stability) is, of course, greater than U^* by an amount which depends, *inter alia*, on productivity change. Thus $\tilde{U}$ might be, say, 5 per cent. We might take this value, or the 7 per cent estimated for the pre-1914 period, as the lower limit of the range. The structural maladjustment of the inter-war period might well cause $\tilde{U}$ to have been much greater than this. Given, however, that excess demand was negative at least sometimes, which will scarcely be denied, $\tilde{U}$ must be less than our most extreme observations. Thus we might set an upper limit of, say, 20 per cent.

Table III.5   Estimates of η and $\tilde{U}$ from preferred equations (Gold Standard off)

	Pre data	break	Post data	break
Equation reference	η	$\tilde{U}\%$	η	$\tilde{U}\%$
O.L.S.				
1. III.3.b3	$-1\cdot798$	16·6	$-0\cdot826$	43·6
2. III.3.b4	$-1\cdot748$	17·37	$-1\cdot306$	27·1
C.N.L.S.				
3. III.4.1	$-1\cdot815$	16·3	$1\cdot536$	21·6
4. III.4.3	$-1\cdot728$	17·8	$-1\cdot426$	24·0

Before turning to the results, reported in Table III.5, there are two further points that require notice. The first is that η is the ratio of two regression coefficients, whence a point estimate outside the acceptable range is not conclusive evidence against the model. The second is that our equations include a dummy variable for the data break, which allows two estimates of η from each equation, as well as revealing errors-in-variables: wages[28] were not correctly measured! If the dispersion of unemployment is not constant, $\tilde{U}$ and η are, of course, not constant. So we can only conclude that, using the dummy to split the period, we obtain two point estimates of $\tilde{U}$, themselves functions of the observed dispersions. What is discouraging about the estimates reported in III.5 is that $\tilde{U}$ is larger in the later period, after the data break. We should expect structural maladjustment to have diminished over the period as a whole rather than to have increased.[29] It also appears that the estimate of $\tilde{U}$ obtained from equation III.3.b.3 is quite unacceptable. This equation in fact gave the poorest fit in Table III.3.b: the consequence of omitting $\dot{p}/p$ is a preposterous estimate of $\tilde{U}$. We have already noted, however, that if the effect of $\dot{p}/p$ is to kink the reaction function, the equations used in Table III.5 are bad approximations.

---

[28] And we may recall, sadly, that even if wages were correctly measured, our specification of $\dot{w}/w$ leaves much to be desired. We may refer again to the problems of estimating equation III.2 above.

[29] A substantial part of the structural maladjustment after world war one was due specifically to the collapse of the export markets for coal and textiles. The problem should have diminished with the passage of time alone (allowing the relocation or retirement of highly specific workers).

.7 From the last remark, it follows that we do not wish to use these estimates to determine whether excess demand were positive or negative in our test of the kinky model. Instead, we adopted an iterative procedure to search for $\tilde{V}$. The model may be written

$$\frac{\dot{w}}{w} = \left(\alpha + \beta^1\left(\frac{\dot{p}}{p}\right)^1\right)x \quad \text{for } V < \tilde{V} \qquad \text{(III.3.a)}$$

$$\frac{\dot{w}}{w} = \left(\alpha + \beta^{11}\left(\frac{\dot{p}}{p}\right)^{11}\right)x \quad \text{for } V > \tilde{V} \qquad \text{(III.3.b)}$$

We have assumed that α is the same whether excess demand is positive or negative. Making our usual transformation, we have

$$\frac{\dot{w}}{w} = -\alpha + \frac{\alpha}{\eta}V - \beta^1\left(\frac{\dot{p}}{p}\right)^1 - \beta^{11}\left(\frac{\dot{p}}{p}\right)^{11} + \frac{\beta^1}{\eta}\left(\frac{\dot{p}}{p}\right)^1 V + \frac{\beta^{11}}{\eta}\left(\frac{\dot{p}}{p}\right)^{11}V$$

$$\text{(III.4)}$$

An O.L.S. estimate of III.4 would lead to overidentification of η, whence CNLS was used. Assuming that $\beta^1 = \beta^{11}$ leads to the equation reported as 1 in Table III.4, where β is badly determined.

The results are given in Table III.6 (where the asymptotic standard errors are given in brackets). Initially, observations of negative excess demand were taken to be those with the highest 7, highest 12, highest 19 and highest 27 unemployment rates. The experiment continued by moving one observation at a time from positive to negative excess demand. We have to report the startling result that the residual variance is minimised when the number of quarters in which excess demand is taken to be negative is 7 (or 8: since $\dot{p}/p = 0$ in the eighth observation, the results are identical). We find that β^1 and β^{11} have the predicted signs, although the statistical significance of $(\beta^1 - \beta^{11})$ is not very high.[30]

Comparing this result with those reported in Table III.4 above, it is hard to draw a firm conclusion. The model of uniform slope change, equation 1, gives the worst result. A combination of kinky and expectations would doubtless give the best result, if any manageable form could be found.

Let us now return to our estimates of $\tilde{U}$. It was convenient to report on η^{-1} rather than η itself in Table III.5. Assuming 7 observa-

[30] We also in fact ran III.4 by O.L.S., assuming 7 observations with negative excess demand. η is, as already noted, overdetermined. Residual variance was slightly reduced to 0·23794. Neither β^1 nor β^{11} was significantly different from zero. Nonetheless, it is rather alarming that their signs were reversed.

Table III.6 'Kinky' for inter-war period, Gold Standard off, C.N.L.S.

Number of observations designated as 'depression'*	Residual variance	α	η^{-1}	β^1	β^{11}	γ (data dummy)	$(\beta^1-\beta^{11})$	Minimum V for 'depression'
4.	0·35670	5·6536 (1·0829)	−0·57114 (0·019322)	0·55629 (0·24829)	−2·5581 (1·9632)	0·98680 (0·25628)	3·1144 (1·95048)	−1·60
5.	0·32974	5·1373 (1·0606)	−0·57886 (0·02122)	0·62451 (0·23150)	−3·0830 (2·4467)	0·94338 (0·24718)	3·7075 (2·4176)	−1·62
6.	0·29347	4·9612 (0·98742)	−0·57982 (0·019806)	0·66027 (0·21785)	−3·5316 (2·5317)	0·94639 (0·23147)	4·1919 (2·5006)	−1·64
7.	0·29278	4·9372 (0·97988)	−0·58030 (0·019588)	0·66116 (0·21669)	−3·5909 (2·5617)	0·94467 (0·23057)	4·2521 (2·5314)	−1·65
8.	0·29278	4·9372 (0·97988)	−0·58030 (0·019588)	0·66116 (0·21669)	−3·5909 (2·5617)	0·94467 (0·23057)	4·2521 (2·5314)	−1·75
9.	0·29721	5·1275 (1·0445)	−0·57477 (0·020777)	0·66912 (0·22849)	−2·9785 (2·2269)	0·97582 (0·23829)	3·6476 (2·1965)	−1·76
10.	0·29907	5·1704 (1·0789)	−0·57384 (0·22242)	0·66860 (0·23197)	−2·8728 (2·2871)	0·98023 (0·24452)	3·5414 (2·2513)	−1·80
11.	0·30434	5·2694 (1·1369)	−0·57033 (0·021957)	0·66746 (0·24209)	−2·5473 (2·0441)	1·0198 (0·23337)	3·2148 (2·0048)	−1·81
12.	0·30871	5·3671 (1·1440)	−0·56914 (0·22917)	0·66125 (0·24718)	−2·3881 (2·0104)	1·0199 (0·24194)	3·0494 (1·9659)	−1·88
13.	0·31474	5·4721 (1·1838)	−0·56744 (0·024340)	0·65618 (0·25378)	−2·2015 (2·0108)	1·0259 (0·25244)	2·8577 (1·9622)	−1·90
14.	Omitted since $V = $ −1·91 as in 15							
15.	0·34717	5·8968 (1·2343)	−0·55778 (0·020856)	0·62477 (0·28321)	−1·3805 (1·3733)	1·1278 (0·24524)	2·0053 (1·3518)	−1·91
19.	0·39126	6·5360 (1·1813)	−0·55121 (0·016156)	0·48212 (0·30120)	−0·52715 (0·84383)	1·2544 (0·24886)	1·0093 (0·8395)	−2·08
27.	0·86965	0·21860 (1·1953)	−0·43312 (0·00784)	15·189 (8·8380)	−1·2605 (0·45592)	1·9451 (0·32468)	16·454 (8·8052)	−2·26

* In descending order of V.

tions with negative excess demand, the direct CNLS estimate of η is -1.723 (asymptotic standard error 0.0582). This gives $\tilde{U}$ at roughly 17·9 per cent (neglecting the effect of the data dummy). This is within the range of values reported in Table III.5. It appears, then, that if the addi-log model is to be taken seriously, these estimates of $\tilde{U}$ must also be taken seriously. It may be that the structural maladjustment of the inter-war period, which we failed to capture with the moments model, is now quantified via the addi-log model. If, of course, these estimates of $\tilde{U}$ are at all reliable, we should have to conclude that the location of the macro-Phillips curve in the inter-war period was very unfavourable to a simple Keynesian cure for unemployment.

IV The post-war period

.1 Our experiments in the post-war period are determined by our two main objects: to enquire further into the importance of dispersion effects or *structure*, and to test alternative explanations of the role of the *intruders* ($f(0)$ equal or not equal to zero). We therefore had no desire to complicate our investigations by considering the effects of Governments' wages policy. We accordingly followed the distinction made by Lipsey and Parkin [18] between 'policy-off' and 'policy-on' periods, and estimated only on the former. Their 'policy-off' period is 1950.4–1955.4 *and* 1957.1–1961.2. It unfortunately turns out that the estimated relationships for these two disjoint sub-periods are significantly different: the hypothesis that we are dealing with two samples from the same population is not acceptable.[31]

From the present point of view, this is a nuisance, but not a surprising one. Whatever the 'true' market adjustment mechanism may be, it is not to be expected that, after it has been suspended, it immediately starts to operate again as though there had been no interruption. Thus suppose that, for a period, wages policy has been effective in keeping $\dot{w}/w$ below what it would otherwise have been.[32] What happens when 'the dam breaks'? Is there some stored-up, or

---

[31] This was noticed independently by Sumner [26]. Since he reports fully, we need not re-examine the Lipsey-Parkin results here. The results of distinguishing the two sub-periods are reported in the Tables. For further criticism of Lipsey and Parkin [18], see Godfrey in Johnson and Nobay [14], The work was also extended in Parkin [19].

[32] Lipsey and Parkin in fact conclude that wages policy has sometimes had the opposite, or perverse, effect, and made $\dot{w}/w$ higher than it would otherwise have been. This result requires re-examination in the light of the results obtained by Sumner and Godfrey since, of course, it depends on their estimates of parameters on the pooled data.

integral effect? We have no theory to tell us, but, in so far as real wages will have been falling, or rising less fast than workers might otherwise have expected, a back-log effect, for a time at least, seems quite plausible. We can make no attempt on this problem in the present paper. We have made free use of devices to estimate separately for the two sub-periods in an attempt to conduct efficient tests of the hypotheses in which we are interested in spite of the shift of some of the parameters. (As a small additional precaution, we did drop the first observation after a policy-on period and the last before one.)

We report here our O.L.S. results with the moments and addi-log models, and our non-linear experiments with the latter. Details of data are reported in the Appendix, but, except where noted, they are identical with those used by Lipsey and Parkin, and by Sumner. Definitions of rate of change variables are unchanged from those used above. As usual, we experimented with both the regional and industrial data in constructing σ^2 and V. As we expected, the regional data give better results than the industrial data. Since the results are not qualitatively different, we only report the regional results. We have not used the rate-of-change variable V^*, since we find rate-of-change effects unimportant, nor the spill-over variable V^2, due again to its high correlation with V. More important, we have no 'kinky' experiment post world war two. The reason for this is that we can obtain no reliable estimate of η for this period.

.2 The results of fitting the moments and addi-log models to the whole policy-off period, with and without an intercept dummy, are reported in Table IV.1. It will be noticed that the dummy for the sub-period is significant, that lagged values of V are significant, and that, when the dummy is introduced, σ^2 is not significant.

Instead of using slope dummies, it was convenient to 'stack' the variables, entering them separately for the two sub-periods. When this was done, the intercept dummy ceased to be significant, and was accordingly dropped. Results are reported in Table IV.2. The instability of the coefficient of $\dot{p}/p$ is alarming: it appears to be both smaller, and much less well determined, in the earlier sub-period than in the later. Coefficients on the other variables do not vary sufficiently to justify the stacking procedure. We therefore repeated the O.L.S. regressions, stacking only $\dot{p}/p$. Results are given in Table IV.3.

We still find alarming instability in the coefficient of $\dot{p}/p$: it is small in the earlier sub-period, and one-half or more in the later. We have

Table IV.1 Post-war O.L.S. results, 1950.4–1955.4 and 1957.1–1961.2. Moments and addi-log models. (D is an intercept dummy for the second sub-period.)

Dependent variable $\dot{w}/w$	Const.	D	U^{-1}	U^{-1}_{-1}	σ^2	$\dot{p}/p$	V	V_{-1}	$\bar{R}^2$	D.W.	ESS
1.	0·7166 (1·13)		3·0907 (3·00)			0·5292 (8·10)			0·837	1·3455	30·1245
2.	−3·1773 (2·02)		6·7032 (4·06)		4·8439 (2·67)	0·4784 (7·57)			0·865	1·4187	24·8964
3.	−3·0488 (1·93)		5·7697 (2·96)	1·0292 (0·90)	4·3459 (2·29)	0·4668 (7·22)			0·869	1·3948	24·2934
4.	2·1919 (3·23)	−1·1464 (3·66)	2·0985 (2·27)			0·4734 (8·14)			0·882	1·6341	21·6237
5.	0·1473 (0·08)	−0·9312 (2·53)	3·9246 (2·08)		2·1988 (1·11)	0·4608 (7·80)			0·887	1·5771	20·8457
6.	0·5787 (0·29)	−1·0018 (2·73)	2·4122 (1·11)	1·4350 (1·36)	1·3036 (0·63)	0·4432 (7·42)			0·893	1·6091	19·7003
7.	−0·8341 (0·27)					0·6352 (10·91)	−2·9964 (1·08)		0·801	1·1746	36·6541
8.	−2·8486 (0·79)					0·6208 (10·42)	−1·2237 (0·38)	−3·6120 (10·9)	0·808	1·1479	35·4210
9.	−0·6381 (0·26)	−1·3980 (4·51)				0·5127 (9·49)	−3·8236 (1·71)		0·876	1·6020	22·9181
10.	−3·6063 (1·31)	−1·4819 (4·97)				0·4840 (9·07)	−1·2510 (0·51)	−5·3432 (2·08)	0·889	1·6766	20·2693
11.	−2·2014 (0·71)					0·6241 (10·73)		−4·2528 (1·50)	0·806	1·1551	35·5720
12.	−2·9445 (1·22)	−1·4816 (5·02)				0·4875 (9·31)		−5·9979 (2·73)	0·889	1·6859	20·4271

no explanation of this phenomenon (but remark again on the errors-in-variables problem). All three experiments confirm that, when attention is given to the sub-division of the periods, σ^2 is not significant. The lagged value of V is considerably more important than the current value in all three tables (which is not true of U^{-1}). We are, of course, using the FQD definition of rates of change, and have no *a priori* reason for picking the quarter in which level variables should enter.

The results reported in Tables V.2 and V.3 are unsatisfactory in another fashion: the constant term is poorly determined. Both models require that it be negative. In addition, in the addi-log model, the ratio of the constant to the coefficient of V is η, when we derive our estimate of $\tilde{U}$. From these results, we can obtain no useful estimate of $\dot{U}$ (although we may suspect $\tilde{U}$ to have been outside the range of observation).

In Table IV.4 we report the results of adding three intruders to the linear regression model: ρ (deviation of productivity from trend), ΔTU (change in union strength) and π (profits). (Detailed descriptions of these variables will be found in the Appendix.) As can be seen, none of them has any explanatory power. (We also experimented with the first difference of the profit series, stacked, without obtaining any significant results.)

.3 We now turn to the nonlinear models discussed in I above. We report (in Table IV.5) on six equations. These are:
(1) The addi-log model with the addition of price expectations (as in equation 1 of Table III.4: the Koyck transform was employed);
(2) The slope change model, equation I.18, with $\dot{p}/p$ additive ($\dot{w}/w = -\alpha + \alpha/\eta \cdot V - \beta z + \beta/\eta \cdot Vz + \delta\dot{p}$) in which z is the trade-union strength variable;
(3) Equation I.18 with $\dot{p}/p$ for z;
(4) Equation I.18 with profits for z;
(5) Equation I.12, in which the $x:U$ transformation is altered by ρ, with $\dot{p}/p$ additive;
(6) A combination of I.12 and I.18, with $\dot{p}/p$ for z.

In view of the finding, already reported, that the two post-war sub-periods differ, all six equations were fitted with all variables 'stacked' (entered separately for the two sub-periods), and with V and $\dot{p}/p$ only stacked. Results are generally better when all variables are stacked, although not qualitatively different, whence these are the results

Table IV.2   Post-war O.L.S. results. All variables stacked. (Note: the
for the two sub-periods, and

Dependent variable w/w	Const.	$1U^{-1}$	$2U^{-1}$	$1U_{-1}^{-1}$	$2U_{-1}^{-1}$	$1\dot{p}/p$	$2\dot{p}/p$	$1\sigma^2$
1.	1·5566	1·9353	2·6220			0·3067	0·5064	
	(2·42)	(1·46)	(2·91)			(2·04)	(8·12)	
2.	−1·5894	6·1726	5·1658			0·1926	0·4946	2·2589
	(0·78)	(2·28)	(2·75)			(1·20)	(8·03)	(1·10)
3.	1·8213			2·3369	2·6603	0·2371	0·4862	−1·3127
	(2·37)			(1·62)	(0·301)	(1·38)	(8·06)	(0·94)
4.	−1·1612	4·9043	2·6969	1·2287	2·5576	0·1405	0·4757	1·3355
	(0·58)	(1·74)	(1·20)	(0·74)	(1·89)	(0·79)	(7·87)	(0·63)
5.	−1·2249					0·4084	0·5337	
	(0·49)					(3·25)	(9·01)	
6.	−3·8304					0·3583	0·5105	
	(1·60)					(2·97)	(9·14)	
7.	−4·4517					0·3606	0·5073	
	(1·60)					(2·91)	(8·81)	

reported. In view of the O.L.S. results, we also fitted all six equations using V_{-1} in place of V, but without any modification to the results worth reporting.

Table IV.5 is alarming: it suggests that the only important variable is $\dot{p}/p$, which does most of the work of explanation almost irrespective of how it entered, while nothing else matters. Equation 1, employing the Koyck transform, appears 'best' again, but our reservations were expressed in III above. Equations 2, 3 and 4, in which the intruder variables alter the slope of the reaction function, are unsuccessful, but also lend no support to the hypothesis that the intruders, other than $\dot{p}/p$, are significant. The introduction of ρ to the $U:x$ transformation itself adds nothing. It does, however, improve the fit when the effect of $\dot{p}/p$ is to change the slope of the reaction function (compare equation 6 with equation 3). We obtain no estimate of either α or η, and hence cannot estimate $\tilde{U}$, although we may suspect that U has not exceeded $\tilde{U}$ in the sample period. (In equation 1, η was not estimated

notation $1x$, $2x$ means that the variable has been centred separately two coefficients estimated.)

$2\sigma^2$	$1V$	$2V$	$1V_{-1}$	$2V_{-1}$	$\bar{R}^2$	D.W.	ESS
					0·885	1·5669	21·0927
4·1014 (1·76)					0·897	1·4488	19·0050
−0·3913 (0·34)					0·901	1·6064	18·3924
2·8198 (1·20)					0·910	1·4932	16·6407
	−3·3098 (1·47)	−4·2428 (1·89)			0·880	1·5408	22·2749
			−5·7227 (2·59)	−6·6763 (3·04)	0·895	1·6315	19·3019
	−2·5345 (0·72)	−0·1216 (0·04)	−3·7392 (1·03)	−7·1171 (2·21)	0·897	1·6309	18·9847

separately in order to save degrees of freedom. Columns 3 and 4 of Table IV.5 give the estimate of α/η for this equation.)

We may note that the results of equation 1 are consistent with our O.L.S. results in one important respect. The expectation-forming parameter, λ, is significant in both sub-periods, while δ, the coefficient of expected inflation in the determination of $\dot{w}/w$, is significant only in the second. This confirms the impression of a significant change in behaviour between the two sub-periods: the second appears to be dominated by the expectation of inflation. On the whole, the excess demand variables do not appear to have much explanatory power.

.4 It would be hasty to conclude 'there is no Phillips curve': equations 1, 2 and 3 of Table IV.3, for example, are perfectly respectable Phillips curves of the conventional, augmented type. There is, however, serious evidence of instability, suggesting fundamental specification error in all the models tested here.

Table IV.3 Post-war O.L.S. results. $\dot{p}/p$ only stacked.

Dependent variable $\dot{w}/w$	Const.	U^{-1}	U^{-1}_{-1}	$1\dot{p}/p$	$2\dot{p}/p$	σ^2	V	V_{-1}	$\bar{R}^2$	D.W.	ESS
1.	1·3245 (2·33)	2·7108 (3·05)		0·2186 (2·16)	0·5277 (9·43)				0·884	1·4869	21·4958
2.	−0·9905 (0·61)	4·8250 (2·93)		0·2464 (2·44)	0·4993 (8·59)	2·7421 (1·51)			0·891	1·4737	20·1056
3.	1·6644 (2·23)		2·7562 (3·20)	0·1557 (1·52)	0·5121 (9·57)	−0·8488 (0·86)			0·895	1·5398	19·3330
4.	−0·3800 (0·24)	2·7735 (1·43)	1·9093 (1·84)	0·1853 (1·80)	0·4812 (8·45)	1·4604 (0·77)			0·901	1·5218	18·1754
5.	−1·3814 (0·53)			0·2567 (2·36)	0·6100 (12·32)		−3·8963 (1·66)		0·863	1·2596	25·3355
6.	−4·0323 (1·58)			0·2010 (1·90)	0·5879 (12·35)			−6·3628 (2·74)	0·878	1·3301	22·4397
7.	−4·6430 (1·59)			0·1981 (1·85)	0·5847 (12·02)		−1·1568 (0·45)	−5·7558 (2·12)	0·880	1·3219	22·3047

Table IV.4 Post-war O.L.S. results. Equations with intruders

Dependent variable $\dot{w}/w$	Const.	$1\dot{p}/p$	$2\dot{p}/p$	$1V_{-1}$	$2V_{-1}$	1ρ	2ρ
1.	-3·3788 (1·17)	0·3583 (2·83)	0·5013 (8·61)	-5·3150 (2·00)	-6·2864 (2·39)	-0·0159 (0·41)	0·0750 (0·65)
2.	-2·8926 (1·11)	0·3098 (2·27)	0·4668 (4·78)	-5·0211 (2·14)	-6·0031 (2·57)		
3.	-3·6047 (1·47)	0·3389 (2·64)	0·5345 (8·57)	-6·6516 (2·19)	-4·6715 (1·50)		

Dependent variable $\dot{w}/w$	$1\Delta TU$	$2\Delta TU$	1π	2π	$\bar{R}^2$	D.W.	ESS
1.					0·897	1·6227	18·8869
2.	1·7836 (0·87)	1·7597 (0·59)			0·899	1·6627	18·6751
3.			-0·0060 (0·55)	0·0125 (0·92)	0·899	1·6857	18·6141

Table IV.5 Post-war C.N.L.S. results. All variables stacked. (Asymptotic standard errors in brackets.)

Dependent variable $\dot{w}/w$	α_1	α_2	η_1 $(\alpha/\eta)_1$	η_2 $(\alpha/\eta)_2$	λ_1	λ_2	δ_1	δ_2
1 (Expected prices)	−4·90680 (4·39777)	−0·893620 (3·03639)	−6·98423 (3·98011)	−3·91752 (2·72283)	0·417709 (0·190600)	0·848577 (0·205332)	0·0827475 (0·350574)	0·542170 (0·0621687)
2 (Slope change: unions)	−1·39146 (5·68021)	0·667701 (2·86870)	1·17972 (9·79360)	−0·165464 (0·607488)			0·336452 (0·143937)	0·455001 (0·108308)
3 (Slope change: $\dot{p}/p$)	0·796241 (3·43588)	−1·29619 (1·58128)	−0·271895 (0·882992)	−0·649663 (1·26449)				
4 (Slope change: profits)	−1·23068 (4·66031)	5·30541 (8·60461)	0·75259 (0·13074)	−2·20157 (1·77292)			0·42381 (0·13756)	0·61124 (0·06710)
5 ($\xi\rho$)	4·72746 (6·68285)	−2·48491 (4·41820)	−0·728833 (0·352120)	2·63799 (15·7442)			0·368196 (0·144592)	0·525630 (0·0614697)
6 ($\xi\rho$ and slope change $\dot{p}/p$)	−0·44694 (0·637846)	−0·332752 (0·389292)	0·226085 (0·428503)	0·127582 (0·157798)				

Dependent variable $\dot{w}/w$	β_1	β_2	ξ_1	ξ_2	ESS	$\bar{R}^2$	D.W.
1 (Expected prices)					16·37954	0·89036	1·78598
2 (Slope change: unions)	−1·44206 (6·72753)	0·510953 (2·18954)			20·77859	0·86092	1·63218
3 (Slope change: $\dot{p}/p$)	0·128432 (0·538154)	−0·195400 (0·249359)			22·29999	0·86006	1·46328
4 (Slope change: profits)	0·00115 (0·00417)	−0·07691 (0·07688)			20·15873	0·89059	1·67300
5 ($\xi\rho$)			−0·0055694 (0·006291)	0·182822 (0·900203)	21·19011	0·85815	1·46277
6 ($\xi\rho$ and slope change $\dot{p}/p$)	−0·345967 (0·173040)	−0·370926 (0·146872)	−0·0018678 (0·022366)	0·0546619 (0·341975)	20·44651	0·86314	1·55934

V   The cross-section distribution of unemployment

.1 We subjected our cross-section unemployment data to statistical tests of fit, in order to shed some light on its distributional properties, and in the hope of testing the suggestion put forward by one of us in an earlier paper (Archibald in Phelps [22]) of 'stochastic stability' in the structure of excess demand. The reason is as follows: if we postulate a probability density function for excess demand and a transformation from x to U, we can derive a probability density function for unemployment by change of variables, and test for goodness of fit. Once the appropriate density function is accepted, we reverse the change of variables and obtain the parameters of the transformation and of the distribution of excess demand. Repetition for successive time periods should yield the story of the structure of excess demand in quantitative form.

Two obvious candidates which would describe the nature of excess demand adequately but without undue complexity are the two-parameter distributions, the Gamma and the Normal. The properties of the Gamma explain its attraction, since excess demand as defined in I.1 and I.2 is a continuous variable confined to the positive half of the real line, and its distribution can be made to look very skewed or rather Gaussian by variations in the magnitudes of the parameters of the Gamma. Tests of the unemployment data, based on the hypothesis that excess demand does have a Gamma distribution, and using transformation (I.5), necessitate tedious numerical approximations since the derived density function of unemployment is not amenable to simple tests of fit. Consequently, the hypothesis that unemployment could be described by a Gamma distribution was tested directly. The transformation (I.5) itself suggests the appropriateness of testing the goodness of fit of excess demand to the Normal distribution, i.e. testing the log of percentage unemployment for normality.[33]

---

[33] Theoretically, the Normal distribution is defined over the entire real range, hence acceptance of the hypothesis of log normal unemployment would appear to imply inappropriate bounds on both unemployment and excess demand as defined. The same argument also applies to our excess demand density function based on unemployment having a Gamma distribution. However, in practice, the sample range of the data is the only relevant fact; the density function of a variable may lie anywhere inside the range, e.g. crop yields are described as normal variables. If excess demand does have a Normal distribution then by definition the log of percentage unemployment is also normally distributed, i.e. percentage unemployment is log normal and lies in the positive half of the real line.

.2 Details of data used will be found in the Appendix, but for the understanding of what follows, it is essential that some characteristics be known.

For the inter-war period, 1927–39, we have two sets of cross-section unemployment data, for each year, by counties and by towns. The former give some 60 observations (not constant, due to changing aggregations of smaller counties), the latter give some 700 observations, and both are exhaustive.

For the post-war period, there are apparently no reliable data on a town or county basis. From 1960, we are able to obtain reasonably consistent data for each year that we think worth using.[34] We again have two sets of data, 'small' and 'large'. The 'small' set itself is not consistent over time. For each of the first four years, we have the published data for 90 towns. For 1967–69 we have a published selection of Travel to Work Areas, giving about 170 observations for each year. For each of the intervening years, 1964–66, we have added to the 90 towns some 60 additional observations, designed to be roughly consistent with the Travel to Work Areas subsequently used. This is the 'small' set, neither exhaustive nor random. The 'large' set for these years is provided by the Employment Exchange data, some 640 observations (until 1968 when new Travel to Work Areas led to a new grouping with some 470 observations). It is important to know that the 'large' set, although exhaustive, already contains some aggregation. Thus, suppose that two or more Labour Exchanges are aggregated to provide a town—or Travel to Work Area—observation in the 'small' set. They are not disaggregated when we go to the 'large' set. Thus we may describe the 'large' set as consisting of the (relatively large) elements of the 'small' set plus a large number of small (single Exchange) observations.

.3 We may report summarily that the Gamma distribution is not acceptable. Results of Chi-square tests for log normality are, however, confusing (tabulated results will be found in the Appendix[35]). The hypothesis of log normality applied to the 'small' data sets is in each year acceptable (at the 10 per cent level). Applied to the 'large'

[34] It would, of course, be possible to analyse the industry distribution, using the Minimum List Classification, with some 150 observations. We have not done this.
[35] We tested the Gamma distribution on the 'small' and 'large' data sets. We only reported results with the 'small' data set. With the 'large' set it was rejected in every case.

data sets, however, it is only acceptable for four years (out of a total of 26) at the 5 per cent level. We must ask if this is not a refutation of our postulated transformation and how, in any case, it can occur.

We have some explanation to offer, and a crude test of the explanation. It will be recalled that we have everywhere made the aggregation assumption that $n_i = n_j$, all i, j. In any case in which this assumption is seriously violated, a normal distribution of excess demand will not generate a log-normal distribution of unemployment: the distribution will be distorted due to the fact that U_i will not be equal to U_j, even if x_i and x_j are equal. Now, the elements of our 'small' data sets are all aggregates of Labour Exchanges. The required assumption here is that η be the same for towns (say, Liverpool and Southampton) or for counties. It appears that whatever inequalities exist, they are not quantitatively important for the present purpose. The 'large' sets consist, however, of the elements of the small sets plus about ten times as many small elements. We suggest that it is at this level that we encounter inequalities between the η's that distort the observed distributions.

We devised a rough-and-ready test of this hypothesis, simply by arbitrarily averaging the 'large' data sets: we aggregated them into groups of ten elements each, taking them in order and paying no attention to geography or to whether the elements themselves were aggregates or not. We then repeated our Chi-square tests. The results were better than for the 'large' sets, worse than for the 'small'. A

Table V.1 Summary of chi-square tests of log normality in the distribution of unemployment for each of the given years

Set	Inter-war (13 years)
'Small'	Accept everywhere at 10%
'Large'	Accept 4 times at 5%
Arbitrary small	Accept 9 times at 5%

Set	Post-war (16 years)
'Small'	Accept everywhere at 10%
'Large'	Accept nowhere at 5%
Arbitrary small	Accept 8 times at 5%

summary of the position is set out in Table V.1 (for detail, see the Appendix). The results appear to be consistent with our aggregation argument, but not conclusive. If they were accepted, it would suggest a moral for the regression approach of the last three sections: it pays to disaggregate—but not too far if one has to assume equality of the micro-parameter!

.4 It would have been desirable to utilize the information gleaned from the distribution tests in our examination of the structure of excess demand over time. This is, however, possible only if we make some arbitrary assumptions about the properties of the density function of excess demand. The likelihood function of excess demand suggested by the tests and derived from transformation I.5 is one in three parameters, η, and the first two moments of the distribution of unemployment, but it can be canonically reduced into a function in two parameters.[36] Hence, it is possible to estimate uniquely only two of the three unless we assume knowledge about the third. We could assume specific values of the moments of the distribution of excess demand and hence pinpoint η, or assume knowledge of the distribution of these moments, and, via Bayesian statistics, derive estimates of η. Both methods require information which is arbitrary, and hence are inconclusive.

We could, of course, use the estimates of η from the regression results to shed more light on the behaviour of excess demand. Thus using the point estimate $\bar{\eta}$ we could derive a series of observations on the first two moments of the distribution of excess demand. Given our uncertainty about the point estimates of $\bar{\eta}$, we have not thought this exercise worth conducting.

---

[36] The moments of the distribution of percentage unemployment for each year were calculated from the ungrouped cross-section data used in the distribution tests. Given equations I.1, I.2 and I.5, we have excess demand defined as

$$x = \frac{\log U - \log 100}{\eta} - 1$$

If the mean and variance of the log of percentage unemployment are μ and σ^2 respectively, then V.1 and V.2 are the corresponding moments of the distribution of excess demand,

$$E(x) = \frac{\mu - \log 100}{\eta} - 1 \qquad (V.1)$$

$$\text{Var}(x) = \frac{\sigma^2}{\eta^2} \qquad (V.2)$$

VI   Conclusion

There is little to add by way of conclusion. The post-war period, in particular, is very poorly explained. The attempt to distinguish between three sorts of intruders (intercept, slope and expectations) has been partially successful: the price-expectations hypothesis is consistent with the data, as is inter-war 'kinky'. For the post-war period, at least, the aggregation or 'structuralist' hypothesis is poorly supported. This, in particular, means that the optimism expressed in earlier papers by one of the present authors (Archibald [1 and 2]) as to the magnitude of favourable shifts in the Phillips curve to be attained by a policy of equalising regional unemployment levels must be severely qualified. The conclusion is, then, generally inconclusive. More work is required (and much, indeed, has already been done: see particularly Brechling [6]). In particular, given the importance of prices, perhaps we should admit that the problem of simultaneity is too much for us, and that the single-equation approach should be given up.

Appendix   Data used in statistical analysis

I   Pre-1914: 1892–1913

Cost of living index. The series constructed by Bowley is apparently the only available series covering our period (A. L. Bowley, *Wages and Income in the United Kingdom Since 1860*, Cambridge, 1937).

Wage series. Three wage series were collected and all investigations run on all three:

(i) Compiled by the Labour Department of the Board of Trade. This was an unweighted average of reported wages in five sectors (*Eighteenth Abstract of Labour Statistics*, 1926, *British Parliamentary Papers* [henceforth *B.P.P.*] 1926, vol. XXIX).
(ii) Bowley's series (*op. cit.*).
(iii) Phelps-Brown and Hopkins, partly based on a series compiled by G. Wood and partly on the Labour Department series (H. Phelps-Brown and S. Hopkins, 'The Course of Wage Rates in Five Countries 1860–1939', *Oxford Economic Papers*, 1950).

Much has been written on the relative merits of these series, especially the latter two (the unweighted averaging suggests the Labour Department series is inferior). Results for both these series are therefore reported in the text.

National Unemployment. Compiled by the Labour Department of the Board of Trade from Union returns relating to 14 Industrial groupings, an annual figure being obtained by averaging the monthly percentage (*18th Abstract of Labour Statistics*, as above).

Industrial disaggregations. In order to calculate the variance about mean unemployment of the sum-of-the-logs for each year, percentage unemployed and the number of employees is needed for each group into which the data is divided. The employee figure, expressed as a fraction of the total number of employees, gives the group unemployment percentage its weighting.

All labour data in this period were compiled from Union returns and so are only relevant to the unionised labour force. A complete listing of union membership, which in this period must be used in place of total employees, classified by Industry but not otherwise aggregated, is available back to the 1880's in the *Annual Report by the Chief Labour Correspondent of the Board of Trade on Trade Unions*. From 1892 the Industrial groupings are aggregated into 20 divisions (*B.P.P.* 1901, vol. xxxiv; *B.P.P.* 1906, vol. cxiii; *B.P.P.* 1912–1913, vol. xlvii). In view of the time that would have been required to process the earlier data, 1892 was adopted as the starting year. The Labour Correspondent's reports were discontinued in 1913, giving 1910 data as the latest published. From 1911, aggregated membership for the 20 groupings is published in Part C of the *Report of the Chief Registrar of Friendly Societies on Trade Unions* (*B.P.P.* 1912–1913, vols. lxxxi and lxxxii; *B.P.P.* 1913, vol. lvii; *B.P.P.* 1914, vol. lxxvi).

In fact we were only able to use five groupings. As noted above, national unemployment figures were compiled from reported percentage unemployment of union members by industry. The disaggregated percentage unemployment data were published in different breakdowns at different times in our period but are available consistently throughout 1892–1913 only on the five groups: building trade, printing trade, furnishing trade, engineering, shipbuilding and metal trade, and other trades (listed as coal mining, textiles, clothing, paper, leather, glass pottery, tobacco). Figures used are yearly averages of monthly percentages (Fifteenth, Sixteenth and Eighteenth *Abstracts of Labour Statistics B.P.P.* 1912–1913, vol. cvii; *B.P.P.* 1914, vol. lxxx; *B.P.P.* 1926, vol. xxix).

The nearest corresponding membership weighting for these five groups from the Industry membership figures is to combine the groups building and construction, printing and paper trade, woodwork and furnishing, metal engineering and shipbuilding. This does involve some discrepancies and also an overlap with the unemployed other trades group: we were unable to reconstruct from these groupings the published national percentage unemployment! This indicates the suspect nature of the data used here to construct σ^2 and V.

II   Inter-war: 1924(2)–1938(3)

Working class cost of living. Compiled by the Ministry of Labour. Retail prices weighted throughout period according to 1914 'Working Class' pattern of consumption (published monthly in the *Ministry of Labour Gazette* [hereafter referred to as *M.L.G.*]).

Weekly wage rate. Compiled by the Ministry of Labour. To June 1934 weighted according to the full-time Wages Bill in 1924 for 32 industries. From June 1934 a new series based on the Wages Bill of that month has been calculated since the war by the Ministry. This series covers 69 industries (a series for 1920–34 based on 69 industries has also been calculated, but only for end June and December). Given the change in the range of industries covered and the likelihood that by 1934 the 1924 weightings would be obsolete, a dummy for the data break was introduced as explained in the text (22nd *Abstract of Labour Statistics* for pre-June 1934, then *M.L.G.* April 1958).

Market disaggregations. Two breakdowns of the U.K. labour force were available, one by region and one by industry (*M.L.G.* monthly, regions pre-1926 21st *Abstract of Labour Statistics*).

The table of insured persons registered as unemployed gave unemployment numbers and percentages by 25 industries, and the unemployment summary of Insured industries by district corresponding numbers for 9 and at the latter end of the period 10 regions, which were aggregated to 8 to keep consistent boundaries throughout the period. Total employees on these breakdowns were obtained by the Ministry at the annual exchange of all Insurance Cards at each July. Employee figures for quarters 1, 3 and 4 were extrapolated from these by taking the figure for quarters 1 and 3 as equal to the July figure, and quarter 4 as half the sum of the previous and next counts.

During the period here covered, the National Insurance Scheme was gradually extended, and as far as possible we kept the data consistent. In several other cases of changes in the law (e.g. the Anomalies Regulation and the Transitional Payments Scheme, both of 1931), and in Ministry procedures, no such adjustment was possible. In these cases checks were run on the data, and in no case was any such change significant.

National unemployment. The mean value of percentage unemployment each month was obtained by the Ministry from the industrial data rather than the regional data (the Special Scheme insured were never regionally disaggregated). (For the regional data pre-1926, where Northern Ireland figures were obtainable only by subtraction of the Great Britain regions total from an industrially compiled United Kingdom total, the resulting figures may be inconsistent.)

Definition of the quarters. Given that the one 'true' Employee figure each year was for July, this month was used as the centre of quarter 2 and the other quarters correspondingly defined (thus, quarter IV is December, January, February). For wage, price and unemployment series, each quarter's figures were the average of the relevant three monthly figures. Disaggregated data referred to the mid-month of the quarter.

The end dates used may appear arbitrary. To an extent they are, although not of our volition. Consistent wage, price and unemployment series are available only back into late 1923, and so, given some of the rate of change definitions tried and the need to earmark the first observation only as a lag for the second observation, the starting quarter becomes 1924(2).

Similarly, as we do not want to make use of any observation after 1939(2), 1938(3) becomes the last quarter we could calculate.

III   Post-war 1950(4), 1957(1)–1961(2)

A post-war moments model has already been tested on annual data (see Archibald [2]). For the present investigation this model was reconstructed on a quarterly basis, for the Lipsey–Parkin 'Policy-Off' periods only (see text) and utilising more disaggregated unemployment data.

As some of the data we required were the same as those already calculated for Lipsey–Parkin [18], we have gratefully used their figures for the following series:

Index of retail prices, all items (*Monthly Digest of Statistics*).
Index of weekly wage rates, for all industries and services (*Monthly Digest of Statistics*).
Percentage of labour force unionised, annual figures with quarterly observations interpolated (*Ministry of Labour Gazette*).
Percentage of the registered labour force wholly unemployed (*Ministry of Labour Gazette*).
Output per man obtained from the Index of Industrial Production.
Monthly Digest of Statistics and the Index of Industrial Production employees (total manufacturing, mining, quarrying, construction, gas, water, electricity) (*Ministry of Labour Gazette*).

In all cases, except the unionised labour force, quarterly figures were obtained by the averaging of monthly figures. The quarters referred to in this period are January–March, etc.

Details of series constructed or collected by ourselves are as follows:

Productivity ρ was obtained by calculating the deviation of output per man from trend over the period 1950(4)–1969(3). The trend was generated by the following preferred equation:

Output per man = $72.42 + 0.040t + 0.005t^2 - 0.13D_1 - 1.74D_2 - 8.97D_3$
$\qquad\qquad\quad$ (56·6) (6·0) $\quad$ (6·2) $\quad$ (0·13) (1·7) $\quad$ (8·7)

$$\bar{R}^2 = 0.970, \text{ D.W.} = 0.485$$

(where the D's are quarterly dummies).

Profits. Gross company profits, excluding public corporations and enterprises, were obtained from *Times Review of Industry* (London and Cambridge Economic Service: Bulletins) and *Economic Trends*, with overlap for the four quarters of 1955 for series splicing. For the relation between the two series see *Times Review of Industry* (March 1959, Bulletin, p. xi).

Disaggregated data. For addi-log and moments calculations.

(i) From the *Ministry of Labour Gazette* Industrial Analysis of Numbers Unemployed and Numbers of Employees tables, giving a breakdown of these categories by Standard Industrial Classification Minimum List Heading (163 observations to 1959(2), then 153).

For the first three quarters of each year the end-May employee count figure was used, and for the fourth quarter the mean of the previous and next count. Due to the Standard Industrial Classification reclassification of the 1959 Employee figures such a procedure became impossible for 1958(4)–1959(2), and the mid-1958 figures were used.

(ii) From the tables of Employee Population and of Numbers Unemployed in the United Kingdom: Regional Analysis, as published in the *Ministry of Labour Gazette.* We aggregated the Eastern and Southern regions in the earlier part of the period to give 11 consistent observations for the whole period. The method of Employee series interpolation was as outlined for the Industrial series above.

The problem of the unemployed category 'not classified by industry', a category wrongly omitted by the Ministry of Labour in the corresponding Employee tables, was solved as before (Archibald [2], p. 131) by distributing persons in this category over all other categories according to the Employee weights corresponding.

IV   The Distributions

We were able to use, and indeed required to use, more finely disaggregated data to investigate the cross-section distributions than we used for the time series analysis.

Regional dispersion data. From the beginning of 1927 until mid-1939 the Ministry of Labour published monthly a *Local Unemployment Index* in pamphlet form. This gave, for the preceding month, unemployed persons as a percentage of insured employees by town by county, for Great Britain, being exhaustive, as far as is ascertainable, from 1929. This gave us the choice of either an average of over 700 town observations, constituting the 'large' data set of the text, or about 60 counties, constituting the 'small' set of the text (until 1931 three aggregations, 'Rest of Highlands', 'Rest of Lowlands', 'Rest of Wales', were published in lieu of about 20 counties and in the interests of consistency we continued computing and using figures for those aggregations even when these counties became individually available in 1931).

Our investigations used the figures for each July, 1927 to 1939. The employee figure used by the Ministry to obtain per cent unemployed was one year out of date. Where we met this problem with the data used in the regression equations we recomputed using the 'correct' employee figure. Here, several other data inconsistencies made us decide this solution was not feasible, and the figures were used as published.

The worst of these inconsistencies is due to the fact that the unemployment figure used until 1937 in conjunction with the insured employee figure was of all registered unemployed, and of course, although they could receive no unemployment benefit, non-insured work people were entitled to register at employment exchanges in the hope of obtaining employment. The percentage unemployment figure published and used therefore overestimated percentage unemployment among insured workpeople, at least until 1937.

Post-war. The published post-war data are largely unsatisfactory for the demands of our investigation. For the 1950's numbers unemployed in some 90 towns (these towns being presumably selected on some non-random basis) are published, but, due to other data deficiencies, it is not possible to obtain a

Table A.1 Results of χ^2 tests of goodness of fit of percentage unemployment to the gamma and lognormal distributions, the 'small' data set

Critical Region Year (no. of observations)	Gamma 0·10		0·05		Lognormal 0·10		0·05	
	A	R	A	R	A	R	A	R
1927 (59)			✓✓✓		✓✓			
1928 (60)	✓				✓✓			
1929 (61)	✓✓				✓✓			
1930 (61)			✓	✓	✓			
1931 (61)	✓✓				✓✓			
1932 (61)	✓✓				✓✓			
1933 (61)	✓✓				✓			
1934 (61)	✓✓				✓			
1935 (61)	✓		✓✓	✓	✓✓			
1936 (61)	✓✓				✓✓			
1937 (61)	✓✓✓				✓✓			
1938 (61)	✓✓✓				✓✓			
1939 (61)	✓✓✓				✓✓			
1960 (90)	✓✓				✓✓			
1961 (90)			✓✓✓		✓✓			
1962 (90)	✓		✓✓		✓✓			
1963 (87)			✓✓✓		✓			✓
1964 (158)			✓✓		✓			
1965 (155)			✓✓✓		✓			
1966 (164)			✓✓		✓			✓✓
1967 (173)	✓✓				✓			
1968 (172)	✓				✓			
1969 (172)			✓✓		✓✓			

Notes to Tables A.1, 2 and 3

(i) To reduce the possible distortion in the results due to the sensitivity of the χ^2 test to the patterns of class intervals, alternative groupings were tested. This occasionally produced varied decisions, as the table demonstrates.

(ii) A ✓ in column 'A' denotes a χ^2 value less than the critical value (for the relevant region), indicating acceptance of the hypothesis. A ✓ in column 'R' denotes a χ^2 value in the critical region, indicating rejection of the hypothesis.

(iii) The number of ticks for each period represent the number of different interval groupings tested. The number of variations are limited by the 'amenability' of the data.

(iv) Note that acceptance at the 10 per cent level implies acceptance at the 5 per cent level; but duplication in the table is omitted.

(v) Significance tests on measures of skewness, kurtosis and Pearson's Beta coefficients were made. Reliable tests require more observations than are afforded by the 'small' set, so while limited importance can be attached to the results (whence details are not included) they did generally support the hypothesis of lognormal unemployment in that set.

Tables A.2 and 3   Results of χ^2 tests of goodness of fit of percentage unemployment to the lognormal distribution

A.2 The 'large' data set Critical region 0·05			A.3 The 'arbitrary' data set Critical region 0·05		
Year (no. of observations)	A	R	Year (no. of observations)	A	R
1927 (638)	✓		1927 (64)	✓	
1928 (649)		✓ ✓ ✓	1928 (65)	✓	
1929 (664)		✓ ✓	1929 (67)	✓	
1930 (671)		✓	1930 (68)		✓
1931 (710)		✓	1931 (71)		✓
1932 (725)	✓		1932 (73)	✓	
1933 (744)		✓ ✓	1933 (75)	✓	
1934 (755)		✓	1934 (76)		✓
1935 (758)		✓	1935 (76)	✓	
1936 (762)	✓		1936 (77)	✓	
1937 (769)	✓		1937 (77)	✓	
1938 (770)		✓ ✓	1938 (77)		✓
1939 (757)		✓ ✓	1939 (76)		✓
1963 (641)		✓ ✓	1963 (65)		✓
1964 (636)		✓ ✓	1964 (64)		✓ ✓
1965 (634)		✓ ✓	1965 (64)	✓	✓
1966 (640)		✓ ✓ ✓	1966 (64)	✓ ✓	
1967 (640)		✓ ✓	1967 (64)	✓	✓
1968 (474)		✓ ✓	1968 (48)	✓ ✓	
1969 (474)		✓ ✓	1969 (48)		✓ ✓

percentage figure (as is required). For 1960–66 the published figures relate to percentages unemployed and include not only the 90 towns but a large number of Development District towns as well. To include all the latter would, of course, severely bias the sample, whence the procedure employed was to pick out the 90 towns selected by the Ministry as 'important' in the 1950's and analyse these for 1960–62. In 1967 the published sample was increased to 173 towns, and from 1968 the figures relate to newly-defined 'Travel to Work Areas' (except that London relates to the G.L.C. area, and we had to obtain figures for the London Travel to Work Area separately from the Department of Employment), of which a sample of 172 areas is published. These data were used as published for these years (there being no noticeable bias toward high unemployment areas), and the 90 towns selection used for the years 1960–62. Adding reconstructed data as below for 1963–66 gave us a series which is denoted as the 'small' set in the text.

We also made use of unpublished Ministry of Labour/Department of Employment and Productivity data of percentage unemployment for every Employment Exchange (or groups of Exchanges in large centres) in the country, computed from 1963. This gives approximately 640 observations until 1968 when, with the introduction of the new Travel to Work Areas, the number of separate observations dropped to about 470. This source gave us our 'large' set of the text, and a sub-set for the period 1963–66 (based on the 1967 listing of 173 towns, and reconstructed back to 1963 excepting several minor omissions made at the time of collection) completed the 'small' set.

For all these series, June figures were used each year, except 1968 where the use of July allowed us to use the improved Exchange area definitions. It should also be noted that in all cases the employee figure used to calculate percentages unemployed were one year out of date. All data relate to Great Britain.

References

[1] Archibald, G. C., 'On Regional Economic Policy in the U.K.', paper delivered at the annual meeting of the Midwestern Economic Association, March 1968, published in *Essays in Honour of Lord Robbins*, ed. B. A. Corry and M. H. Peston, London, Weidenfeld and Nicolson (1972).

[2] Archibald, G. C., 'The Phillips Curve and the Distribution of Unemployment', *American Economic Review, Papers and Proceedings*, Vol. LIX, No. 2 (May 1969).

[3] Brechling, F. P. R., 'The Relationship Between Output and Employment in British Manufacturing Industries', *Review of Economic Studies*, Vol. XXXII, No. 3 (July 1965).

[4] Brechling, F. P. R., 'Trends and Cycles in British Regional Unemployment', *Oxford Economic Papers*, Vol. 19, No. 1 (March 1967).

[5] Brechling, F. P. R., 'The Trade-Off Between Inflation and Unemployment', *Journal of Political Economy*, Vol. 76, No. 4, Part II (July/August 1968).

[6] Brechling, F. P. R., 'Wage Inflation and the Structure of Regional Unemployment', Ch. 7 below. First published, University of Essex Discussion Paper No. 40 (1972).

[7] Corry, B. A. and Laidler, D. E. W., 'The Phillips Relation: A Theoretical Explanation', *Economica*, Vol. XXXIV (May 1967).

[8] Friedman, M., 'The Role of Monetary Policy', *American Economic Review, Papers and Proceedings*, Vol. LVIII, No. 1 (March 1968).

[9] Hines, A. G., 'Trade Unions and Wage Inflation in the United Kingdom', 1893–1961, *Review of Economic Studies*, Vol. 31 (1964).

[10] Hines, A. G., 'Wage Inflation in the United Kingdom, 1948–62: A Disaggregated Study', *Economic Journal*, Vol. 79 (1969).

[11] Hines, A. G., 'The Phillips Curve and the Distribution of Unemployment', *American Economic Review*, Vol. LXII (1972).

[12] Goldberger, A. S., *Econometric Theory*, New York, John Wiley (1964).

[13] Hansen, B., 'Excess Demand, Unemployment, Vacancies and Wages', *Quarterly Journal of Economics*, Vol. XXXXIV, No. 1 (Feb. 1970).

[14] Johnson, Harry G. and Nobay, A. R. (eds.), *The Current Inflation*, London, Macmillan (1971).

[15] Keynes, J. M., 'The Economic Consequences of Mr. Churchill', reprinted in *Essays in Persuasion*, London, Macmillan (1931).

[16] Kuh, E., 'A Productivity Theory of Wage Levels—An Alternative to the Phillips Curve', *Review of Economic Studies*, Vol. XXXIV, No. 4 (Oct. 1967).

[17] Lipsey, R. G., 'The Relation Between Unemployment and the Rate of Change of Money Wage Rates in the the United Kingdom, 1862–1957: A Further Analysis', *Economica*, Vol. XXVII, (Feb. 1960).

[18] Lipsey, R. G. and Parkin, J. M., 'Incomes Policy: A Re-appraisal', *Economica*, Vol. XXXVII (May 1970). Reprinted as Ch. 4 in M. Parkin and M. T. Sumner (eds.), *Incomes Policy and Inflation*, Manchester, Manchester University Press (1972).

[19] Parkin, J. M., 'Incomes Policy: Some Further Results on the Determination of the Rate of Change of Money Wages', *Economica*, Vol. XXXVII (Nov. 1970). Reprinted as Ch. 5 in M. Parkin and M. T. Sumner (eds.), *Incomes Policy and Inflation*, Manchester, Manchester University Press (1972).

[20] Phelps, E. S., 'Phillips Curves, Expectations of Inflation and Optimal Unemployment Over Time', *Economica*, Vol. XXXIV (August 1967).
[21] Phelps, E. S., 'Comment', *Journal of Political Economy*, Vol. 76, No. 4, Part II (July/Aug. 1968).
[22] Phelps, E. S., *et al.*, *Microeconomic Foundations of Employment and Inflation Theory*, New York, Norton (1970).
[23] Phillips, A. W., 'The Relation Between Unemployment and the Rate of Change of Money Wage Rates in the United Kingdom, 1861–1957', *Economica*, Vol. XXXV (Nov. 1958).
[24] Samuelson, P. A., *Foundations of Economic Analysis*, Harvard University Press (1947).
[25] Simler, N. J. and Tella, A., 'Labour Reserves and the Phillips Curve', *Review of Economics and Statistics*, Vol. 50 (1968).
[26] Sumner, M. T., 'Aggregate Demand, Price Expectations and the Phillips Curve', Ch. 9 in M. Parkin and M. T. Sumner (eds.), *Incomes Policy and Inflation*, Manchester, Manchester University Press (1972).
[27] Taylor, J., 'Hidden Unemployment, Hoarded Labor, and the Phillips Curve', *Southern Economic Journal*, Vol. XXXVII, No. 1 (July 1970).
[28] Thirlwall, A. P., 'Demand Disequilibrium in the Labour Markets and Wage Rate Inflation in the United Kingdom', *Yorkshire Bulletin of Economics and Social Research*, Vol. 21, No. 1 (May 1969).
[29] Thirlwall, A. P., 'Types of Unemployment: With Special Reference to "Non-Demand-Deficient" Unemployment in Great Britain', *Scottish Journal of Political Economy*, Vol. 16 (1969).
[30] Thirlwall, A. P., 'Regional Phillips Curves', *Bulletin of the Oxford University Institute of Economics and Statistics*, Vol. 32, No. 1 (1970).
[31] Thomas, R. L. and Stoney, P. J. M., 'Unemployment Dispersion as a Determinant of Wage Inflation in the U.K. 1925–66', *The Manchester School*, Vol. XXXIX, No. 2 (June 1971). Reprinted as Ch. 11 in M. Parkin and M. T. Sumner (eds.), *Incomes Policy and Inflation*, Manchester, Manchester University Press (1972).
[32] Tobin, J., 'Inflation and Unemployment', *American Economic Review*, Vol. LXII, No. 1 (March 1972).
[33] Vanderkamp, J., 'Wage Adjustment, Productivity and Price Change Expectations', *The Review of Economic Studies*, Vol. XXIX(1) (Jan. 1972).

J. I. Foster[1]

Chapter 6 The relationship between unemployment
and vacancies in Great Britain
(1958–72): some further evidence

I Introduction

1 Summary

It has been widely recognised that there has been a shift in the
relationship between unemployment and vacancies (henceforth the
UV relationship) in Great Britain since late 1966. The purpose of this
paper is to isolate the causes of this shift.

The plan of the paper is as follows:

(i) a brief discussion of the current state of knowledge concerning
the causes of the UV shift;
(ii) a reconsideration of the idea that the UV shift can be attributed
to increased 'shaking-out' behaviour by firms since late 1966;
(iii) consideration of the importance of demographic changes in
labour supply arising from the post-war 'birth bulge'; and
(iv) conclusions and policy implications.

The conclusions reached can be summarised. The evidence contained in the paper suggests that the UV shift in late 1966 can be
attributed to two main factors. First, the abnormal demographic
increase in young, inexperienced labour at that time. Second, the
introduction of Redundancy Payments legislation, which encouraged
employers to shake-out older, less efficient workers. Furthermore,
this legislation encouraged a polarisation of redundancies towards
very young and very old employees. The introduction of earnings
related benefits was found to be only of minor importance in explaining the UV shift.

[1] I would like to thank J. M. Parkin, D. Purdy and M. T. Sumner for their
helpful comments on earlier drafts of this paper. However, I remain responsible
for any errors or other shortcomings.

2 The current state of knowledge

In a recent note, Foster [2] commented on an attempt by Gujarati [3] to explain why a shift in the relationship between unemployment and vacancies, in the latter part of 1966, was attributable to the introduction of the Redundancy Payments Act (1965) and the National Insurance Act (1966). This legislation, Gujarati felt, had encouraged an increase in voluntary unemployment.

Foster had two main criticisms of this work. First of all, the 'evidence' produced only demonstrated that there had been a shift of the UV relationship, which could have been attributed to a number of potential causal factors—there was no real justification for isolating the above legislation as the reason for the shift. Second, there were several reasons why this legislation might not have had the impact on voluntary unemployment that Gujarati suggested. It was concluded that Gujarati's article contributed little to the solution of the UV shift problem, and that a more careful examination of potential causal factors would be necessary before anything positive could be said about the origin of the shift.

Since then, Bowers, Cheshire, Webb and Weeden [1] have conducted a thorough investigation of several causal factors. They demonstrate fairly conclusively that a 'supply side' explanation of the UV shift, such as that suggested by Gujarati, is not supported by the available evidence. They conclude that the level of unemployment since late 1966 is not extraordinary provided productivity improvements and demand conditions are taken into account. However, the causes of this observed improvement in productivity were not analysed, mainly because their intention was to demonstrate that a 'supply side' explanation was not valid, rather than to examine the plausibility of 'demand side' explanations. Consequently, we are still left with several potential causal factors on the 'demand side' to choose from (see Bowers et al. [1], p. 77, para. 2).

A further contribution has been made by Taylor [10], who concentrates on a 'demand side' explanation of the shift. He suggests that the UV shift might be due to a 'shake-out' of labour caused by a change in the labour hoarding behaviour of firms. Thus, there is a transfer of labour, previously hoarded, on to the unemployment register after late 1966. This, of course, would result in an increase in the productivity of employed labour. Consequently, Taylor's explanation is a special case of the Bowers et al. general conclusion that there has been an acceleration in the rise of labour productivity in the late 1960's. His work, then, represents a first step in identifying which 'demand side' causal factors are important in explaining the UV shift.

In this paper a 'demand side' explanation of the UV shift is suggested, based on the approach contained in Foster [2]. The concept of a 'shake-out' of labour is considered carefully and incorporated, but in a different way from Taylor, whose explanation of the UV shift is regarded as deficient in certain respects. In addition, certain important demographic changes in the labour force in the late 1960's are taken account of. The explanation offered is guided by the Bowers et al. systematic rejection of 'supply side' explanations and is intended as an extension of that work. Consequently, the over-riding concern is with isolating the most important determinants of the UV shift, rather than leaving the reader with several causal factors to choose from.

II   The shake-out reconsidered

1   Estimates of 'hoarded unemployment'

In view of casual empiricism, indicating that firms have increased their redundancies in the recent past, and more specific sample evidence on redundancies by Mackay [7] and Mackay and Reid [8], it is somewhat surprising to find that Gujarati [4], in his reply to Taylor [10], so readily discounts the 'shake-out hypothesis' as an explanation of the UV shift. Taylor's explanation is cast in a very informal way which makes it difficult to evaluate. Consequently, it would be worthwhile, as a point of departure, to take a closer look at his approach and conduct some simple empirical tests.

Using labour productivity data, Taylor obtains aggregate estimates of hoarded unemployment (see Statistical Appendix) which he adds to registered unemployment to obtain a 'true' estimate of unemployment. This estimate, he maintains, is the most appropriate one to use as a proxy for excess demand in the labour market, since 'true' unemployment will be unaffected by a shift of hoarded unemployment on to the register.

Consequently, two empirical questions come to mind. First, what sort of UV relationship do we get using Taylor's re-estimation of unemployment? Second, is this relationship the same for post-1966 (iii) and pre-1966 (iv) periods? A log-linear relationship was specified between 'true' unemployment and notified vacancies. The specification and results for the period 1959 (i)–1971 (ii) are shown in Table 1.

Table 1

Specification		$\log_{10} U_{Tt} = \alpha_1 + \alpha_2 \log_{10} V_{Rt}$			
Reg. no.	Period	α_1	α_2	$\bar{R}^2$	D.W.
1	1959(i)–1966(iii)	0·7901* (0·027)	−0·5839* (0·1863)	0·227	0·61
2	1966(iii)–1971(ii)	0·7846* (0·080)	−0·581 (0·5365)	0·009	0·27
3	1959(i)–1971(ii)	0·7889* (0·024)	−0·5734* (0·1670)	0·180	0·48

where U_{Tt} = 'true' unemployment

  = $U_{Ht} + U_{Rt}$

where U_{Ht} = hoarded unemployment

  U_{Rt} = registered unemployment

and V_{Rt} = notified vacancies.

Comparing the results for the 1959(i)–1966(iii) period with those using only registered unemployment and notified vacancies (see Table 2), it is clear that the addition of hoarded unemployment to registered unemployment has led to a considerable deterioration in the UV fit for the pre-1966(iv) period. All that can be said is that the estimated coefficients do remain much the same for both periods indicating that there was no shift in the UV relationship. However, the overall poor quality of the results indicate that the relationship is seriously misspecified.

The main reason for the poor fit is not that 'true unemployment' is necessarily a bad measure of unemployment, but that Taylor has only considered one dimension of the hoarding issue. When employers decide to hoard labour, not only is such labour unregistered unemployment, but also, when there is a cyclical upswing in product demand, the existence of this hoarded labour means that there is no need to notify vacancies, as would occur in a situation where the same labour was on the unemployment register. Consequently, registered vacancies tend to understate 'true' vacancies when demand increases, i.e. the additional vacancies that would have arisen, had there been no labour hoarding, must be added.

Thus, given only estimates of hoarded unemployment, there is insufficient information to estimate the 'true' UV relationship. The correct relationship to test would be 'true' unemployment against 'true' vacancies. Now, Taylor has already warned us that his estimates of hoarded unemployment may not be wholly reliable (see Taylor [10], pp. 1356–60). Obviously, any calculation of 'hoarded' vacancies would also be subject to similar potential measurement errors.

Given these problems, it would, perhaps, be best not to pursue the above approach further.[2] In the next section I shall suggest how Taylor's hypothesis can be taken account of using only registered data. However, before further tests of the empirical validity of his hypothesis can take place, there are some problems with his rationalisation of the movements in registered unemployment after 1966(iii) that must be discussed.

In all discussions of labour hoarding, it is clearly stated that such behaviour is a cyclical phenomenon (see Taylor [10], p. 1354, para. 3). The quasi-fixity of labour is identified as a short-run phenomenon and Taylor gives several good reasons why this should be so.

If, then, labour hoarding is a cyclical phenomenon which has diminished in its extent since late 1966, one would expect to see registered unemployment rising to a higher peak than before in a downswing of aggregate demand. In an upswing unemployment should fall more rapidly and return to a level that one would have expected previously for a given peak in aggregate demand. Consequently, there is a prediction of increased 'shaking-out' and 'shaking-in' behaviour by firms over the cycle after late 1966.

The observed UV shift certainly accords with the increase in cyclical shake-out but not with the shake-in. In the 1967–8 upswing in aggregate demand one would have expected to see some decline in registered unemployment as labour shaken-out in late 1966 was re-employed. There is no evidence that this happened, in fact registered unemployment kept rising over the period in question.

It is not surprising, then, that Taylor had some difficulty in explaining these movements in terms of his dishoarding hypothesis (see Taylor [10], pp. 1362–3). His resulting explanation appears tentative and *ad hoc* in construction. Gujarati, in his reply to Taylor, readily exposes this vagueness in empirical justification.

[2] This does not mean that Taylor's 'hoarded unemployment' estimates are not useful in other contexts. For example, Taylor [11] has used his estimates of 'true' employment as a proxy for excess demand for labour, in his studies of the 'Phillips curve', with considerable success.

Table 2

Specification		$\log_{10} U_{Rt} = \alpha_1 + \alpha_2 \log_{10} V_{Rt}$			
Reg. no.	Period	α_1	α_2	$\bar{R}^2$	D.W.
1	1959(i)–1966(iii)	0·090* (0·006)	−0·771* (0·039)	0·93	0·83
2	1966(iii)–1971(ii)	0·234* (0·028)	−0·707* (0·185)	0·43	0·13
3	1959(i)–1971(ii)	0·120* (0·016)	−0·936* (0·109)	0·61	0·09

In order to explain the movements in registered unemployment after late 1966 the idea of firms shaking-out labour needs to be extended to include the possibility that firms have also been shaking-out labour independently of the cyclical position of the economy. Although the causes of these two types of shake-out, which I shall discuss later, are not altogether independent of each other, I shall consider each separately since the effects are likely to be different in each case.

2 The dual shake-out hypothesis

(a) Cyclical shake-out

In Foster [2] it was demonstrated that the simple UV relationship was misspecified (see Table 2) because it tended to shift outwards and inwards over the demand cycle. The reason why this comes about is because, for example, at the beginning of an upswing in demand, vacancies will rise as firms begin to demand labour. The level of unemployment will not show an appreciable change immediately since it takes time to allow for job search and other frictional barriers to be overcome. Thus the UV curve will shift outwards.

However, these cyclical changes will be reflected by an alteration of the rate of change in unemployment. Thus a better specification[3] of the UV relationship is as follows:

$$V_R = f(U_R, \dot{U}_R) \tag{1}$$

[3] The rationale for this specification is discussed more fully in Phelps [9] and Hanson [5].

The relationship was specified as log-linear and fitted data from 1959(i) to 1966(iii). The results for this time period (see below in Table 3) were very satisfactory showing little evidence of the serial correlation problem that arose in the straight UV specification.

It is not necessary to include hoarded unemployment (or hoarded vacancies) in this specification for two reasons.

First, provided firms' hoarding policies remained constant over the pre-1966(iv) period, as Taylor suggests, then there should be a good fit between registered unemployment and registered vacancies. In a cyclical downswing, a cyclical shake-out would occur and registered unemployment would increase. In addition some labour would be hoarded, causing hoarded unemployment to rise. The important point is that firms' hoarding behaviour remained unchanged.

Second, any changes in hoarding behaviour that do occur should be taken into account in the above re-specification of the UV relationship. To illustrate this let us return to the firm at the beginning of an upswing in demand and look more closely at the sequence of events. The first likely action by the firm is to begin to utilise its hoarded labour. It may do this even before it recognises that the upswing is underway and not just a temporary increase in demand. As it recognises that the upswing is underway and that hoarded unemployment is declining it will begin to notify vacancies which it will anticipate filling by the time the hoarded labour is utilised and overtime is being worked.

Now, if the firm changes its hoarding behaviour so that more labour than previously is dishoarded in the downswing, the upswing will be entered with lower stocks of hoarded labour. Thus, this labour will be used up and the overtime situation reached more quickly than before. There will be a larger number of vacancies than before for a given level of aggregate demand. However, registered unemployment will fall faster than before for two reasons. First, firms will attempt to fill vacancies more quickly than before, assuming they dislike making excessive overtime payments. Second, in a situation of high unemployment workers will be eager to be re-employed and vacancies will be applied for quickly. For these reasons, labour market frictional delays will be shorter and unemployment will fall faster than previously.

Consequently, any outward shift of the UV curve caused by a change in cyclical hoarding policy should be taken account of in the above specification.

If there has been such a change since 1966(iii) then there should be little change in the fit over the 1966(iii) to 1971(ii) period—since the UV shift will be accounted for by greater fluctuations in the rate of change of unemployment. In Foster [2] it was observed that this was not the case. This is spelt out when the complete results are inspected (Table 3). In the post-1966(iii) period the coefficient on $(\log_{10} U_{Rt} - \log_{10} U_{Rt-1})$ increases and that on U_{Rt} declines. When subjected to a 'Chow' test there is evidence that the fits for the two periods are not part of the same relationship. This is further emphasised by the poor quality of the 'whole period' fit.

It can be concluded then that a 'cyclical shake-out' explanation of the UV shift by itself is inadequate since the above fit is not the same over both periods. Despite the inadequacy of a 'cyclical shake-out' explanation by itself, it may be that the UV shift can still be partly attributed to such a change after 1966(iii).

A more detailed examination of the above results shows that the post-1966(iii) fit yields a D.W. of 0.75, suggesting that the relationship is misspecified. It is possible that this misspecification arises because an increase in cyclical dishoarding is not the only type of shake-out that has occurred since 1966(iii). This possibility will now be considered.

(b) *Non-cyclical shake-out*

Apart from the possibility that there has been a cyclical shake-out of labour since 1966(iii), there is also the possibility that a shake-out

Table 3

Specification	$\log_{10} V_{Rt} = \alpha_1 + \alpha_2 \log_{10} U_{Rt}$ $+ \alpha_3(\log_{10} U_{Rt} - \log_{10} U_{Rt-1})$				
Reg. no.	Period	α_1	α_2	α_3	$\bar{R}^2$	D.W.
1	1959(i)–1966(iii)	0·0963* (0·0107)	−1·1858* (0·0571)	−0·3763* (0·1473)	0·939	1·47
2	1966(iv)–1971(ii)	0·1416* (0·0519)	−0·8038* (0·1485)	−0·7535* (0·2475)	0·618	0·75
3	1959(i)–1971(ii)	0·0306 (0·0197)	−0·6250* (0·0788)	−0·2287 (0·2560)	0·594	0·16

of a non-cyclical nature has occurred. It is plausible to suppose that firms hold stocks of underutilised labour even at a peak of product demand. This will arise because some types of employees are difficult to dishoard under any circumstances. Such labour will characteristically exist in the 'overhead' area of the firm's activities where the contribution of individual workers is more difficult to calculate. In a cyclical downturn it is relatively easy to dishoard unskilled production workers whose workload is directly sensitive to demand. With the 'overhead' workers, a situation prevails where their workload is less related to the state of product demand, but, owing to the interdependence of tasks, an individual cannot be easily dishoarded because of the disruptive effect on the department involved. What is required is a thorough investigation and reorganisation of tasks before labour can be dishoarded. Bearing in mind that the workload of such workers is much less responsive to demand changes and the cost of such investigatory exercises is high, cyclical changes in demand are unlikely, by themselves, to encourage a reduction of these unused man-hours.

Since 1966(iii) there have been certain encouragements to firms to shake-out labour they would otherwise have held on to, underutilised, even at a demand peak. In Section III I shall detail these encouragements and discuss indications that a steady non-cyclical shake-out may have taken place since 1966(iii). Such a shake-out would be likely to be fairly slow since it takes time to set up 'organisation and methods' departments to pin-point underemployed labour and to devise ways of reallocating workloads in order to release individual workers.

To get some indication of the extent of such a shake-out, Taylor's estimates of hoarded unemployment can be utilised. Now, although it has been pointed out, above, that this data is not very helpful in testing whether or not there was a change in cyclical hoarding behaviour since 1966, such data are still useful in accounting for cyclical movements in the UV relationship in the pre-1966(iv) period.

It has already been observed that as vacancies increase at the beginning of a cyclical upswing, hoarded labour declines. Therefore, given that cyclical hoarding behaviour remained unchanged in the pre-1966(iv) period, movements in labour hoarding should explain the cyclical shifts in the UV relationship (Table 4).

The similarity of this result with that using the rate of change of registered unemployment as the additional independent variable is

Table 4

Specification	$\log_{10} V_{Rt} = \alpha_1 + \alpha_2 \log_{10} U_{Rt} + \alpha_3 \log_{10} U_{Ht}$				

Reg. no.	Period	α_1	α_2	α_3	$\bar{R}^2$	D.W.
1	1959(i)– 1966(iii)	0·180* (0·021)	−1·162* (0·050)	−0·116 (0·028)	0·954	1·50

striking. When both variables are included in the UV specification (see Table 5 below) for this period, they are found to be multicollinear, confirming that they both measure the same cyclical influences.

In the post-1966(iii) period there is also the possibility that non-cyclical shake-out is important. If such a shake-out took place there would be a steady decline in hoarded labour and a steady increase in registered unemployment over time. If it is assumed that this relationship can be specified as log-linear,[4] then,

$$\log_e U_{YRt} = \beta_1 - \beta_2 \log_e U_{Ht} \qquad (2)$$

where U_{YR} = that part of registered unemployment attributable to non-cyclical shake-out, and, in addition,

$$\log_e U_{Rt} = \log_e U_{ZRt} + \log_e U_{YRt} \qquad (3)$$

where U_{ZR} = that part of registered unemployment that would have prevailed without non-cyclical shake-out.

If it is further assumed that V_R is related only to U_{ZR} and not to U_{YR}, then the log-linear relationship hypothesised earlier becomes:

$$\log_e V_{Rt} = \alpha_1 - \alpha_2 \log_e U_{ZRt} - \alpha_3 (\log_e U_{ZRt} - \log_e U_{ZRt-1}) \quad (4)$$

from (2) and (3),

$$\log_e U_{ZRt} = \log_e U_{Rt} - \beta_1 + \beta_2 \log_e U_{Ht} \qquad (5)$$

[4] The relationship between hoarded and registered unemployment was specified as log-linear, since, as this 'disguised' unemployment is reduced, one would expect an increasing proportion to find their way to the employment exchanges. For example, a firm can commence its reorganisation by removing married female labour, by natural wastage and early retirements. However, to reduce labour to successively lower levels, the firm must increasingly resort to making redundant workers who will remain in the labour market and go onto the register.

substituting (5) in (4) and assuming that

$$(\log_e U_{ZRt} - \log_e U_{ZRt-1}) \simeq (\log_e U_{Rt} - \log_e U_{Rt-1})$$

then,

$$\log_e V_{Rt} = \alpha_1 - \alpha_2 (\log_e U_{Rt} - \beta_1 + \beta_2 \log_e U_{Ht})$$
$$\qquad\qquad - \alpha_3 (\log_e U_{Rt} - \log_e U_{Rt-1}) \quad (6)$$
$$= \alpha_1 + \alpha_2\beta_1 - \alpha_2 \log_e U_{Rt} - \alpha_2\beta_2 \log_e U_{Ht}$$
$$\qquad\qquad - \alpha_3 (\log_e U_{Rt} - \log_e U_{Rt-1}) \quad (7)$$

Let $\alpha_1 + \alpha_2\beta_1 = \gamma_1,$

$$\alpha_2 = \gamma_2,$$
$$\alpha_3 = \gamma_3,$$
$$\alpha_4 = \alpha_2\beta_2$$

then the reduced form equation is:

$$\log_e V_{Rt} = \gamma_1 - \gamma_2 \log_e U_{Rt}$$
$$\qquad - \gamma_3 (\log_e U_{Rt} - \log_e U_{Rt-1}) - \gamma_4 \log_e U_{Ht} \quad (8)$$

However, using U_{Ht} to take account of non-cyclical shake-out presents some problems when the second sub-period regression is estimated, since it has been already observed that there is a relationship between V_{Rt} and U_{Ht} due to cyclical shake-out. It is unlikely that cyclical hoarding will cease completely in the second sub-period, but earlier evidence suggests that it may be substantially reduced.

In an effort to overcome this difficulty the relationship is specified between V_{Rt} and U_{Ht-1}. In the first sub-period, such a relationship should continue to pick up cyclical effects, but in the second sub-period, if stocks of hoarded labour are lower than previously, vacancies should increase much earlier. Thus the cyclical relationship, if any, will tend to be between V_{Rt} and U_{Ht} rather than U_{Ht-1}.

This one quarter lag before the effects of non-cyclical shake-out affects registered unemployment is quite acceptable since there are several reasons to expect a delay before some of these redundant employees registered. First, the type of worker affected would be likely to be unfamiliar with unemployment and his rights to benefit. Given that a redundancy payment may have been received, such workers may be confident that they would find another job quickly and not bother registering as unemployed. Non-eligibility may have discouraged immediate registration in some cases, particularly amongst women. Also, it is not always easy for a firm to indulge in non-cyclical shake-out by direct redundancies, since there is strong Trade Union opposition to such drastic moves. Therefore, an indirect alternative of simply not replacing staff lost through natural wastage can be resorted to. Such a policy will tend to affect new entrants to the labour force most of all. However, it is this group which is composed of many individuals who are not entitled to unemployment benefit and therefore have little incentive to register.

After one quarter of a year's unemployment, one would expect most to have registered to assist in finding a job and/or to receive unemployment benefit.

If there is indeed non-cyclical shake-out in the post-1966(iii) period, two distinct predictions can be made about the nature of the results. First of all, the constant should be larger than in the pre-1966(iv) period since $\gamma_1 = \alpha_1 + \alpha_2\beta_1$. Second, the multi-collinearity observed between $\log U_{Ht}$ and $(\log U_{Rt} - \log U_{Rt-1})$ in the first period should not be observed in the second period. The complete specification and results are shown in Table 5.

Both predictions as to the nature of the results in the post-1966(iii) period were confirmed. The constant almost doubles in size and there is no evidence of multi-collinearity between $\log U_{Ht-1}$ and $(\log U_{Rt} - \log U_{Rt-1})$. Thus there is some indication that non-cyclical shake-out has occurred since 1966(iii) in addition to any cyclical shake-out that may have occurred. However, despite the fact that the inclusion of

Table 5

Specification	$\log_{10} V_{Rt} = \alpha_1 + \alpha_2 \log_{10} U_{Rt}$ $+ \alpha_3(\log_{10} U_{Rt} - \log_{10} U_{Rt-1}) + \alpha_4 \log_{10} U_{Ht-1}$					
Reg. no.	Period	α_1	α_2	α_3	α_4	$\bar{R}^2$	D.W.
1	1959(i)–1966(iii)	0·1503* (0·0262)	−1·1198* (0·0611)	−0·1872 (0·1619)	−0·0860* (0·0386)	0·947	1·64
2	1966(iv)–1971(ii)	0·2871* (0·0424)	−0·9211* (0·0941)	−0·4946* (0·1603)	−0·1545* (0·0296)	0·855	1·17
3	1959(i)–1971(ii)	0·2031* (0·0374)	−0·6225* (0·0638)	−0·2366 (0·2263)	−0·2386* (0·0469)	0·735	0·49

U_{Ht-1} to take account of non-cyclical shake-out, has led to a noticeable improvement in the results, the Durbin-Watson statistic of 1·17 still indicates that the relationship is underspecified.

In addition, the 'Chow' test rejects the hypothesis that the estimated coefficients in the two sub-period regressions are the same, indicating that the two sub-period fits are not part of the same relationship. Visual inspection of the whole period regression, with its poor fit, serious misspecification and biassed coefficients emphasises this instability.

To conclude this section, then, the evidence discussed above suggests that there may have been two types of shake-out in operation in the post-1966(iii) period, of a cyclical and non-cyclical nature. Why this should have occurred will be considered in the next section. However, the remaining problems of misspecification and instability indicate that some other factor of importance has been excluded from consideration.

III   The effects of demographic changes on the supply and demand for labour

In this section I attempt to analyse the effect of demographic changes on unemployment rates. Since these changes are related to the 'shake-out' factors already discussed, I shall discuss the causes of such a 'shake-out', as well, in this section.

First, each causal factor will be discussed, showing how firms' demand will be influenced.

1   The 'birth bulge'

From 1939 to about 1952 the birthrate in Britain deviated considerably from its long-run upward trend (see Figure 1). In the early war years the birthrate fell well below trend, but by 1942 this situation had reversed and there began a rapid increase in the birthrate that reached its peak in 1947. Any investigation of unemployment in the latter part of the 1960's should take this demographic phenomenon into consideration.

(a) *The point of impact*

It takes fifteen years to complete a minimum education and leave school. However, it takes much longer to make an impact on the unemployment figures. In general, fifteen-year-olds either choose to continue with education, enrol in an apprenticeship scheme or

Figure 1 Movements in the annual birthrate, 1933–56

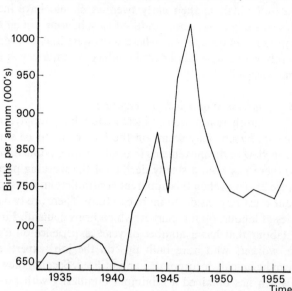

training scheme. Traditionally, this process takes about five years to complete. Consequently, an individual is about twenty years old, or over, before he is a fully fledged member of the labour force.

Even when there are large numbers of school-leavers the likelihood of unemployment in the 15–20 age group is small. The government supports students in further education and subsidises the training of apprentices in industry. Consequently, firms are encouraged to train apprentices, since there are more potential benefits than costs from doing so. In terms of the birthrate data, the decline in the birthrate in the early war years meant that in the early 1960's there was a shortage of trained apprentices and graduates. The above-trend birthrates of 1942 to 1944 resulted in an increase in the availability of trained labour in 1962 to 1964, which would be eagerly employed to augment previous shortages. There was a decline in the birthrate in 1945, consequently the supply of trained workers in 1965 should have been absorbed.

In 1966 there was a large number of individuals attaining the age of twenty. This time it is unlikely that firms could cope with the increased supply, particularly when they were in the downswing of a recession. Two effects can be suggested. First, unemployment amongst individuals in their early twenties should have increased. Second, firms might have been induced to substitute young workers for old workers, in occupations where skills were low. Consequently, such an inflow of young labour could induce unemployment in other age groups as well.

(b) *The importance of age disaggregation*

The idea that there has been an increase in labour supply, resulting from unemployment may seem, on the face of it, to be somewhat puzzling in view of the movements in total working population. Since 1966(iii) there has been a steady decline of the working population (see Figure 2). To explain this apparent contradiction, firms' demand for labour must be considered more carefully. There are two distinct categories of labour, on the market, which firms demand. First, they require labour that has a number of years experience on a specific job—i.e. workers who have built up 'on the job' expertise. Such labour can be quickly incorporated and utilised. Second, they require labour which has obtained a minimum familiarity with productive techniques but possesses no accumulated knowledge of the peculiarities and problems of specific jobs. This labour can be introduced gradually to specific jobs which will be vacated through retirements, etc.

The first type will, typically, be demanded when there are short run increases in product demand since there is no time to bring in-

Figure 2   Movements in quarterly seasonally adjusted
working population, 1965(i)–1972(i)

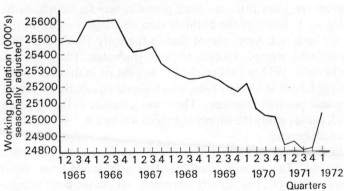

Figure 3 Movements of the 20–24 population per annum (1957–73)

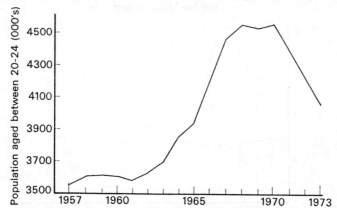

experienced workers up to their full potential. The second type will tend to be demanded on a longer run basis.

Consequently, newly qualified/trained labour cannot be easily substituted for older more experienced labour except where the work involved is of a very unskilled nature. Thus a situation where there is an excess supply of inexperienced labour and an excess demand for experienced labour is perfectly plausible.

To look at changes in the working population alone, then, does not tell us much about the effect of the 'birth bulge' on unemployment rates, since other factors may be operative on working population simultaneously. What is required is a disaggregation of working population and unemployment data to focus on the relative movements in supply and demand for labour of different experience types.

The 20–24 age group was selected as representative of 'inexperienced' labour as far as firms are concerned. In Figure 3 the numbers each year in this age group are plotted over time. The slump below trend in the early 1960's is clearly shown, recovery, through compensating above trend observations, not being complete until about 1965. There follows a steep rise to a peak in 1969.

However, if the proportion of the working population in this age group is calculated, a somewhat different graph is revealed (see Figure 4). Despite the decline in numbers in this group after 1969, there is no decline in the proportion of working population. In addition, when absolute numbers are rising in 1966 to 1969, the proportion is rising even faster.

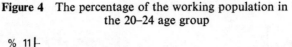

Figure 4   The percentage of the working population in the 20–24 age group

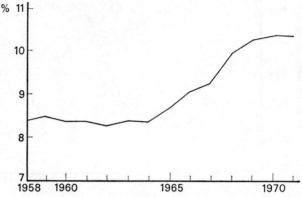

The implication of this, then, is that there has been an absolute decline in numbers in older age categories. It has already been noted that total working population has declined since 1966(iii), so the absolute decline must have outweighed the absolute increase in the younger groups. Before going on to analyse movements in unemployment for different age groups the reasons for this decline in working population amongst older age groups must be investigated.

2   Social security legislation
In 1965–6 the Labour Government, concerned with balance of payments problems, committed itself to encouraging a shake-out of labour which could be made available to exporting industries. To cushion the impact on those shaken-out, the Redundancy Payments Act was introduced to make good loss of 'property' rights; and the National Insurance Act to ease the hardship of the resulting unemployment, by introducing a system of earnings related benefits.

The Redundancy Payments Act (1965) made provision for repayments of a certain proportion of redundancy payments by firms (see Table 6). For employees made redundant aged over forty years, the additional half-week's wages paid was recovered in full from the Redundancy Fund. This introduced an immediate incentive for firms to polarise their redundancies.

From time to time, in the past, redundancies had to be made in cyclical downswings. The introduction of this Act immediately made

Table 6

Age group	Redundancy payments (for each year of service)	Employer's rebate (for each year of service)	Net contribution by employers	Incremental contribution by employers
Under 1965 Act				
18–21 inclusive	$\frac{1}{2}$ W.P.	$\frac{1}{3}$ W.P.	$\frac{1}{6}$ W.P.	–
22–40 inclusive	1 W.P.	$\frac{2}{3}$ W.P.	$\frac{1}{3}$ W.P.	$\frac{1}{6}$ W.P.
41–64 inclusive	$1\frac{1}{2}$ W.P.	$1\frac{1}{6}$ W.P.	$\frac{1}{3}$ W.P.	0
Under 1699 Act				
18–21 inclusive	$\frac{1}{2}$ W.P.	$\frac{1}{4}$ W.P.	$\frac{1}{4}$ W.P.	–
22–40 inclusive	1 W.P.	$\frac{1}{2}$ W.P.	$\frac{1}{2}$ W.P.	$\frac{1}{4}$ W.P.
41–64 inclusive	$1\frac{1}{2}$ W.P.	$\frac{3}{4}$ W.P.	$\frac{3}{4}$ W.P.	$\frac{1}{4}$ W.P.

it in a firm's interest to make redundant either older, less efficient, workers or the very young, who didn't qualify for payments, or only qualified for small amounts.

However, not only did this legislation encourage a polarisation of 'usual' redundancies, but also encouraged 'non-cyclical' redundancies. The introduction of such payments offered a relatively inexpensive way of making redundant older and more inefficient long service workers. In the past, employers were reluctant to make redundant such workers because of the probable hardship that would be suffered and trade union opposition to such manoeuvres. Voluntary contributions could be made, but an adequate sum, comparable to that paid after the Act, represented a sizeable cost to the firm involved. After the 1965 Act employers only had to bear about 22 per cent of such a sum. With the redundant worker receiving this tax free lump sum, plus earnings related benefits in unemployment, employer concern about hardship was significantly reduced. Also, Trade Union opposition to redundancies was muted, since in many cases employees wanted to be made redundant in order that they could qualify for a sizeable redundancy payment.

Before non-cyclical redundancies can be made, investigations must be made by firms to isolate likely candidates, and devise ways of redistributing the workload among remaining employees. Therefore, despite the fact that the Redundancy Payments Act came into force in December 1965, there would be little immediate effect on registered unemployment figures. As was mentioned earlier, such a non-cyclical shake-out would take place gradually over time beginning about a year after the legislation was introduced. Also, the introduction of earnings related benefits, as was mentioned acted as an additional encouragement to employers to make redundant older workers. The oldest workers who were made redundant, being near retirement, had two strong incentives to remove themselves from the working population. First, there is evidence (see Hauser and Burrows [6]) that involuntary workers in the oldest age groups characteristically find re-employment very difficult even when there is a high demand for labour. Second, these workers qualify for near-maximum redundancy payments. The effect of these early retirements would be to reduce the working population. The working population tends to fall in a recession in any case—this effect will cause it to fall further than normal.

This reduction in working population, by itself, will tend to increase the unemployment rate even though the level of unemployment is unchanged. The introduction of the 1969 Redundancy Rebates Act should have altered this tendency to some extent. This Act reduced the incentive to make older employees redundant (see Table 6), and encouraged the removal of the youngest workers in a cyclical downswing.

3   A disaggregation of unemployment by age
To get some indication as to whether or not the demographic and policy changes discussed above had the effects suggested, the proportional shares of total male unemployment attributable to different age groups, (18–25, 26–40, 41–64) over time were computed (see Figure 5).

The first point to note is the sharp change between July 1966 and January 1967. The 41–65 group experienced a 10 per cent decline in their share of unemployment. The other two groups increased their share by 5 per cent. However this increase was more severe for the 18–25 group (36 per cent as compared with 21 per cent for the 26–40 group).

This sudden change is consistent with earlier discussions. Older workers made redundant leave the working population, thus reducing their share of unemployment, there is a demographic increase in the young group, causing its share to increase. In addition, the middle group has increased its proportion, probably because of the decline

Figure 5 Movements in the proportional shares of total male
unemployment attributable to different age groups
(Jan. 1965–July 1972)

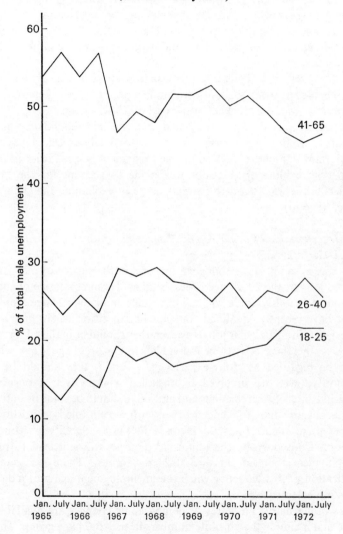

in working population and the fact that there may be some substitution of younger workers for older workers in unskilled occupations, by firms, in an attempt to reduce their wage bills.

From January 1967 to July 1969 the proportional shares continue to move appropriately. The oldest group's share rising as progressively younger workers over 40 are shaken out and register rather than retire. The youngest group maintains its increased share as demographic increases continue. The middle group's share declines to its earlier level.

After 1969, and the change in legislation, there is a steady decline in the oldest group's share as young workers are shaken out in preference to older workers in the cyclical downswing.

These graphical inspections, then, indicate that redundancy payments legislation and demographic increases in labour inflow may be important in any explanation of unemployment rates. Earlier in the paper an exploratory attempt was made to account for the first effect, but it was found to be inadequate in explaining the changes since 1966(iii).

4   Incorporation of demographic changes into formal specification of UV relationship

To take account of an abnormal increase in the supply of inexperienced labour, the 20–24 age group is taken as representative of such labour. Obviously, there will be individuals in the over 24 age groups that have recently 'qualified' but not in a position where they are specialists in a particular job. However, they should be in the minority.

Also, there are likely to be individuals in the 20–24 age group who can be regarded as 'fully-experienced'. Again, they should be a minority, who are involved in unskilled work. Given a positive relationship between earnings and age, there should be some incentive to substitute young for older workers in these unskilled occupations when there is an abnormal increase in the availability of young labour. Consequently, the abnormal increase will still lead to unemployment, but not in the 20–24 age group. There was some indication of this tendency when the unemployment/age group data was inspected earlier.

Two alternative measures of demographic changes are available. The first is simply the absolute numbers in the 20–24 age group. This data can be computed directly from the U.K. birth statistics and gives the most accurate profile of population changes.

The second is the percentage of the working population aged between 20 and 24. This measure has the advantage that it only accounts for changes in the numbers of individuals actually available for work. This percentage is, of course, sensitive to changes in the working population that occur in other age groups. An increase in early retirements in the older age groups, suspected in the previous section, due to redundancy payments legislation would result in an increase in its value. Consequently shake-out of older workers should also be reflected in the movements of this percentage.

(a) *Absolute changes in the 20–24 population*
If there is a positive relationship between unemployment and demographic changes, and this relationship is specified as log-linear, then:

$$\log_e U_{LRt} = \beta_1 + \beta_2 \log_e L_{At} \tag{9}$$

where, U_{LR} is that part of registered unemployment attributable to demographic increases, and, L_A is the population aged between 20 and 24.

Now, if

$$\log_e U_{Rt} = \log_e U_{LRt} + \log_e U_{ZRt} \tag{10}$$

where U_{ZRt} is that part of registered unemployment that would have prevailed given no demographic changes.

Then,

$$\log_e U_{ZRt} = \log_e U_{Rt} - \log_e U_{LRt} \tag{11}$$

Substituting for $\log_e U_{LRt}$ from (9):

$$\therefore \log_e U_{ZRt} = \log_e U_{Rt} - \beta_1 - \beta_2 \log_e L_A \tag{12}$$

Assuming that it is U_{ZRt} rather than U_{Rt} that is related to V_{Rt}, then the log-linear relationship hypothesised earlier becomes:

$$\log_e V_{Rt} = \alpha_1 - \alpha_2 \log_e U_{ZRt} - \alpha_3 (\log_e U_{ZRt} - \log_e U_{ZRt-1}) \tag{13}$$

Assuming that $(\log_e U_{ZRt} - \log_e U_{ZRt-1}) \simeq (\log_e U_{Rt} - \log_e U_{Rt-1})$ and substituting for $\log_e U_{ZRt}$ from (12), then,

$$\log_e V_{Rt} = \alpha_1 - \alpha_2 \log_e U_{Rt} + \alpha_2\beta_1$$

$$+ \alpha_2\beta_2 \log_e L_A - \alpha_3 (\log_e U_{Rt} - \log_e U_{Rt-1}) \tag{14}$$

Let $\gamma_1 = \alpha_1 + \alpha_2\beta_1$

$\quad\;\; \gamma_2 = \alpha_2$

$\quad\;\; \gamma_3 = \alpha_3$

$\quad\;\; \gamma_4 = \alpha_2\beta_2$

Then the reduced form is:

$$\log_e V_{Rt} = \gamma_1 - \gamma_2 \log_e U_{Rt}$$
$$- \gamma_3(\log_e U_{Rt} - \log_e U_{Rt-1}) + \gamma_4 \log_e L_A \quad (15)$$

This relationship was tested over the 1959(i)–1971(ii) period and the results were shown in Table 7.

The estimated coefficient on L_A is of the appropriate sign and significant in all three periods.

Despite its significance in the first sub-period there is little increase in the explanatory power of the regression. This is as expected, since there is little upward trend in the L_A series over this sub-period—in a growing economy all such 'inexperienced' labour would be demanded and the impact of increases in L_A would be small. Thus the estimated coefficient in this sub-period is much smaller than in the second sub-period. The only noticeable impact of the inclusion of L_A over this period is to change the sign of the constant and remove its significance.

In the second sub-period, there is a greater improvement in the results. In particular the $\bar{R}^2$ increases from 0.617 to 0.738. In addition, the inclusion of L_A in the specification has altered the values of the estimated coefficients. That on U_{Rt} has moved closer to its value in the first sub-period regression.

Table 7

Specification		$\log_{10} V_{Rt} = \alpha_1 + \alpha_2 \log_{10} U_{Rt}$ $+ \alpha_3(\log_{10} U_{Rt} - \log_{10} U_{Rt-1}) + \alpha_4 \log L_{At}$					
Reg. no.	Period	α_1	α_2	α_3	α_4	$\bar{R}^2$	D.W.
1	1959(i)–1966(iii)	−1·641 (0·832)	−1·119* (0·063)	−0·393* (0·139)	0·497* (0·237)	0·946	1·470
2	1966(iv)–1971(ii)	−7·634* (2·691)	−0·911* (0·128)	−0·202 (0·280)	2·191* (0·758)	0·738	0·878
3	1959(i)–1971(ii)	−4·750* (0·389)	−0·927* (0·046)	−0·405* (0·126)	1·383* (0·112)	0·903	0·785

The estimated coefficient on $\dot{U}_R$ has become non-significant in the second sub-period. This is due to multi-collinearity between L_{At} and $\dot{U}_R$. This implies that firms' cyclical hoarding policy has been influenced by the demographic increase in the 20–24 population after 1966(iii). This certainly accords with the idea that the existence of a large pool of unemployed labour encourages firms to hold lower stocks of unemployed man-hours. Earlier speculation that firms have biassed cyclical shake-out towards the young age groups receives some support from this evidence.

Although the inclusion of L_A does not increase the explanatory power of the sub-period regressions a great deal, there has been a noticeable improvement in the 'whole period' result. Inclusion of L_A has removed the perverse coefficient estimates found earlier and improved the $\bar{R}^2$ and D.W. statistic. However, the D.W. statistic continues to indicate that the relationship is misspecified. In addition, the 'Chow test' continues to reject the hypothesis that the same relationship exists in both sub-periods.

To take some account of the existence of non-cyclical shake-out, U_{Ht-1} is again included in the specification. The complete specification and results are shown in Table 8. The results in the first sub-period are similar to those in Table 5, with evidence of multi-collinearity between U_{Ht-1} and $\dot{U}_R$. The addition of L_A to the specification has improved the $\bar{R}^2$ and D.W. by only a small amount.

The results for the second sub-period are more interesting. The inclusion of U_{Ht-1} has removed the significance of the estimated coefficient on L_A found in Regression 2 in Table 7. Again, this implies that firms' dishoarding behaviour has been influenced by the plentiful supply of young, inexperienced labour, encouraging them, irrespective

Table 8

$$\log_{10} V_{Rt} = \alpha_1 + \alpha_2 \log_{10} U_{Rt} + \alpha_3(\log_{10} U_{Rt} - \log_{10} U_{Rt-1}) + \alpha_4 \log U_{Ht-1} + \alpha_5 \log L_A$$

Reg. no.	Period	α_1	α_2	α_3	α_4	α_5	$\bar{R}^2$	D.W.
1	1959(i)–1966(iii)	−1·575* (0·769)	−1·054* (0·064)	−0·205 (0·151)	−0·085* (0·036)	0·493* (0·219)	0·954	1·713
2	1966(iv)–1971(ii)	−2·726 (2·351)	−0·944* (0·094)	−0·323 (0·207)	−0·130* (0·035)	0·843 (0·658)	0·861	1·182
3	1959(i)–1971(ii)	−4·016* (0·365)	−0·885* (0·039)	−0·153 (0·119)	−0·117* (0·026)	1·195* (0·103)	0·932	1·113

of cyclical considerations, to reduce their stocks of unutilised labour of this type. However, the inclusion of U_{Ht-1} in this sub-period leads to a noticeable improvement in the $\bar{R}^2$ and D.W. indicating that non-cyclical shake-out also occurred for reasons other than this demographic change.

The 'whole period' result has also improved through the inclusion of U_{Ht-1}. In this regression the estimated coefficient on L_A remains very significant and is unaffected by the inclusion of U_{Ht-1}. Inspection of the corresponding result in Table 5 emphasises the importance of L_A in the 'whole period' regression. However, the D.W. statistic continues to indicate positive first order serial correlation and the 'Chow' test continues to reject the hypothesis that the same relationship exists in both sub-periods.

In conclusion, the use of the crude population statistics has only resulted in a partial improvement in explaining the UV shift. This is not surprising since the relevant data, as far as the labour market is concerned, are working population statistics, not the whole population. However, the significance of L_A, particularly over the whole period, gives an indication of the importance of demographic changes.

(b) *Changes in the proportion of the working population aged between 20 and 24*

The percentage of the working population aged between 20 and 24 (L_p) was incorporated into the UV specification in the same way as with L_A. Again, the relationship between registered unemployment and L_p was specified as log-linear. The complete specification and results were as shown in Table 9.

As with L_A, the main impact of introducing L_P, in the first sub-

Table 9

$$\log_{10} V_{Rt} = \alpha_1 + \alpha_2 \log_{10} U_{Rt} + \alpha_3(\log_{10} U_{Rt} - U_{Rt-1}) + \alpha_4 \log_{10} U_{Ht-1} + \alpha_5 \log_{10} L_{Pt}$$

Reg. no.	Period	α_1	α_2	α_3	α_4	α_5	$\bar{R}^2$	D.W.
1	1959(i)–1966(ii)	−1·285* (0·557)	−1 034* (0·065)	−0 219 (0·148)	−0 099* (0·035)	1·542* (0·598)	0·956	1·829
2	1966(iii)–1971(ii)	−1·128* (0·289)	−1·270* (0·100)	−0·548* (0·144)	+0·022 (0·037)	1·448* (0·293)	0·908	2·10
3	1959(i)–1971(ii)	−1·640* (0·167)	−1·032* (0·049)	−0·257* (0·126)	−0·048 (0·030)	1·889* (0·170)	0·927	1·041

period, is to alter the sign of the constant. The results show a slight improvement using L_P rather than L_A probably due to the fact that L_P is concerned with movements in the working population rather than the population as a whole.

The second sub-period result is more interesting, since the inclusion of L_P rather than L_A has resulted in a substantial improvement in the results. The $\bar{R}^2$ has increased from 0.861 to 0.908 and the D.W. statistic from 1.182 to 2.100. In addition, the inclusion of L_P has removed the significance of the estimated coefficient on U_{Ht-1}. This multi-collinearity between U_{Ht-1} and L_P suggests that shake-out behaviour can be accounted for in the movements of L_P. Therefore some important characteristics of shake-out behaviour by firms can be inferred.

Firstly, shake-out can affect the size of L_P if some of the redundant labour, not in the 20–24 age group, remove themselves from the working population. This removal will increase L_P. The age group most likely to remove themselves from the working population is that composed of individuals nearing retirement, for reasons discussed earlier.

Secondly, the existence of a substantial supply of labour, encouraging firms to reduce stocks of such labour, has already been discussed when the impact of L_A on U_R was being investigated. The size of L_P will increase due to increases in L_A, and this shake-out inducement will also be picked up by L_P.

Thus, the decline in importance[5] of U_{Ht-1} in the second sub-period suggests that shake-out, particularly of the non-cyclical type, has been concentrated in two age-groups—those containing very old and young members of the working population.

The whole period fit, again, is similar, in terms of explanatory power to that using L_A (see Table 8). The significance of U_{Ht-1} is again removed and that on $\dot{U}_R$ re-established. Thus U_{Ht-1} can be removed from the specification without changing the results. This reinforces the conclusion that shake-out has been biased towards specific age groups.

However, despite these improvements, the 'Chow' test still rejects the null hypothesis that the estimated coefficients in the three regressions are the same.

---

[5] Removal of U_{Ht-1} from the specification has no effect on the results in the second sub-period. The $\bar{R}^2 = 0.911$ and D.W. statistic $= 2.14$.

(c) *An increase in the duration of unemployment*

Despite the rejection of Gujarati's 'supply side' explanation of the UV shift, there are likely to be some effects on the duration of unemployment arising because of the introduction of earnings related benefits. The effect of these benefits is not to induce direct voluntary unemployment, but to simply enable a worker, made redundant, to conduct a more thorough job-search than otherwise. Such behaviour in redundancy, must inevitably result in some increase in the average duration of unemployment.

It must be emphasised that the impact of this increase is inadequate by itself to explain the UV shift.[6] There has been no tendency for the proportional share of unemployment of those unemployed for over 26 weeks[7] to decline dramatically after 1966(iii), as would be expected if earnings related benefits were the sole cause of an increase in registered unemployment. Also, evidence cited by Weeden [1] and Mackay and Reid [8] indicates, as suggested, that there has only been a slight increase in the duration of unemployment due to the introduction of these benefits.

To take account of any effect on unemployment duration, of the introduction of earnings related benefits, a dummy variable (D_B), operative from 1966(iv), is introduced into the whole period regression. Also, U_{Ht-1} is dropped on the grounds that it has a very small non-significant estimated coefficient in the second sub-period and whole period regressions. In addition, three seasonal dummy variables are included in the specification to take account of the artificial way in which the L_P series is constructed.[8] The complete specification and results were as shown in Table 10.

[6] Inclusion of a dummy variable from 1966(iv) in the straight UV specification yields an $\bar{R}^2$ of 0·85 but a D.W. statistic of 0·56.

[7] The maximum period that these benefits are paid is 26 weeks.

[8] This series is only available at mid-yearly intervals, so, in order to convert to quarterly observations, a simple interpolation was undertaken. It was assumed that third quarter was when demographic changes affected labour supply. It is in this quarter when most individuals leave school and enrol in various types of training schemes, apprenticeships, etc. Consequently, most individuals will complete this training in a third quarter and make themselves available for full-time work. With this in mind the mid-yearly observation was taken as that for third and fourth quarter of that year and first and second quarter of the next year. The resultant 'step-like' series is an oversimplification for several reasons. First of all, there are likely to be some increases in L_P at other times in the year, since individuals also leave school and contract apprenticeships in other quarters. Secondly, the impact on U_R of a given change in L_P, due to demographic increases in supply, in third quarter is likely to be much larger than in subsequent quarters when individuals gradually find themselves employment. Thirdly, L_P can increase in all quarters due to the effect of a decline in the working population in older age groups.

Table 10

		$\log_{10} V_{Rt} = \alpha_1 + \alpha_2 \log_{10} V_{Rt} + \alpha_3(\log_{10} U_{Rt} - \log_{10} U_{Rt-1})$						
Specification			$+ \alpha_4 \log L_{Pt} + \alpha_5 D_B + $ (S.D.'s)					
Reg. no.	Period	α_1	α_2	α_3	α_4	α_5	$\bar{R}^2$	D.W.
1	1959(i)–1966(iii)	−0·850 (0·596)	−1·135* (0·059)	−0·509* (0·139)	1·026* (0·512)	—	0·952	1·674
2	1966(iv)–1971(ii)	−1·209* (0·209)	−1·280* (0·109)	−0·607* (0·127)	1·528* (0·233)	—	0·936	2·009
3	1959(i)–1971(ii)	−1·093* (0·183)	−1·129* (0·039)	−0·521* (0·096)	1·284* (0·197)	0·076* (0·016)	0·950	1·664

The estimated coefficient on D_B is positive and significant. However, the smallness of the coefficient indicates that the impact of earnings related benefits on the UV relationship is not large, but their inclusion reduces the serial correlation problem found earlier in the whole period regressions. In addition the 'Chow' test is satisfied—indicating that there is no significant difference between the estimated coefficients in each regression.

(d) *A re-estimation of the UV relationship including post 1971(ii) data*

Earlier estimation was handicapped by the fact that Taylor's hoarded unemployment data was only available until mid-1971. Now that U_{Ht-1} has been dispensed with, the specified UV relationship can be re-estimated using additional observations on later quarters.

Some deterioration can be expected with this re-estimated fit, since the impact of the 'bulge' first felt on the 20–25 age group in 1966(iii) will correspondingly be felt on the over 25 age group in 1971(iii). Therefore, any impact on unemployment caused by this change will not be accounted for in the specification.

The re-estimated results, using data up to 1972(ii) were as shown in Table 11.

These re-estimated results exhibit similar characteristics to those over the shorter period. As expected, the D.W. statistic declines due to the omission of the 'bulge' effect in the over 25 age group. No attempt will be made to incorporate this secondary 'bulge' effect here, except to point out that it is necessary to take it into account after 1971(ii).

To conclude this section, the evidence discussed suggested that

Table 11

$$\log_{10} V_{Rt} = \alpha_1 + \alpha_2 \log_{10} U_{Rt} + \alpha_3(\log_{10} U_{Rt} - \log_{10} U_{Rt-1})$$
$$+ \alpha_4 \log L_{Pt} + \alpha_5 D_B + (3 \text{ S.D.'s})$$

Reg. no.	Period	α_1	α_2	α_3	α_4	α_5	$\bar{R}^2$	D.W.
1	1959(i)–1966(iii)	−0·850 (0·596)	−1·135* (0·059)	−0·509* (0·139)	1·026* (0·512)	— —	0·952	1·674
2	1966(iv)–1972(ii)	−1·026* (0 236)	−1·074* (0 064)	−0·645* (0·146)	1·267* (0·249)	— —	0·943	1·556
3	1959(i)–1972(ii)	−1 163* (0·1826)	−1 101* (0·036)	−0·540* (0·098)	1·351* (0·197)	0·069* (0·016)	0·956	1·527

much of the observed UV shift in late 1966 can be attributed to demographic increases in labour supply. Furthermore, the shake-out suspected in the previous section, was found to be biased towards the very young and very old age groups. The introduction of earnings related benefits played only a minor role in explaining the UV shift.

IV   Conclusions
The evidence contained in this paper suggests that the primary determinants of the 'UV shift', after 1966(iii), were demographic changes in the late 1940's and redundancy payments legislation.

The former factor resulted in an excess supply of 'inexperienced' labour after mid-1966. Firms were unable to accommodate this increase and unemployment resulted. Also the large pool of this type of labour encouraged firms to reduce their stocks of such labour. Inclusion of this effect into the UV specification contributes importantly to removal of the 'shift' effect. In addition, visual inspection of the movements in unemployment by age groups reinforces this conclusion.

In earlier work (see, for example, Mackay and Reid [8]) attention has been concentrated on the effect of the second factor on the supply of labour. There has been little or no evidence that its introduction has encouraged voluntary unemployment. In this paper, redundancy payments legislation has been regarded as encouraging unemployment through its effect on the 'demand-side' rather than the 'supply-side'.

To understand the impact of this legislation on firms' demand for labour, it was necessary conceptually to separate 'shake-out' behaviour into cyclical and non-cyclical components. It was found that the Redundancy Payments Act (1965) encouraged a polarisation of cyclical shake-out into the youngest and oldest age groups. In addition, this Act encouraged non-cyclical shake-out of, almost exclusively, the oldest employees.

The Redundancy Rebates Act (1969) was introduced to reduce these incentives to make redundant the oldest workers. The new rebate structure (see Table 6) certainly reduced the incentive to bias cyclical shake-out towards oldest workers. However, the incentive for non-cyclical shake-out remained since the 50 per cent, rather than 22 per cent, employer contribution to redundancy payments was still an attractive incentive to remove certain very old and relatively inefficient workers. However, the main impact of this change in legislation was to encourage cyclical shake-out of the youngest workers, since in absolute and relative terms the cost to the firm of removing this type of labour was least. Furthermore, such a move would receive Trade Union approval since they have always supported a L.I.F.O. policy with respect to redundancies.

Unfortunately, such an encouragement could hardly have been introduced at a more inappropriate time, since there already existed a situation where there was an abnormal level of young unemployment due to the demographic effects discussed above. In addition, a cyclical downswing commenced in 1969, so the impact on young unemployment was immediate.

The inadequacies of redundancy payments legislation as a means of compensating redundant workers for the loss of their jobs has been discussed elsewhere (see [6, 8]). In this paper, the evidence suggests that this legislation also had adverse effects on employer behaviour, encouraging them to be age selective in their shaking-out.

This indicates that the Government did not anticipate labour market problems arising out of the demographic changes discussed. What is surprising is that, in terms of education and training, these changes were taken into account and additional facilities provided, but there was no policy to induce employers to employ the products of these supported training schemes.

Consequently the UV shift after 1966(iii) can be directly attributed, firstly, to a lack of Government policy to deal with an abnormal demographic change in the working population. Secondly, to the introduction of a redundancy payments policy which was inappropriate in terms of its objectives and had a redundancy inducing effect which was inequitably spread over the age distribution of the employed population.

Statistical appendix

1   Data series used in estimation of UV relationship

Quarter	(1) Unemployment registered (U_R) (%)	(2) Vacancies registered (V_R) (%)	(3) Unemployment hoarded (U_H) (%)	(4) Population aged 20–24 (L_A) (000's)	(5) % of W.P. aged 20–24 (L_P) (%)
1958 (iv)	1·915	0·510	8·2	2891	8·4
1959 (i)	1·876	0·541	9·9	2891	8·4
(ii)	1·842	0·590	5·0	2891	8·4
(iii)	1·750	0·690	5·8	2907	8·5
(iv)	1·648	0·771	2·5	2907	8·5
1960 (i)	1·450	0·836	3·0	2907	8·5
(ii)	1·393	0·908	4·3	2907	8·5
(iii)	1·322	0·968	4·8	2889	8·4
(iv)	1·260	0·998	5·4	2889	8·4
1961 (i)	1·171	0·968	6·0	2889	8·4
(ii)	1·182	0·964	5·8	2889	8·4
(iii)	1·221	0·952	6·4	2861	8·4
(iv)	1·340	0·849	8·1	2861	8·4
1962 (i)	1·411	0·748	8·6	2861	8·4
(ii)	1·600	0·658	7·6	2861	8·4
(iii)	1·780	0·562	6·8	2897	8·3
(iv)	1·941	0·510	8·9	2897	8·3
1963 (i)	2·178	0·510	11·0	2897	8·3
(ii)	2·067	0·544	7·2	2897	8·3
(iii)	1·942	0·568	5·2	2981	8·4
(iv)	1·764	0·677	4·1	2981	8·4
1964 (i)	1·532	0·794	3·1	2981	8·4
(ii)	1·409	0·838	3·5	2981	8·4
(iii)	1·455	0·885	4·0	3157	8·4
(iv)	1·296	0·978	3·4	3157	8·4
1965 (i)	1·201	0·997	3·6	3157	8·4
(ii)	1·192	1·035	5·2	3157	8·4
(iii)	1·259	1·040	5·7	3257	8·7
(iv)	1·192	1·086	5·6	3257	8·7
1966 (i)	1·089	1·101	6·0	3257	8·7
(ii)	1·101	1·058	6·8	3257	8·7
(iii)	1·243	0·987	7·2	3440	9·1
(iv)	1·623	0·819	9·2	3440	9·1
1967 (i)	1·821	0·740	9·0	3440	9·1
(ii)	1·990	0·661	8·7	3440	9·1
(iii)	2·114	0·660	8·6	3654	9·3
(iv)	2·115	0·698	7·1	3654	9·3
1968 (i)	2·150	0·695	6·2	3654	9·3
(ii)	2·141	0·732	5·4	3654	9·3
(iii)	2·167	0·749	4·1	3681	10·0
(iv)	2·107	0·800	2·7	3681	10·0
1969 (i)	2·104	0·783	3·7	3681	10·0
(ii)	2·056	0·800	2·7	3681	10·0
(iii)	2·170	0·794	3·4	3740	10·3
(iv)	2·161	0·790	4·3	3740	10·3

1 Data series used in estimation of UV relationship (continued)

		(1)	(2)	(3)	(4)	(5)
Quarter		Unem-ployment registered (U_R) (%)	Vacancies registered (V_R) (%)	Unem-ployment hoarded (U_H) (%)	Population aged 20–24 (L_A) (000's)	% of W.P. aged 20–24 (L_P) (%)
1970	(i)	2·225	0·757	5·0	3740	10·3
	(ii)	2·240	0·746	5·0	3740	10·3
	(iii)	2·236	0·739	4·8	3603	10·4
	(iv)	2·324	0·707	4·6	3603	10·4
1971	(i)	2·582	0·603	5·0	3603	10·4
	(ii)	2·868	0·515	3·6	3603	10·4
	(iii)	3·152	0·478	—	3375	10·4
	(iv)	3·368	0·476	—	3375	10·4
1972	(i)	3·502	0·493	—	3375	10·4
	(ii)	3·345	0·533	—	3375	10·4

Note: The unemployment and vacancy rates are percentages of the working population.
Sources:
Series (1), (2) and (5) were constructed using data from the *Department of Employment Gazette* (H.M.S.O.).
Series (3) was kindly supplied by J. Taylor, University of Lancaster.
Series (4) was constructed using data on live births from the *Annual Abstract of Statistics* (H.M.S.O.).

2 Data series used in figures

Figure 1—as in (4) above.

Figure 2—used quarterly deseasonalised working population statistics taken from *Department of Employment Gazette* (H.M.S.O.).

Figure 3—as in (4) above.

Figure 4—as in (5) above.

Figure 5—computed from half-yearly breakdown of unemployment by age groups in *Department of Employment Gazette* (H.M.S.O.).

References

[1] Bowers, J. K., Cheshire, P. C., Webb, A. E. and Weeden, R., 'Some Aspects of Unemployment and the Labour Market, 1966–71', *National Institute Economic Review*, No. 62 (Nov. 1972), pp. 75–88.
[2] Foster, J. I., 'The Behaviour of Unemployment and Unfilled Vacancies: Great Britain, 1958–1971—A Comment', *Economic Journal*, No. 329 (March 1973), pp. 192–201.
[3] Gujarati, D., 'The Behaviour of Unemployment and Unfilled Vacancies: Great Britain, 1958–1971', *Economic Journal* (March 1972), pp. 195–204.
[4] Gujarati, D., 'A Reply to Mr. Taylor', *Economic Journal* (Dec. 1972), pp. 1365–8.

[5] Hanson, B., 'Excess Demand, Unemployment, Vacancies and Wages', *Quarterly Journal of Economics*, 84 (1970), pp. 1–23.

[6] Hauser, M. M. and Burrows, P., *The Economics of Unemployment Insurance*, London, Allen and Unwin (1969).

[7] Mackay, D. I., 'After the Shake-Out', *Oxford Economic Papers 24* (1972), pp. 89–110.

[8] Mackay, D. I. and Reid, G. L., 'Redundancy, Unemployment and Manpower Policy', *Economic Journal* (Dec. 1972), pp. 1256–72.

[9] Phelps, E. S., 'Money-Wage Dynamics and Labour Market Equilibrium', *Journal of Political Economy 76* (1968), pp. 678–711.

[10] Taylor, J., 'The Behaviour of Unemployment and Unfilled Vacancies: Great Britain, 1958–1971. An Alternative View', *Economic Journal* (Dec. 1972), pp. 1352–64.

[11] Taylor, J., 'Incomes Policy, the Structure of Unemployment and the Phillips Curve: the United Kingdom Experience, 1973–70', in M. Parkin and M. T. Sumner (eds.), *Incomes Policy and Inflation*, Manchester, Manchester University Press (1972).

F. P. R. Brechling[1]

Chapter 7 Wage inflation and the structure of regional unemployment

I Introduction

An important implication of classical monetary theory is that, if fully expected and adjusted to, the rate of inflation cannot have an influence on real economic activity. In the context of the Phillips curve discussions, this basic, classical conclusion has recently been re-established by neoclassical writers, such as Mortensen [11] and Phelps [13]. According to them, any trade-off that may exist between unemployment and inflation must be caused by adjustment lags, money illusion, and similar frictions which disappear in long-run equilibrium. Any such trade-off is, thus, strictly temporary and, indeed, illusory. Only one rate of unemployment—the natural rate of unemployment—is compatible with a constant rate of inflation. Any attempt by governments to attain a permanently lower or higher rate of unemployment by ordinary fiscal or monetary methods would lead to ever-increasing rates of inflation or deflation. The mechanism through which the Phillips curve becomes unstable is the generation of and adjustment to inflationary expectations. Although the logic of this classical approach cannot be faulted, the empirical evidence on the manner in which expectations are generated and adjusted to

[1] In revising the earlier version of this paper, presented to the NBER Conference, I have had the benefit of detailed comments from Chris Archibald, Bernard Corry and Dan Hamermesh. Moreover, I have attempted to deal with some of the points raised by the official discussants, Charles Holt and Robert Lucas. I am especially indebted to Chris Archibald, who has influenced my thinking on structural unemployment problems over a period of years. The collection of regional unemployment data, some of which were used for this paper, was financed by a grant from the Manpower Administration, U.S. Dept. of Labor (Grant No. 91-15-70-07). The paper was written while I was at the University of Essex, on leave from Northwestern University. I would also like to acknowledge a Ford Foundation Faculty Fellowship, which allowed me to devote all of my time toward research during the academic year 1970–1.

is not strong (see Lucas and Rapping [10], Solow [16], and Brechling [5]).

The neoclassical models mentioned above describe the behaviour of only a single market. There is one wage change which, in the long run, is fully anticipated and fully adjusted. The short-run and long-run behaviour of multimarket models, on the other hand, does not seem to have been studied much in this context. All published studies on multimarket models appear to be based on the assumption of stable individual market Phillips curves. In a seminal article [9], Lipsey showed that dispersions of sectoral unemployment rates may affect the aggregate Phillips curve. The first published empirical investigations of this problem seem to be those of Archibald [1]; more recently, Thomas and Stoney [17] have made an important contribution in this area. Both Archibald and Thomas and Stoney found that the dispersion of regional unemployment rates tends to have a positive influence on the aggregate Phillips curve. Moreover, some estimates of the reduction in wage inflation which might be achieved by reducing the dispersion of unemployment are quite sizeable (see Archibald [2]).

In this paper an attempt will be made to combine the neoclassical and the multisector approaches. The concepts of the short-run and long-run Phillips curves will be developed in a multisector framework and the effects of changes in the distribution of sectoral unemployment rates upon the aggregate short-run and long-run Phillips curves will be examined. In Section II, the conditions which lead to three different types of long-run Phillips curves will be described: (1) in the long run expected wage changes become equal to actual wage changes in each and every sector and no intersectoral relationships in the expectation-generating process are allowed; (2) in the long run expected wage changes in each sector become equal to the *mean* actual wage change; and (3) in the long run there is a general dependence of each sectoral expected wage change on possibly all actual wage changes, but actual wage changes remain constant over time. It will be shown that the long-run Phillips curve and, hence, the 'natural' level of unemployment can be affected by the distribution of sectoral unemployment rates only under (2) and (3). Under (2) the 'non-linear aggregation hypothesis' is obtained according to which the aggregate long-run Phillips curve is shifted by changes in the dispersion of sectoral unemployment rates. Under (3) the 'dynamic market interdependence hypothesis' is obtained according to which the aggregate long-run Phillips curve varies with shifts of sectoral unemployment between sectors with strong and weak expectational leadership.

In Sections III, IV, and V, the results of the empirical examination of the two hypotheses will be reported. The dependent variable is the change in total straight-time hourly earnings in U.S. manufacturing and the unemployment data refer to states. In contrast to some previous findings, the non-linear aggregation hypothesis has received very little empirical support in the present study (Section III). Two distinct versions of the dynamic market interdependence hypothesis have been examined. First, regions with *low unemployment* have been assumed to be the strong expectational leaders, but no empirical support has been found for this assumption (Section IV). Second, a simple model of migration has been developed which predicts that regions with high relative earning levels should exert strong expectational leadership. Some empirical support has been found for this proposition (Section V). It would appear that the Western and South-western states exert a much stronger influence on total wage changes than other regions.

Although the conclusions presented in this paper must be regarded as tentative, they do suggest that there may be a strong intersectoral element in the typical expectation-generating process in labour markets: the expected wage change in sector i being influenced not only by its own past actual wage changes, but also by (past and present) wage changes in sector j. Such intersectoral relations are both plausible and supported by casual empiricism. It would appear, therefore, that they ought to be incorporated into our models of wage and price formation. The present paper reports on an attempt to reformulate the Phillips curve analysis accordingly.

The approach of this paper suffers from the same theoretical short-comings as most previous Phillips curve inquiries. The single-equation specification is the most serious disadvantage. Strictly, it is valid only if all the regional unemployment rates are exogenous, say, that they are controlled without error by government policy. Moreover, the change in consumer prices is also taken to be exogenous. The exact size of the simultaneous equation bias which arises from these mis-specifications can only be determined by building and fitting a more general model. In the present case, such a model would have to explain regional unemployment rates and wage levels as well as all the well-known macrovariables and, hence, its construction would present formidable problems and absorb substantial resources. Hence, a more limited approach has been adopted in order to obtain some approximate results which might be refined later on.

II   Short-run and long-run Phillips curves and the mean 'natural' rate of unemployment

In this section, the relationship between the distribution of sectoral unemployment rates and the short-run and long-run Phillips curves will be discussed from a formal point of view. There are two reasons for this discussion: first, it would appear that several plausible definitions of the long-run and, hence, of the 'natural' rate of unemployment are available in multi-sector models, and, second, since long-run Phillips curves cannot be estimated directly, their characteristics can only be inferred from short-run Phillips curves and this requires a formal framework of their interrelationship.

Throughout the paper the following symbols will be used:

$$w_{it} = 100 \frac{W_{it} - W_{it-1}}{\frac{1}{2}(W_{it} + W_{it-1})} \tag{1}$$

The lower case w_{it} stands for the *percentage* change of wages in sector i. The average percentage wage change (w_t) is the weighted sum of w_{it}:[2]

$$w_t = \sum a_i w_{it} \tag{2}$$

where the a_i are the sectoral weights[3] and $\sum a_i = 1$.

Proportionate excess demands for labour in each sector are defined as:

$$X_{it} = \frac{D_{it} - S_{it}}{S_{it}} \tag{4}$$

which can range between -1 (for large S_{it}) and ∞ (for large D_{it}). Moreover, there exists a generally non-linear monotonic transformation, such that

$$g_i(u_{it}) = X_{it} \tag{5}$$

where u_{it} is the unemployment (percentage) rate in sector i. It will be

[2] Throughout the paper the subscript reference under $\sum$ has been omitted when it is obvious what is being summed.
[3] In the empirical work w_t will be approximated by the percentage change in aggregate wages because, at this time, sectoral wage series on a quarterly basis are not readily available for the period studied (1950–69).

assumed that $g_i'(u_{it}) < 0$ and $g_i''(u_{it}) \geq 0$.[4] Aggregate unemployment is defined as:

$$U_t = \sum a_i u_{it} \qquad (6)$$

The percentage change in average prices is denoted by a lower case p_t:

$$p_t = 100 \frac{P_t - P_{t-1}}{\frac{1}{2}(P_t + P_{t-1})} \qquad (7)$$

Expected wage changes will be denoted by w_{it}^e for sector i and by $w_t^e = \sum a_i w_{it}^e$ for the mean expected wage change and, similarly, p_t^e stands for the expected percentage change in prices.

It will frequently be convenient to use matrix notation. The symbols $\tilde{a}$, $\tilde{w}_t$, $\tilde{X}_t$, $\tilde{u}$ and $\tilde{w}_t^e$ will be used to describe the $n \times 1$ vectors of the a_i, w_{it}, X_{it}, u_{it} and w_{it}^e.

The system of Phillips curves with which we shall be concerned can now be written in matrix notation:

$$\tilde{w}_t = B\tilde{X}_t + k_0 p_t + C(\tilde{w}_t^e - k_0 p_t^e) \qquad (8a)$$

or

$$(\tilde{w}_t - k_0 p_t) - C(\tilde{w}_t^e - k_0 p_t^e) = B\tilde{X}_t \qquad (8b)$$

where B and C are $n \times n$ matrices and k_0 is an $n \times 1$ vector of parameters. Both actual and expected wage changes are measured as deviations from the actual or expected price changes. The reasoning underlying this assumption is that both current and expected wages change with prices owing to cost-of-living allowances and, hence, this part of the wage change should not be attributed to excess demand or other factors in the wage determination process.

The aggregate wage change w_t can be obtained by pre-multiplying (8a) by the row vector of weights $\tilde{a}'$:

$$w_t = \tilde{a}'\tilde{w}_t = \tilde{a}'BX_t + \tilde{a}'k_0 p_t + \tilde{a}'C(\tilde{w}_t^e - k_0 p_t^e) \qquad (9)$$

Equations (8) and (9) describe a system of short-run Phillips curves. They are similar to the single equation used by Phelps [13], for instance, but they allow for the possibility of intersectoral relationships.

---

[4] The discussion in the papers by Corry and Laidler [6], Vanderkamp [18] and Holmes and Smyth [8] has shown that this transformation need not be constant through time. Moreover, there are plausible arguments which lead to different signs of the derivatives.

In order to keep the exposition simple, let us assume that both B and C are diagonal. This means that the wage determination process in sector i depends only on its own excess demand (X_{it}) and its own expected wage change (w_{it}^e). While there is little (or no) theory on this subject, such an assumption does not seem to be too implausible. The intersectoral relationships which have thus been removed will be reintroduced below through an intersectoral expectation generating process.

Let us now turn to a discussion of the 'long-run' Phillips curves which correspond to the system of short-run curves in equations (8) and (9). In the single equation approach of, say, Phelps [13] or Brechling [5], two conditions characterise the long run: first, employers and employees have adapted their expected wage changes to equal the actual wage changes and, second, in the wage-fixing process, actual wage changes are adjusted fully to expected wage changes. When price changes are also included, then a third condition requires that expected price changes equal actual price changes. For instance, let the single short-run Phillips curve be $w_{kt} = b_k X_{kt} + k_0 p_t + c_k(w_{kt}^e - k_0 p_t^e)$. The three conditions for the long run are: (i) $w_{kt}^e = w_{kt}$, (ii) $c_k = 1$, and, (iii) $p_t^e = p_t$. As a consequence the long-run Phillips curve becomes $0 = b_k X_{kt}^*$, and the unemployment rate corresponding to $X_{kt}^* = 0$ (since $b_k > 0$), namely u_{kt}^*, is the 'natural' unemployment rate. At this level of unemployment wage changes are not determined, but they are constant. In other words, the second derivative of wages with respect to time is zero. If $u_{kt} < u_{kt}^*$ then actual wage changes will always exceed expected wage changes and, hence, w_{kt} will keep rising. Similarly if $u_{kt} > u_{kt}^*$, w_{kt} will keep falling. The adjustment of w_{kt}^e to w_{kt} and of w_{kt} to w_{kt}^e is the cause of the instability.

It would appear that in a multisector framework stable long-run Phillips curves may exist in at least three different sets of conditions that describe different adjustments of expected to actual wage changes. First, a long-run set of Phillips curves may be said to exist if (i) expected wage changes equal actual wage changes in each and every sector, that is, $\tilde{w}_t^e = \tilde{w}_t$, (ii) actual wage changes are fully adjusted to expected wage changes, so that, $C - I$ and, (iii) expected price changes equal actual price changes, so that, $p_t^e = p_t$. This definition of the long run is a simple extension of the single-equation definition discussed in the previous paragraph and it does not allow for any inter-sectoral relationships. If the conditions are satisfied, equation (8) collapses to:

$$0 = B\tilde{X}_t^* \qquad (10)$$

Since B is not a null matrix, equation (10) implies that excess demand must be zero in each and every sector. Let $\tilde{u}_t^*$ correspond to $\tilde{X}_t^* = 0$, then the mean 'natural' rate of unemployment is $U_t^* = \tilde{a}'\tilde{u}_t^*$. Moreover, if $g_i(u_t) = g_j(u_t)$ for all i and j, then equation (10) implies identical 'natural' unemployment rates for all sectors and $U_t^* = u_t^*$. Since this definition of the long-run Phillips curves implies a unique set of sectoral 'natural' unemployment rates, there can be no separate influence of the distribution of unemployment upon the mean 'natural' rate of unemployment. The reason for this result is that all sectoral interdependences have been assumed away: there are n separate markets each of which must be in long-run equilibrium. While this definition may correspond to the classical long run, it is based on some restrictive assumptions which may not be appropriate in most present-day Western societies. We know, for instance, that over considerable periods of time sectoral unemployment dispersions are substantial and that the relative ranking of sectors within these dispersions remain remarkably constant.[5] Hence, if the $g_i(u_t)$ are similar for all i, the evidence that the system converges to a state in which all $X_{it} = 0$ is very weak indeed.

The second definition of the long run is based on a slightly different assumption about the formation of expected wage changes. It is now assumed that the expected wage change in sector i is adjusted to and finally set equal to the mean of actual wage changes, so that, in the long run $w_{it}^e = w_t$ for all i. If actual wage changes are again fully adjusted to expected wage changes, so that $C = I$ and $p_t^e = p_t$, then equation (9) reduces to:

$$0 = \tilde{a}'B\tilde{X}_t^* = \sum a_i b_{ii} X_{it}^* \qquad (11)$$

According to equation (11), the second definition of the long-run implies that the weighted mean of the X_{it} be equal to zero. This condition can, of course, be satisfied by a large number of vectors of $\tilde{X}_t^*$, and, hence, corresponding vectors $\tilde{u}_t^*$. Consequently, there will also be a large number of possible mean 'natural' unemployment

[5] For regional unemployment in Britain, see the evidence given by Brechling [4]. In the U.S. the evidence is very similar.

rates U_t^*. It is now meaningful to ask which vector $\tilde{X}_t^*$ or $\tilde{u}^*$ leads to the minimum mean 'natural' rate? Formally, the problem can be stated:

Minimise

$$U_t^* = \tilde{a}'\tilde{u}_t^*$$

subject to

$$0 = \tilde{a}'B\tilde{X}_t$$

and

$$X_{it} = g_i(u_{it}) \quad i = 1, \ldots, n$$

The ith and jth terms in the corresponding Lagrange function are: $L = \cdots a_i u_{it}^* + a_j u_{jt}^* \cdots + \lambda(\ldots a_i b_{ii} g_i(u_{it}^*) + a_j b_{jj} g_j(u_{jt}^*)\ldots)$. After differentiation with respect to u_{it}^* and u_{jt}^*, setting the results equal to zero, and eliminating λ the necessary first-order condition for a minimum is obtained as $b_{ii} g_i'(u_{it}^*) = b_{jj} g_j'(u_{jt}^*)$. Moreover, if $b_{ii} = b_{jj}$ and $g_i(u_t) = g_j(u_t)$, then $u_{it}^* = u_{jt}^*$ and, hence, $X_{it}^* = X_{jt}^*$ for all i and j and, in that case, equation (11) implies that all excess demands must be zero.[6] An essential element of this argument is that the $g_i(u_{it})$ functions are non-linear. If the $g_i(u_{it})$ functions are all linear, then the solution either lies at a corner (if $b_{ii} \neq b_{jj}$ or $g_i' \neq g_j'$) or there is no unique minimum (if $b_{ii} = b_{jj}$ and $g_i' = g_j'$).[7] Hence this case is very similar to the familiar aggregation of identical convex individual market Phillips curves of Archibald [1] and Lipsey [9], which leads to the conclusion that the minimum pressure on wages is achieved when there is zero dispersion in unemployment rates. The above analysis has led to an analogous conclusion: with identical Phillips curves (that is, $b_{ii} = b_{jj}$ and $g_i(u_t) = g_j(u_t)$ for all i and j), the minimum mean 'natural' rate of unemployment is achieved when there is zero dispersion in sectoral unemployment rates and then the corresponding excess demands are all zero ($\tilde{X}_t^* = 0$). Since the non-linearity of the $g_i(u_{it})$ functions is crucial to this case, it will be referred to as the non-linear aggregation hypothesis. In Section III of

___

[6] The second-order conditions for a minimum are satisfied if $g_i''(u_{it}) > 0$ for all i.

[7] As Archibald has pointed out [1] and as will be argued below, changes in the distribution of unemployment rates may affect the aggregate Phillips curve, even if the individual Phillips curves are linear. Convexity, however, is necessary for a unique interior solution.

this paper the non-linear aggregation hypothesis will be subjected to empirical tests.

Let us now turn to a third definition of the long run and the mean 'natural' rate of unemployment. It is postulated that, in the long run, expected wages changes adjust to and become equal to a linear function of some or all actual wage changes: namely $\tilde{w}_t^e = H\tilde{w}_t$ where H is an $n \times n$ matrix which in general need not be diagonal.

As before, $C = I$ and $p_t^e = p_t$, so that equation (8) becomes:

$$\tilde{w}_t = DB\tilde{X}_t \qquad (12)$$

and the mean wage change is

$$w_t = \tilde{a}'\tilde{w}_t = \tilde{a}'DB\tilde{X}_t \qquad (13)$$

where $D = (I - CH)^{-1}$. Because of the general expectational sectoral interdependence, there is no reason why D should be diagonal. Hence, w_{it} may be affected by X_{jt} independently of X_{it}, because w_{it}^e is influenced by w_{jt}. Even if there is zero excess demand in sector i, wages in i may rise because wages in j are rising. This expectational interaction will be referred to as dynamic market interdependence.

Because of the complex expectational interdependence, equations (12) and (13) no longer imply a unique set of 'natural' unemployment rates which are compatible with any constant $\tilde{w}_t$. In other words, according to this third definition of the long run a trade-off between unemployment and (constant) wage changes is possible. But this does not mean that the question of the influence of the dispersion of sectoral unemployment rates on the position of the trade-off curve has become irrelevant. It can be rephrased as follows: for a given mean wage change, which dispersion of sectoral unemployment rates would lead to a minimum mean unemployment rate? Or:

Minimise

$$U_t = \tilde{a}'\tilde{u}_t$$

subject to

$$w_t = \tilde{a}'DB\tilde{X}_t$$

and

$$g_i(u_{it}) = X_{it} \quad i = 1, \ldots, n$$

The kth and jth terms of the corresponding Lagrange function are:

$$L = \cdots a_k u_{kt} + a_j u_{jt} \cdots$$

$$+ \lambda(w_t \cdots - b_{kk} g_k(u_{kt}) \sum_i a_i d_{ik} - b_{jj} g_j(u_{jt}) \sum_i a_i d_{ij} \cdots)$$

After differentiation with respect to u_{kt} and u_{jt}, equating to zero and eliminating λ, the first-order conditions turn out to be

$$a_j g_k'(u_{kt}) b_{kk} \sum_i a_i d_{ik} = a_k g_j'(u_{jt}) b_{jj} \sum_i a_i d_{ij} \quad j,k,i = 1, \ldots, n \quad (14)$$

If D were the identity matrix, then $\sum_i a_i d_{ik} = 1$ for all k and hence this condition would be the same as for the non-linear aggregation hypothesis. The expressions $\sum_i a_i d_{ik}$ measure the own and cross effects of the u_{kt} which arise because of the expectational dynamic market interdependence. Even if $b_{kk} = b_{jj}$ and $g_k(u_t) = g_j(u_t)$, the optimum dispersion of sectoral unemployment rates is likely to be non-zero because the sectors with relatively strong own and cross effects should have relatively high unemployment rates, for mean unemployment to be at a constrained minimum.

It should perhaps be pointed out that the dispersion of sectoral unemployment rates may have an influence on the constrained mean unemployment even if the $g(u)$ functions are linear and identical, so that their derivatives disappear from equation (14). In that case, however, the optimum solution is likely to be at a corner. Let us illustrate this case by means of a two-sector example. In Figure 1, let u_1 be measured along the vertical and u_2 along the horizontal axes. There are minimum levels of unemployment, below which u_1 and u_2 cannot fall. The straight line $u_1 = (1/a_1) U - (a_2/a_1)u_2$ is an iso-U curve which represents the objective function. The constraint—that is, the combinations of u_1 and u_2 which yield a mean wage change of $\bar{w}$— is derived from $\bar{w} = (a_1 d_{11} + a_2 d_{21}) b_{11} g(u_1) + (a_1 d_{12} + a_2 d_{22}) b_{22} g(u_2)$. Let $g(u) = \alpha + \beta u$ for both sectors and $b_{11} = b_{22}$, then the linear constraint can be written as $u_1 = \gamma_0 - \gamma_1 u_2$ where (to make economic sense) γ_0 must be a positive constant and $\gamma_1 = (a_1 d_{12} + a_2 d_{22})/ (a_1 d_{11} + a_2 d_{21})$. Thus, γ_1 is the ratio of the weighted own and cross effects of the two unemployment rates which stem from the expectational dynamic interdependence. It is clear from Figure 1, that there may be three solutions: (i) If sector 1 has relatively large own and cross effects, so that $\gamma_1 < a_2/a_1$ then the solution lies at u_{2min} and u_{12}. (ii) If $\gamma_1 = a_2/a_1$, so that the slopes of the constraint and objective

Figure 1   Two-sector example

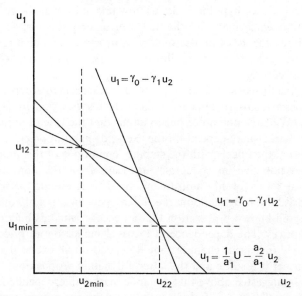

function coincide, there is no unique solution. (iii) If sector 2 has relatively large own and cross effects, so that $\gamma_1 > a_2/a_1$, then the solution lies at $u_{1\min}$ and u_{22}. This analysis can be extended to n sectors. In $n-1$ sectors the u_i will lie at $u_{i\min}$, while u_1 is determined by the constraint. Sector 1 will be the one for which

$$\frac{\sum_{i=1}^{n} a_i d_{i1}}{\sum_{i=1}^{n} a_i d_{ik}} > \frac{a_1}{a_k} \quad k = 2, \ldots, n$$

These results are quite plausible; in order to achieve the constrained minimum of the mean unemployment rate, the sector with the strongest own and cross effects (arising from the expectational dynamic market interdependence) should have a relative high unemployment rate while all other sectors are at their minimum rates of unemployment. This implication of dynamic market interdependence is thus different from that of the simple non-linear aggregation hypothesis (with $b_{ii} = b_{jj}$ and $g_i(u_t) = g_j(u_t)$ for all i and j), because the latter implies that all sectoral unemployment rates should be equalised. However, as is shown by equation (14) the two hypotheses are not mutually exclusive.

Having dealt with some of the mechanics of the dynamic market interdependence hypothesis, let us now take a look at the economic reasoning which may underlie it. Unfortunately there is, as yet, no established theory of non-tâtonnement processes to which reference could be made. Hence the following remarks must be tentative and suggestive.

The first formal statement of the 'dynamic market interdependence' hypothesis seems to appear in Samuelson's *Foundations* [15]. He states, 'We have no choice but to admit that the rate of adjustment in one market may depend on the excess demand in *other* markets.' Samuelson then deals with the stability conditions of this model but he does not give an economic justification for the non-zero off-diagonal terms of his adjustment matrix.[8] It should perhaps be emphasised that dynamic market interdependence is not equivalent to the well-known proposition that all excess demands may depend on all prices. The dependence of excess demands on all prices does not imply that price changes should depend on all excess demands. The former is a static and the latter a dynamic proposition.

It was suggested above that dynamic market interdependence may arise from the cross effects in a multisector expectation generating process, which means that w_{it}^e is influenced not only by actual past values of w_i but also by current and past values of w_j. This type of economic justification is particularly plausible in labour markets. Conventional textbooks on labour economics repeatedly refer to such intersectoral relationships (see, for instance, Ross [14]). Indeed, if wage contracts typically last three years, for example, then the own past wage changes may be quite unimportant compared with recent wage changes in other sectors as a determinant of the expected wage change.

Dynamic market interdependence may be an important contributing factor in maintaining conventional wage differentials. If sector i manages to raise its w_{it} relative to w_{jt}, and, thereby, to widen the proportionate difference between W_{it} and W_{jt} employees in j are quick to press for a rise in w_{jt} even if there is ample excess supply in j. In other words, dynamic market interdependence tends to contribute to sluggishness in the adjustment of w_j to X_j. In Sections 4 and 5 the dynamic market interdependence will be examined empirically: First, regions with low unemployment will be assumed to be strong

---

[8] For other examples of this kind of adjustment matrix, see Negishi [12].

expectational leaders and second, a simple migration model will be developed which predicts that regions with high relative earnings should be the expectational leaders.

Unfortunately, the economic justification for dynamic market interdependence given in the past few paragraphs is somewhat vague. But such vagueness is common to most expectational hypotheses. The basic assertion made here is that intersectoral transmissions of expectations may be an important aspect in the whole expectations generating process and, consequently, our models ought to allow for them.

In this section of the paper an attempt has been made to analyse the influence of different distributions of sectoral unemployment rates upon the long-run Phillips curve. Three definitions of the long run have been examined: The first implies a unique sectoral distribution of unemployment rates (such that $X_{it}^* = 0$ for all i) and hence, the distribution cannot be changed. According to the second definition of the long run (which is based on the assumption that $w_{it}^e = w_t$ for all i) does allow for different sectoral distributions, and, with identical non-linear sectoral Phillips curves ($g_i(u_t) = g_j(u_t)$ and $b_{ii} = b_{jj}$ for all i and j) identical sectoral unemployment rates lead to the lowest long-run Phillips curve and, hence, the lowest mean 'natural' level of unemployment. This case is referred to as the non-linear aggregation hypothesis. According to the third definition of the long run, expected wage changes (w_i^e) adjust to present and past actual wage changes in its own (w_i) as well as other sectors (w_j), and, in the long run, all w_i remain constant through time. This is referred to as the dynamic market interdependence hypothesis, and it leads to the conclusion that the lowest long-run Phillips curve is obtained by raising (lowering) unemployment rates in sectors which exert relatively strong (weak) expectational leadership (through their own and cross effects). In the next few sections these two hypotheses will be subjected to further analysis.

III   The non-linear aggregation hypothesis

The fact that identical convex individual market Phillips curves lead to an aggregate curve that is positively related to the dispersion of the sectoral unemployment rates has been recognised for a long time. It was the basis of Lipsey's loops around the Phillips curve [9] and more recently Archibald [1] and Thomas and Stoney [17] have analysed this case.

In his most recent work on this subject [2], Archibald postulates a specific non-linear form for $g(u_{it})$, namely, a log-linear form:

$$X_{it} + 1 = \eta^{-1} \ln u_{it} \quad i = 1, \ldots, n \tag{15}$$

His adjustment matrix—that is, the matrix B in equations (8) and (9)—is Ib and consequently the Archibald analogue to equation (9) would be:

$$w_t = \tilde{a}'\tilde{w}_t = b\eta^{-1} \sum a_i \ln u_{it} - b + k_0 p_t + \tilde{a}'C(\tilde{w}_t^e - k_0 p_t^e) \tag{16}$$

Archibald refers to $V_t = \sum a_i \ln u_{it}$ as the addi-log term and to his approach as the addi-log model.

In the first part of their paper, Thomas and Stoney approximate the identical non-linear individual market Phillips curves $bg(u_{it})$ by a truncated Taylor series. In the present context, such an approximation might be written as:

$$w_{it} = bg(U_t) + bg'(U_t)(u_{it} - U_t) + \tfrac{1}{2}bg''(U_t)(u_{it} - U_t)^2$$
$$+ k_0 p_t + c_{ii}(w_{it}^e - k_0 p_t^e) \tag{17}$$

Summation of this curve over sectors leads to an aggregate Phillips curve:

$$w_t = bg(U_t) + \tfrac{1}{2}bg''(U_t) \operatorname{Var}(U) + k_0 p_t + \tilde{a}'C(\tilde{w}_t^e - k_0 p_t^e) \tag{18}$$

where $\operatorname{Var}(U)$ stands for the variance of sectoral unemployment rates. The operational advantage of the Thomas-Stoney formulation is that various non-linear forms for $g(U_t)$ can be tried without too much computational effort.

In this section, the non-linear aggregation hypothesis will be examined empirically, with U.S. regional data. The aim is to discover the degree of non-linearity of the individual market Phillips curves, because—as was pointed out in Section II—the distribution of sectoral unemployment has no effect on the aggregate long-run Phillips curve if all sectoral Phillips curves are linear and identical. Hence, the determination of the degree of non-linearity is of crucial importance.

The dependent variable is the proportionate change in straight-time hourly earnings in all U.S. manufacturing industries. Although this variable is far from perfect, it seems much preferable to earnings figures with broader coverage.[9] The consumer price index was used for the computation of p_t. Equations (1) and (2) were not used for the computation of w_t, because the w_{it} are not readily available. Instead w_t is defined as $100 \left(\sum a_i W_{it} - \sum a_i W_{it-1} \right)/\frac{1}{2} \left(\sum a_i W_{it} + \sum a_i W_{it-1} \right)$. But p_t was computed according to equation (7). The sectors are thirty-six U.S. states, and the weights (a_i) are based on the labour force.[10] The data are quarterly for the period 1950:I to 1969:II. Seasonal fluctuations were removed by linear shift dummies.

The short-run Phillips curve of equation (9) cannot be estimated directly because data on $\tilde{w}_i^e$ do not exist. Thus, an expectation-generating function has to be postulated. The use of adaptive expectations appears to have become quite conventional in recent years, and, hence, it has been adopted for present purposes:

$$w_t^e - w_{t-1}^e = \eta(w_{t-1} - w_{t-1}^e) \qquad (19)$$

After taking first differences of equation (9), assuming $C = I\delta$ (where δ is a scalar parameter) and substituting out w_t^e we obtain the following second-order difference equations:

$$w_t = b \sum_i a_i[g(u_{it}) - g(u_{it-1})] + k(p_t - p_{t-1})$$
$$+ \eta b \sum_i a_i g(u_{it-1}) + \eta k p_{t-1} + (1 + \eta\delta - \eta)w_{t-1} \qquad (20)$$

where b stands for the (identical) diagonal terms of the matrix B. Moreover, p_t^e was assumed to be related linearly to p_t and, hence, the effects of both p^e and p_t are picked up by k. Equation (20) has been used in an attempt to discover the nature of the non-linearities in the $g(u_{it})$ functions. Four different cases have been examined: (i) For purposes of comparison $g(u_{it})$ has been assumed to be linear. (ii) Archibald's log-transformation was used. (iii) A fairly general non-linear form of the type $bg(u_{it}) = \alpha + \beta u_{it}^{\gamma}$ was assumed and an attempt was made to estimate α, β and γ by means of the Taylor series expansion described in equation (18). (iv) Finally the same non-linear form as under (iii) was assumed and the variable $R_t = \sum a_i u_{it}^{\gamma}$ was computed for a wide range of values of γ and then R_t was

---

[9] Earnings data which include overtime earnings tend to produce marked loops, or rate of change effects. The latter virtually disappear when straight-time earnings are used.

[10] For the other states unemployment rates are not available for the entire sample period. Unemployment by states were collected from *Employment and Earnings*.

used in (20) to find the γ for which the residual variance was at a minimum. Let us discuss these four sets of assumptions in detail:

(i) In the linear case, in which $bg(u_{it}) = \alpha + \beta u_{it}$, equation (20) reduces to

$$w_t = \eta\alpha + \beta(U_t - U_{t-1}) + k(p_t - p_{t-1}) + \eta\beta U_{t-1}$$
$$+ \eta k p_{t-1} + (1 + \eta\delta - \eta)w_{t-1} \tag{21}$$

This equation was fitted to the data and the parameter estimates turned out as follows (asymptotic standard errors are given in brackets):

$$\alpha_1 = 1.46779 \qquad \eta_1 = 1.25893$$
$$(0.45630) \qquad\quad (0.31367)$$

$$\beta_1 = -0.13416 \quad \delta_1 = 0.29818$$
$$(0.05797) \qquad\quad (0.18965)$$

$$k_1 = 0.28045 \qquad R^2 = 0.6576$$
$$(0.10564)$$

In this and all the following equations the Durbin-Watson statistics turned out to be very close to 2 and, hence, they are not reported. The coefficients of the seasonal dummies, most of which turned out to be quite significant are not reported either. This means that the α refers only to one quarter (usually the first one).[11]

The estimates of the above coefficients seem to be roughly in line with earlier findings. The value of β_1 implies that, on the average, if unemployment rises by one percentage point, the quarterly rate of increase in straight-time hourly earnings declines by 0.13 percentage points. This is a rather flat Phillips curve. The estimates of k_1, η_1 and δ_1 are similar to previous findings. Thus, Solow [16] also observed that η_1 tended to be close to unity and δ_1 relatively small. Within the theoretical structure postulated above, this means that expectations are formed very fast but that adjustment to them—as measured by δ_1—is not very strong.

---

[11] Since η is overidentified in equation (21), a non-linear estimating technique was used. The particular programme that was used is based on the Gauss–Newton iterative procedure.

(ii) Next Archibald's addi-log formulation was tried. After equation (16) has been adjusted for the expectation-generating mechanism of equation (19), it becomes identical to equation (21) except that the mean unemployment U_t is replaced by the addi-log term $V_t = \sum a_i \ln u_{it}$. This equation was fitted to the data and the following parameter estimates were obtained:

$$\alpha_2 = -0.41141 \qquad \eta_2 = 1.26238$$
$$(0.49684) \qquad\qquad (0.32143)$$

$$\beta_2 = -0.41024 \qquad \delta_1 = 0.29467$$
$$(0.17692) \qquad\qquad (0.19489)$$

$$k_2 = 0.26526 \qquad R^2 = 0.6596$$
$$(0.10441)$$

The parameter values are again quite plausible. The overall exactness of fit—as measured by the R^2 or the residual variance—however, is virtually the same as in the linear case. Hence, there is no strong reason for preferring the addi-log formulation over the linear one.

(iii) Since Archibald's log-transformation is a non-linearity of a special kind, an attempt was made to use another non-linear form, namely: $bg(u_{it}) = \alpha + \beta u_{it}^\gamma$. By means of the Taylor series expansion described in equations (17) and (18), and by taking the expansion to another term, so as to include the third moment of the distribution of unemployment and after substituting out w_t^e, the following estimating equation is obtained:

$$w_t = \left[1 + \gamma(\gamma - 1) \frac{M_{2t}}{2U_t^2} + \gamma(\gamma - 1)(\gamma - 2) \frac{M_{3t}}{6U_t^3} \right] \beta U_t^\gamma$$

$$- [1 - \eta] \left[1 + \gamma(\gamma - 1) \frac{M_{2t-1}}{2U_{t-1}^2} \right.$$

$$\left. + \gamma(\gamma - 1)(\gamma - 2) \frac{M_{3t-1}}{6U_{t-1}^3} \right] \beta U_{t-1}^\gamma \qquad (22)$$

$$+ k(p_t - p_{t-1}) + \eta k p_{t-1} + (1 + \delta\eta - \eta)w_{t-1} + \eta\alpha$$

M_2 and M_3 stand for the second and third moments of unemployment about their mean. The set of parameters which minimises the residual variance of this equation is as follows (as before, asymptotic standard errors are given in parentheses):

$$\alpha_3 = 2.0531 \qquad k_3 = 0.2708$$
$$(4.0592) \qquad (0.1065)$$

$$\beta_3 = -0.6474 \qquad \eta_3 = 1.2665$$
$$(3.7365) \qquad (0.3269)$$

$$\gamma_3 = 0.4093 \qquad \delta_3 = 0.3002$$
$$(1.6289) \qquad (0.1954)$$

$$R^2 = 0.6581$$

As under (ii) the explained variance is only minutely larger than in the linear case. Moreover, the standard errors of α_3, β_3 and γ_3 are large, which indicates that the residual variance does not change much with changes in these parameters. Various different versions of equation (22) were tried. Thus, M_3 was omitted, η was assumed to be unity, and δ was assumed to be zero. None of these changes in specification changed the basic result, namely that the residual variance turned out to be only minutely lower, or even higher, than in the linear case.

(iv) In the further search for empirical support of the non-linear aggregation hypothesis, the $bg(u_{it})$ were again assumed to be equal to $\alpha + \beta u_{it}^\gamma$ but now γ was obtained by an iterative procedure. The $bg(u_{it})$ functions can be aggregated directly, namely $\sum a_i bg(u_{it}) = \alpha + \beta \sum a_i u_{it}^\gamma$. Thus values of $R_t = \sum a_i u_{it}^\gamma$ were computed for a range of values of γ and then R_t and R_{t-1} were used in place of U_t and U_{t-1} in equation (21). Table 1 contains the estimated values of α_4, β_4, k_4, η_4, δ_4, for each of the assumed values of γ. The residual variance reaches a minimum when $\gamma = -1.9$. It is clear from the last row, however, that the overall goodness of fit is quite insensitive to the value of γ. The highest R^2 is 0.6677 as compared with 0.6576 for the linear model. Thus the last attempt at introducing non-linearities seems to have been marginally more successful than the first two. But it cannot be claimed that non-linear aggregation yields strikingly better results than linear aggregation.

This concludes the discussion of the non-linear aggregation hypothesis. It would appear that for the present sample, neither the addi-log formulation, the Taylor series approximation, nor the search

Table 1 Estimates of α_4, β_4, k_4, η_4 and δ_4 for various assumed values of γ

γ	Assumed γ											
	-2.9	-2.5	-2.3	-2.1	-1.9	-1.7	-1.5	-1.3	-0.9	-0.5	0.5	0.9
α_4	0.9683	0.9751	0.9696	0.9549	0.9298	0.8948	0.8509	0.7976	0.6414	0.2687	1.8929	1.5167
	(0.2529)	(0.2626)	(0.2689)	(0.2748)	(0.2789)	(0.2803)	(0.2786)	(0.2743)	(0.2615)	(0.2875)	(0.6235)	(0.4752)
β_4	0.2082	0.3741	0.4715	0.5668	0.6508	0.7196	0.7753	0.8247	0.9486	1.2753	−0.4871	−0.1689
	(0.0856)	(0.1429)	(0.1774)	(0.2133)	(0.2480)	(0.2798)	(0.3083)	(0.3349)	(0.3980)	(0.5450)	(0.2104)	(0.0730)
k_4	0.3121	0.2965	0.2873	0.2783	0.2703	0.2604	0.2596	0.2570	0.2561	0.2589	0.2728	0.2789
	(0.1021)	(0.1006)	(0.1003)	(0.1002)	(0.1004)	(0.1008)	(0.1012)	(0.1018)	(0.1028)	(0.1036)	(0.1051)	(0.1055)
η_4	1.2214	1.2168	1.2156	1.2166	1.2210	1.2284	1.2373	1.2459	1.2581	1.2627	1.2604	1.2592
	(0.2506)	(0.2558)	(0.2618)	(0.2701)	(0.2800)	(0.2904)	(0.3002)	(0.3085)	(0.3191)	(0.3227)	(0.3176)	(0.3144)
δ_4	0.2840	0.2669	0.2612	0.2590	0.2609	0.2661	0.2729	0.2796	0.2894	0.2936	0.2955	0.2975
	(0.1648)	(0.1698)	(0.1738)	(0.1783)	(0.1828)	(0.1867)	(0.1898)	(0.1921)	(0.1947)	(0.1955)	(0.1927)	(0.1903)
R^2	0.6577	0.6641	0.6663	0.6675	0.6677	0.6671	0.6660	0.6647	0.6625	0.6609	0.6586	0.6578

All values at intervals of 0·2 between −2·9 and 1·5 were tried, but only some of the results are given above. For the unreported cases, the R^2 moves smoothly. No local maxima were found. Standard errors are given in brackets.

technique of Table 1 yield substantially better results than the linear formulation of equation (21). Let us, therefore, turn to an examination of the dynamic market interdependence hypothesis.

IV   Relative unemployment as a determinant of dynamic market interdependence

In this and the following section the dynamic market interdependence hypothesis will be examined. For this purpose, equation (13) or some version of it will be used. It is based on the assumption that expectations are generated quite fast through some multisector process of the type described in Section II. The estimated values of η presented in the previous section tend to support this assumption of fairly fast adjustments in expectations.

Since it is not possible to estimate the elements of the matrix DB directly, certain further assumptions must be made about the nature of the dynamic market interdependence.[12] It is especially appealing to triangularise the matrix DB by some ordering of the sectors, or alternatively to partition DB in accordance with some theoretical criterion.

In the latter part of their paper Thomas and Stoney [17] suggest that some transfer mechanism, similar to the dynamic market interdependence, should operate only from low-unemployment to high-unemployment sectors. The 'leading' sectors are supposed to be the low-unemployment sectors which dominate the wage rate change in the entire system. But there is no transfer from high-unemployment to low-unemployment sectors. This means that if DB were rearranged so that the equations are ranked in ascending order of unemployment, DB would become triangular. One might then devise a weighting scheme by which the low-unemployment sectors are given a much stronger weight than the high-unemployment sectors in an aggregate measure of unemployment. Alternatively one might sub-divide the total number of sectors into one leading group and one following group and see whether leaders and followers have an essentially different influence on aggregate wage changes.

Both triangularisation and partitioning of DB were tried after the

---

[12] Even if the entire vector of wage rate changes $\bar{w}_t$ were readily available, the estimation of the elements of DB would require 36 regression equations with 37 exogenous variables each and 78 observations each. This procedure does not promise too much success.

equations were ranked in ascending order of unemployment.[13] The results were only marginally better than the result of the linear formulation of equation (21), and, hence, they are not reported here. Nor is it really surprising that this procedure should not have worked too well. Although the non-linear aggregation hypothesis is, in general, quite different from the dynamic market interdependence hypothesis, the actual computational procedure is similar when it is assumed that the interdependence operates from low-unemployment to high-unemployment sectors. In both cases, low-unemployment sectors are given a larger weight than high-unemployment sectors; and, since the non-linear aggregation hypothesis has not worked well, this version of the dynamic market interdependence cannot be expected to work well either.

There is another reason for rejecting this particular version of the dynamic market interdependence hypothesis. The states with the lowest unemployment rates between 1950–69 were Colorado, Nebraska, Iowa, South Dakota, Kansas, Wyoming, Wisconsin and Indiana. Although their combined, very low unemployment rate tends to explain total wage changes slightly better than total unemployment, it seems most implausible that these states should set the pace of wage changes for the country as a whole. It was, therefore, decided to abandon the ranking by unemployment and to adopt an approach which is based explicitly on a theory of migration. This will be described in the next section.

V Regional migration and dynamic market interdependence

In this section of the paper an attempt will be made to explain the dynamic market interdependence in terms of regional mobility of labour. The approach is deliberately somewhat non-formal and predominantly suggestive because the development of a complete model of regional migration would be beyond the scope of this paper.

Let us adopt a fairly conventional approach to regional migration. The potential migrant is assumed to have some knowledge of interregional differences in wages (adjusted for cost-of-living differences), in the probabilities of obtaining a job and in non-pecuniary rewards (i.e., attractive environment, weather conditions, etc.). Moreover, he

---

[13] The relative ranking of the state unemployment rates remained remarkably constant over the 20 years of our sample period. Hence, it did not make much difference whether the states were ranked in each quarter or according to some average relative position.

is assumed to have a time horizon and to compute the expected present value of his income stream (inclusive of non-pecuniary rewards) for each region. Let us denote these expected present values by W_i^*. Let W_s^* stand for the expected present value in the region in which he currently resides. The costs of migration are equal to Z_{si}. The potential migrant is assumed to maximise his own expected present income and, hence, he will search among the regions and focus on the one for which the difference $(W_i^* - Z_{si} - W_s^*)$ is largest. Let us subscript that region 1. Clearly, if $(W_1^* - Z_{s1}) > W_s^*$, he will migrate and if $(W_1^* - Z_{s1}) < W_s^*$ he will stay in his present region. The $(W_i^* - Z_{si})$ in all the other regions (i.e. $i \neq 1$, $i \neq s$) are irrelevant to his current migration decision. Moreover, if he already resides in the region 1 he will not even contemplate migration.

Let us now consider the behaviour of the employed in region s. It is assumed that wages are determined in a bilateral bargaining process between employers and employees. Employers have a maximum wage, which is determined by their demand conditions and other prices. They would be bankrupted by a wage settlement above this maximum. Similarly, the employees have a minimum wage below which they will not settle. In the migration approach described above, this minimum employees' wage will be related to $(W_1^* - Z_{s1})$, that is, the net expected present value of income in region 1. In other words, the minimum wage must yield a W_s^* which is, at least equal to $(W_1^* - Z_{s1})$. Let us assume that, in general, employees manage to obtain a better bargain, so that the actual settlement implies $W_s^* > (W_1^* - Z_{s1})$. Now consider a *ceteris paribus* increase in wages in region 1 leading to a rise in W_1^* and, hence, raising the employee's minimum wage in region s. Unless the employees' bargaining power is reduced sufficiently, this will lead to a rise in wages in s. Thus the essence of this version of dynamic interdependence of markets can be summed up as follows: region 1 with high $(W_1^* - Z_{s1})$ determines the minimum acceptable wage in region s and the reason for the interdependence is the threatened or realised migration from region s to region 1.

The question which now arises is: What role does the level of unemployment in region s play in this process? Clearly, employers need not pay the higher wages to their present employees if there is ample local excess supply of labour. To analyse the impact of unemployment, let us adopt Charles C. Holt's approach to the Phillips curve [7]. In Figure 2, let the duration of unemployment be measured

Figure 2   Dynamic interdependence of markets

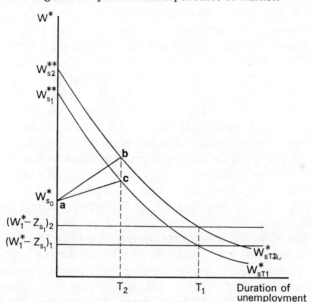

along the horizontal axis and the various expected present values of income along the vertical axis. Let W_{s0}^* correspond to the wage the unemployed person earned in his last job and W_s^{**} to his aspiration wage at the beginning of his job search. The duration of unemployment is proportional to the unemployment rate and is determined by local demand and supply conditions. Suppose the net expected present value of earnings in region 1 were $(W_1^* - Z_{s1})_1$. Then this would impose a limit on the possible level of unemployment in region s represented by T_1. The curves W_{sT1}^* and W_{sT2}^* illustrate how the average worker's acceptance wage declines with the period of his unemployment. If demand and supply conditions generate an unemployment level corresponding to T_2, then the employee will have obtained an increase in wages corresponding to c and the slope of $(a$–$c)$ measures the rate of increase in the expected present value of earnings. Now if expected wages in region 1 increase, one would expect that the entire acceptance wage schedule would move from W_{sT1}^* to W_{sT2}^*, thereby increasing the rate of change in wages. Charles Holt made a very similar assumption when he postulated that the individuals' wage aspiration levels are shifted by general wage

.increases. In the above formulation, wage aspiration levels are shifted not by general wage increases but by wage increases in the region which is most attractive to a potential migrant.

It is clear that the above description of dynamic market interdependence ceases to operate when the employee in question already resides in the region with the highest expected present value of income. Thus if he expects W_1^* and $W_1^* > W_i^*$ for all $i \neq 1$, changes in W_i^* do not effect his bargaining position or acceptance wage because migration would be inefficient in his situation. In other words, this type of dynamic market interdependence is unidirectional in the sense that it transmits wage changes from high to low expected income regions, but not vice versa. If inter-regional differences in the assessment of non-pecuniary rewards and in Z_{s1} are not too large, a general pattern of this dynamic market interdependence may be observable.

In the high-expected-earnings regions, local market forces and wage expectations must, therefore, play the most important part in wage determination. By contrast, in the low-expected-earnings regions, local labour market conditions may play only a minor role, the major impact on wages being brought about by wage changes in the high-expected-earnings regions.

The empirical investigation of the above dynamic market interdependence hypothesis must begin with a ranking of regions according to expected earnings. Accordingly, the straight-time hourly earnings (excluding overtime) were computed for 1953, 1960 and 1966.[14] A somewhat imperfect adjustment was made for the probability of obtaining this wage by multiplying it by $(1 - u_i)$. The states were then ranked in descending order of these expected wages. A number of facts emerged from an examination of these data: (i) With a few exceptions the rankings were very similar in 1953, 1960 and 1966; the relative wage structure does not change rapidly over time. (ii) The spread in expected money wages is quite substantial; for instance in 1960 they ranged from $1.50 to $2.70. (iii) Expected wages are not correlated with unemployment, some high-wage states also have high unemployment and vice versa. (iv) Roughly speaking, the West Coast states have the highest wages, followed by the Midwest,

---

[14] Several commentators on a previous draft felt that the appropriate measure for ranking states should be earnings including overtime earnings, because the latter may be an attraction for potential migrants. In fact, the ranking of states is virtually unaffected by this definitional change.

the East, and the South trailing behind. The evidence on inter-regional differences in the cost of living which is published by the U.S. Department of Labor suggests that the cost of living may be as much as 20 per cent above the average in some Eastern cities, 10 per cent below in the South and not far from the average in the West and North Central America. Adjustment for these regional differences in the cost of living might change the details of the ranking somewhat but the general pattern would not be changed. Because of lack of data, the costs of change (Z_{si}) and the non-pecuniary rewards could not be considered for the ranking. After the states had been ranked, it was decided to partition DB in a specific way. The states were sub-divided into two groups: the leaders with high relative expected wages (subscripted $j = 1, \ldots, m$) and the followers with low relative expected wages (subscripted $k = m + 1, \ldots, n$). Through the dynamic market interdependence the mean wage change of the leaders ($\bar{w}_{1t}$) influences the expected and, hence, the actual wage change among the followers. The leaders, however, do not respond to wage changes among the followers, but instead their expected wages are assumed to be related to their own past unemployment. Thus, in the leading sectors wage changes are assumed to be deter-mined by current and past unemployment:

$$w_{jt} = b_1 g_1(u_{jt}) + c_1 w_{jt}^e + k_1 p_t \tag{23}$$

$$w_{jt}^e = f_1(u_{jt-1}) \quad j = 1, \ldots, m \tag{24}$$

The subscript 1 refers to all leading sectors. The parameters b_1, c_1, k_1, and the functions g_1 and f_1 are assumed to be the same in all m leading sectors. In the following sectors, on the other hand, wage changes are influenced by the mean wage changes in the leading sectors:

$$w_{kt} = b_2 g_2(u_{kt}) + c_{21} w_{kt}^e + k_2 p_t \tag{25}$$

$$w_{kt}^e = c_{22} \bar{w}_{1t} \quad k = m + 1, \ldots, n \tag{26}$$

where $\bar{w}_{1t}$ is the mean of w_{jt}, namely:

$$\bar{w}_{1t} = \frac{\sum a_j(b_1 g_1(u_{jt}) + c_1 f_1(u_{jt-1}))}{\sum a_j} + k_1 p_t \tag{27}$$

After substitution for w_{jt}^e, w_{kt}^e and $\bar{w}_{1t}$, the w_{jt} and w_{kt} in equations (23) and (25) are weighted and summed, and the aggregate mean wage change is obtained as $w_t = \sum a_j w_{jt} + \sum a_k w_{kt}$ (according to an earlier assumption $\sum a_j + \sum a_k = 1$). In order to derive the actual estimating equation, an assumption about the functional forms of the g and f functions has to be made. The results of Section III suggested that non-linear formulations might give marginally better results. Consequently, a simple reciprocal transformation has been used:

$$g_i(u_t) = W_i + u_t^{-1} \quad i = 1, 2 \tag{28}$$

$$f_1(u_t) = \alpha_{11} + u_{t-1}^{-1} \tag{29}$$

After substitution for the g and f functions, the estimating equation becomes:

$$w_t = \alpha + \beta_1 \frac{\sum a_j u_{jt}^{-1}}{\sum a_j} + \gamma_1 \frac{\sum a_j u_{jt-1}^{-1}}{\sum a_j} + \beta_2 \sum a_k u_{kt}^{-1} + k_0 p_t \tag{30}$$

where α consists of a number of terms involving α_1, α_2 and α_{11}, and the other coefficients are related to the basic parameters as follows:

$$
\begin{aligned}
\beta_1 &= b_1(\sum a_j + c_{21} c_{22} \sum a_k) \\
\beta_2 &= b_2 \\
\gamma_1 &= c_1(\sum a_j + c_{21} c_{22} \sum a_k) \\
k_0 &= k_1(\sum a_j + c_{21} c_{22} \sum a_k) + k_2 \sum a_k
\end{aligned}
\tag{31}
$$

Thus, the appropriate estimating equation contains the weighted means of the reciprocals of unemployment rates in the leading sectors and the weighted sum of the reciprocals of unemployment rates in the other sectors. Unfortunately b_1, c_1, k_1 and k_2 cannot be identified. If, however, $c_2 c_3 = 1$, then $\beta_1 = b_1$, $\gamma_1 = c_1$ and $k_0 = k_1 + k_2 \sum a_k$ because $\sum a_j + \sum a_k = 1$.

According to our theoretical arguments, the leading sectors should be the ones with the highest relative earnings. This yields a ranking of states, but it does not provide the number of states that should be included in the group of leading sectors (namely, m). Consequently, equation (20) was fitted eight times, each containing a different number of states in the leading group: m was increased in steps of three. Table 2 shows that the minimum residual variance is reached when the group of leading sectors contains twelve states (namely, Nevada, Washington, California, Oregon, Wyoming, Indiana, Montana, Utah, Arizona, Colorado, Wisconsin and New Jersey). Although the overall exactness of fit—as measured by the R^2 of

Table 2 Parameters of equation (30) for different sizes of leading sector

No. of states in leading sector	α	β_1	γ_1	β_2	k_0	R^2
3	−0·3815	2·8334	−0·9368	0·5961	0·3089	0·7018
	(0·2102)*	(0·9586)	(0·8815)	(0·4693)	(0·0929)	
6	−0·3501	3·7773	−0·1455	−1·5024	0·2849	0·7117
	(0·2019)	(1·1035)	(0·7586)	(0·9602)	(0·0900)	
9	−0·3547	3·7640	−0·1816	−1·6220	0·2880	0·7189
	(0·1980)	(1·0158)	(0·7187)	(0·9429)	(0·0890)	
12	−0·2383	3·7334	0·0064	−3·0388	0·2888	0·7340
	(0·1861)	(0·8707)	(0·6083)	(1·1513)	(0·0865)	
15	−0·1953	3·0840	0·0446	−3·0829	0·2957	0·7193
	(0·1928)	(0·7938)	(0·5691)	(1·3273)	(0·0888)	
18	−0·3480	5·1811	−0·1449	−7·3982	0·3308	0·7132
	(0·2038)	(1·2988)	(0·6888)	(2·5181)	(0·0903)	
21	−0·2133	5·9162	−0·0990	−15·5932	0·2940	0·7164
	(0·1919)	(1·3818)	(0·6877)	(4·4286)	(0·0892)	
24	−0·2169	4·0252	−0·2965	−12·0834	0·3061	0·6992
	(0·1989)	(1·0882)	(0·7124)	(4·2347)	(0·0918)	

*Asymptotic standard errors are given in parentheses.

0·7340—may still not be remarkably high, the residual variance (adjusted for degrees of freedom) is over 20 per cent lower than in the linear formulation of equation (21). Moreover, in comparison with the non-linear aggregation hypothesis, the present dynamic market interdependence hypothesis, based on a theory of migration, appears to work markedly better. Of course, the two hypotheses are not mutually exclusive, but the non-linear aggregation hypothesis does not contribute very much by itself.

One of the striking and unexpected results in Table 2 is that the coefficient of $\sum a_k u_{kt}^{-1}$ is negative (in all but the first regressions) which means that, holding unemployment constant in the 'leading' high-earnings sectors, a rise in unemployment in the low-earnings sectors is associated with a rise in w_t. This sign is not predicted by the theory described earlier in this section. It does point the way to a model in which the difference $(\sum a_j u_{jt}^{-1} - \sum a_k u_{kt}^{-1})$ has a crucial part to play in the determination of w_t. It is interesting that Thomas and Stoney obtained a very similar result (although they ranked their regions by unemployment). They postulated $w_{it} = f(u_{it}) + h(\bar{w}_{jt} - f(u_{it}))$ and estimated h as larger than 2 [17]. Some further preliminary investigations have suggested that the negative signs are attributable to the 'wrong' behaviour of the Southern states: As unemployment rises *ceteris paribus* in the South, wage changes in the country as a whole tend to rise. One possible explanation of this expected sign is that as unemployment in the South rises *relatively* to unemployment in other areas, migration flows from the South increase. If the migrants are employed in areas with relatively high wages, then the mean rate of change of straight-time hourly earnings in the country as a whole may rise. But a more complete model of dynamic market interdependence might produce other reasons for 'wrong' signs. More work on this problem is in progress.

In this section of the paper a model of dynamic market interdependence based on a theory of regional migration has been sketched and some of its implications have been tested. The basic proposition is that regions with high relative expected earnings will influence the pace of wage increases in other regions because of threatened or realised migration. This dynamic market interdependence is unidirectional because there is no tendency to migrate from high-earnings to low-earnings regions. When the sample of states was sub-divided into a high-earnings and a low-earnings group and their mean unemployment rates were allowed to have separate effects on total wage changes, rather better statistical results were obtained than in the linear and non-linear specifications of Section III. Though an unexpected sign is still somewhat puzzling, it looks as though this version of dynamic market interdependence is worth pursuing further.

Conclusions

The influence of the distribution of regional unemployment rates upon aggregate wage inflation has been examined in this paper by looking at two different—but not mutually exclusive—hypotheses: The first has been called the non-linear aggregation hypothesis because it is based—at least, in its empirical applications—on the aggregation of identical convex individual market Phillips curves. The empirical results presented in Section III indicate that non-linear aggregation appears to play only a minor role in the determination of aggregate wage changes. According to the second hypothesis, there exists some dynamic market interdependence which arises from an intersectoral propagation of expectations. Thus, the expected wage change in sector i is allowed to be influenced by actual (present and past) wage changes in sector j, so that the actual wage change in i responds not only to (past and present) market conditions in i but also to those in j. Two versions of the dynamic market interdependence have been examined: In Section IV, it was assumed that regions with relatively low unemployment rates were the 'leaders' which influenced wage changes in other regions. The empirical support for this hypothesis was found to be very weak. In Section V, it was assumed that regions with relatively high average earnings were the 'leaders' which influenced wage changes in other regions. This proposition was derived from a simple theory of migration. Some empirical support for this formulation has been found.

Although the non-linear aggregation and the dynamic market interdependence hypotheses are not mutually exclusive, they do have different implications for economic policy: According to the former, unemployment dispersions should be reduced; while the latter implies that sectors with the strongest own and cross effects, that is, the 'leaders', should be depressed for a reduction in the average Phillips curve.

Two general conclusions have emerged from the analysis: First, conventional textbooks on labour economics and casual empiricism suggest fairly strongly that wage expectations are formed through an intersectoral process. The resulting dynamic market interdependence may lead to extremely slow adjustments to sectoral excess demands and to an inflation-prone wage market. Very little work has been done on the nature of these intersectoral processes. The tentative conclusions reached in this paper suggest that further research effort in this area may well be rewarding.

Second, although U.S. authorities do not pursue an explicit regional unemployment policy, recent experience has shown dramatically that government stabilisation policies may have an uneven impact on regional unemployment rates. Not much is known about the short- and long-run effects of such redistributions of relative unemployment rates. Since it seems desirable that stabilisation policies should be designed with full knowledge of their consequences, it is hoped that the tentative results presented here can be followed up by a more thorough theoretical and empirical analysis.

226   F. P. R. Brechling

References

[1] Archibald, G. C., 'The Phillips Curve and the Distribution of Unemployment', *American Economic Review* (May 1969).

[2] Archibald, G. C., 'Analysis of Regional Economic Policy', in *Essays in Honour of Lord Robbins*, edited by B. A. Corry and M. Peston, London, Weidenfeld and Nicolson (1972).

[3] Archibald, G. C., Kemmis, R. and Perkins, J. W., 'Excess Demand for Labour, Unemployment and the Phillips Curve', Ch. 5 above.

[4] Brechling, F., 'Trends and Cycles in British Regional Unemployment', *Oxford Economic Papers* (March 1967).

[5] Brechling, F., 'The Trade-off between Inflation and Unemployment', *Journal of Political Economy*, Part II (July/Aug. 1968).

[6] Corry, B. and Laidler, D., 'The Phillips Relation: A Theoretical Explanation', *Economics* (May 1967).

[7] Holt, C. C., 'Job Search, Phillips Wage Relation and Union Influence: Theory and Evidence', in *Microeconomic Foundations of Employment and Inflation Theory*, edited by Edmund S. Phelps *et al.*, New York, W. W. Norton (1970).

[8] Holmes, J. M. and Smyth, D. J., 'The Relation between Unemployment and Excess Demand for Labour: An Examination of the Theory of the Phillips Curve', *Economics* (Aug. 1970).

[9] Lipsey, R. G., 'The Relationship between Unemployment and the Rate of Change of Money Wages in the United Kingdom, 1862–1957: A Further Analysis', *Economica* (Feb. 1960).

[10] Lucas, R. E. and Rapping, L. A., 'Price Expectations and the Phillips Curve', *American Economic Review* (June 1969).

[11] Mortensen, D., 'A Theory of Wage and Employment Dynamics', in *Microeconomic Foundations of Employment and Inflation Theory*, by E. S. Phelps *et al.*, New York, W. W. Norton (1970).

[12] Negishi, T., 'Market Clearing Processes in a Monetary Economy', in F. H. Hahn and F. Brechling (eds.), *The Theory of Interest Rates*, New York, Macmillan (1965).

[13] Phelps, E. S., 'Money Wage Dynamics and Labor Market Equilibrium', in *Microeconomic Foundations of Employment and Inflation Theory*, by E. S. Phelps *et al.*, New York, W. W. Norton (1970).

[14] Ross, A. M., *Trade Union Wage Policy*, Berkeley, University of California Press (1950).

[15] Samuelson, P. A., *Foundations of Economic Analysis*, New York, Atheneum Publishers (1965).

[16] Solow, R. M., *Price Expectations and the Behaviour of the Price Level*, Manchester, Manchester University Press (1969).

[17] Thomas, R. L. and Stoney, P. J. M., 'Unemployment Dispersion as a Determinant of Wage Inflation in the U.K., 1925–66', *Manchester School* (June 1971). Reprinted as Ch. 11 in M. Parkin and M. T. Sumner (eds.), *Incomes Policy and Inflation*, Manchester, Manchester University Press (1972).

[18] Vanderkamp, J., 'The Phillips Relation: A Theoretical Explanation—A Comment', *Economica* (May 1968).

R. L. Thomas

Chapter 8 Wage inflation in the U.K.: a multi-market approach

I Introduction

The recent, historically high, rate of wage inflation in the U.K. has led to a re-awakening of econometric interest in this area and to a series of papers in which conclusions of earlier studies by, for example, Phillips [7] and Lipsey [5] are increasingly being questioned. This second generation of wage–price inflation models differs in several important ways from the earlier studies.

Firstly, recent studies regard the price-change variable normally included in the wage equation not as 'a measure of the cost-push element in wage adjustments', (Phillips [7]) but as a proxy for expected price changes. Friedman [2], in particular, denying the existence of money illusion in the wage bargaining process, suggests that the coefficient on the price change variable should be unity thus implying a vertical long-run Phillips curve with no long-run trade off between the level of unemployment and the rate of inflation. Existing empirical evidence for the U.K., however, suggests a price change coefficient of less than unity and one which, moreover, varies in a highly unstable manner from period to period (see for example Sumner [9]).

Another feature of some recent wage inflation models (for example Archibald [1] and Thomas and Stoney [10]) is the attention paid to the dispersion of unemployment across labour markets. One defect of these models is the assumption of identical micro-Phillips curves in all individual markets. Given this assumption the influence of unemployment dispersion on aggregate wage change is the result solely of aggregation over non-linear micro-curves. However it is clear that if this assumption is relaxed then the pattern of unemployment across labour markets will influence aggregate wage change whether the micro-curves are non-linear or not. For example a concentration of high unemployment in markets with 'shallow' Phillips curves will result in a higher aggregate rate of wage change than if the concentration of high unemployment were in markets with 'steep' Phillips curves.

We present in this paper a multi-market model of wage inflation which has two main features. Firstly the market Phillips curves are assumed to be both non-linear and non-identical. In particular the parameters of the market curve are explicitly formulated as functions of the level of unionisation. With the exception of Hines [3], most empirical studies of wage inflation either simply ignore the existence of trade unions or simply assume that variations in union activity are reflected in variations in the size of the coefficients in estimated equations. A major aim of this paper is to assess the effect, if any, of varying unionisation levels on the degree of response of wage changes to changes in the conventional variables (unemployment and expected price changes) in the wage equation.

Secondly attention is paid to the possibility that different labour markets may react differently to a given expected rate of price change. Empirical results suggest strongly that aggregate wage change reacts in a non-linear or 'threshold' manner to price changes. However little attention has been given to the patterns of individual market behaviour implied by a given non-linear aggregate relationship. We consider a number of possible market behaviour patterns and deduce the resultant aggregate relationships.

II   A multi-market model
In this section we develop, first, a market Phillips curve for the case where the expected rate of price change is zero. By aggregating over all markets, a macro curve is derived and then finally, the influence of non-zero expected rates of price change is considered.

The market Phillips curve given a zero expected rate of price change
The market curves in the model have the following general form

$$\Delta W_i = A_i + B_i \log (U_i + \gamma) \quad \gamma = 0 \text{ or } 1 \qquad (\text{II}.1)$$

where ΔW_i and U_i are the rate of wage change and the level of unemployment in the ith market and there are n such markets in all. The use of the log function ensures that, so long as $B_i \leq 0$, the curve has the normal 'Phillips' shape. γ is discussed below.

At this stage the restrictive assumptions $A_i = A = \text{const}$ and

$B_i = B = $ const are normally made. These assumptions may be considerably generalised by making A_i and B_i functions of some relevant labour market variable(s). In this model we develop the case where A_i and B_i and hence the 'slope' and position of the market curve are functions of T_i the percentage of the labour force unionised in market i.

$$\Delta W_i = A(T_i) + B(T_i) \log (U_i + \gamma) \qquad (\text{II.2})$$

The properties of equation II.2 are more easily considered if we assume for the moment that $A(T_i)$ and $B(T_i)$ are both linear functions

$$\Delta W_i = a_1 + a_2 T_i + (b_1 + b_2 T_i) \log (U_i + \gamma) \qquad (\text{II.3})$$

where, since $0 \le T_i \le 1$ and $B_i = b_1 + b_2 T_i \le 0$ we have $b_1 \le 0$ and $b_1 + b_2 \le 0$. Also, since it seems reasonable to suggest that a highly organised labour force in a market is likely to make the rate of wage less responsive rather than more responsive to changes in the level of unemployment in that market we also have $b_2 > 0$.

Equation II.3 implies that for a value of $U_i = U^* = $ antilog $(-a_2/b_2) - \gamma$, the rate of wage change $W_i = a_1 - a_2 b_1/b_2 = $ const, independent of the level of unionisation. For levels of $U_i > U^*$, the rate of wage change is largest in high unionisation markets, while for $U_i < U^*$ the rate of wage change is largest in low unionisation markets.

The value of the intersection point U^* depends on the size of the coefficient a_2 and on the value of γ. Considering the case $\gamma = 1$, then if $a_2 > 0$, we have $U^* < 0$ and equation II.3 defines a family of market Phillips curves as illustrated in Figure 1. On the other hand, if $a_2 < 0$ then $U^* > 0$ and the family of curves is similar to that illustrated in Figure 2.

If, however, $\gamma = 0$, then the intersection U^* is always positive and the market curves are constrained to be similar to those of Figure 2, thus implying that there is always some level of unemployment at which wage change is inversely related to unionisation.

It is difficult to choose on *a priori* grounds between the two formulations represented by Figures 1 and 2. Figure 2 could be interpreted as a cross-sectional analogue of the Lipsey-Parkin [6] idea that separate Phillips curves exist in time series, these curves intersecting at a positive level of unemployment and being less steeply sloped the more the wage-adjustment process is isolated from labour market

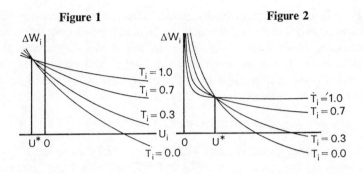

Figure 1

Figure 2

conditions by the operation of incomes policies. In the present context, Figure 2 implies that *given zero expected price changes* there are some relatively low levels of unemployment at which rates of wage change are lowest in high unionisation markets. This is not implausible, since, in a highly unionised labour market the wage bargaining procedure tends to be highly institutionalised and often follows a set pattern. This may have the result that, given a strong excess demand for labour ($U_i < U^*$), the adjustment of wage rates towards their equilibrium values is in fact hindered by long drawn out and set bargaining procedures, this being reflected in a slower rate of wage change than would occur in more competitive markets.

While Figure 2 implies a positive correlation between ΔW_i and T_i only for unemployment levels $U_i > U^*$, Figure 1 implies such a relationship at all levels of unemployment. This formulation, then, implies a tendency, given the level of unemployment, towards an ever-increasing gap between wage levels in high and low unionisation markets. Whether such a tendency is apparent in the U.K. context is obviously a matter which may be empirically investigated. Indeed, it is clear that any choice between Figures 1 and 2 can only finally be made on empirical grounds.

Up to this point, by considering only the special case of equation II.2 where both $A(T_i)$ and $B(T_i)$ are linear functions of T_i, discussion has been restricted to the case where all market curves pass through a single intersection point U^*. However, if either $A(T_i)$ or $B(T_i)$ is given a non-linear form then we have the less restrictive situation where there is no common intersection point. Multiple intersection points will exist lying either to the left or right of the vertical (wage change) axis for $\gamma = 1$, but constrained to lie to the right of the axis if $\gamma = 0$.

The aggregate Phillips curve given a zero expected rate of price change
For the case where $A(T_i)$ and $B(T_i)$ are linear functions of T_i, the aggregate rate of wage change may be obtained by summing equation II.3 over all labour markets.

$$\Delta W = \sum \alpha_i \, \Delta W_i = a_1 + a_2 T + b_1 \sum \alpha_i \log (U_i + \gamma)$$

$$+ \, b_2 \sum \alpha_i T_i \log (U_i + \gamma) \tag{II.4}$$

where ΔW and T are the aggregate wage change and aggregate unionisation level respectively and α_i is the weight assigned to the ith labour market. Taking a truncated Taylor series expansion of $\log (U_i + \gamma)$ about $U + \gamma$ where U is the aggregate unemployment level, and a similar two variable series expansion of $T_i \log (U_i + \gamma)$, this time about T and $U + \gamma$, we have

$$\log (U_i + \gamma) = \log (U + \gamma) + (U_i - U)/(U + \gamma)$$

$$- \tfrac{1}{2}(U_i - U)^2/(U + \gamma)^2$$

$$T_i \log (U_i + \gamma) = T \log (U + \gamma) + (T_i - T) \log (U + \gamma)$$

$$+ \, (U_i - U)T/(U + \gamma)$$

$$- \tfrac{1}{2}(U_i - U)^2 T/(U + \gamma)^2$$

$$+ \, (T_i - T)(U_i - U)/(U + \gamma)$$

Substituting in equation II.4 now yields

$$\Delta W = a_1 + a_2 T + (b_1 + b_2 T) \left[\log (U + \gamma) - \frac{S_u^2}{2(U + \gamma)^2} \right]$$

$$+ \, \frac{b_2 K}{U + \gamma} \tag{II.5}$$

where S_u^2 is the weighted variance of market unemployment levels and $K = \sum \alpha_i (T_i - T)(U_i - U)$ is the weighted covariance of unemployment and unionisation levels. Similar equations may be derived for cases where $A(T_i)$ and $B(T_i)$ are non-linear. *The covariance term in equation II.5 reflects the idea that, given the aggregate level of unemployment, the greater the tendency for market unemployment to be concentrated in high unionisation areas (i.e. markets with shallow Phillips curves), the greater will be the aggregate rate of wage change.*

For the U.K., during the post-war period, aggregate unionisation has remained virtually constant, so that if II.5 is to be estimated from time series data, we may use

$$W = \alpha + \beta\left[\log\left(U + \gamma\right) - \frac{S_u^2}{2(U + \gamma)^2}\right] + b_2\frac{K}{U + \gamma} \quad \text{(II.6)}$$

where $\alpha = a_1 + a_2T = \text{const}$ and $\beta = b_1 + b_2T = \text{const}$.

Alternatively, if separate estimates of b_1 and b_2 are required, we may use

$$\Delta W = \alpha + b_1\left[\log\left(U + \gamma\right) - \frac{S_U^2}{2(U + \gamma)^2}\right]$$
$$+ b_2\left[T\log\left(U + \gamma\right) - \frac{TS_U^2}{2(U + \gamma)^2} + \frac{K}{U + \gamma}\right] \quad \text{(II.7)}$$

The inclusion of the unionisation variable T in the above equations inevitably invites comparison with the models of A. G. Hines [3 and 4]. However there are several important differences between the model presented here and those of Hines. The key variable in the Hines model is ΔT, the change in unionisation—this is assumed to represent union militancy. The only unionisation variable in the present model, however, is the level of unionisation, T, and this is not to be interpreted as a proxy for militancy as such, but simply as reflecting what it obviously measures—the degree to which the labour force is organised. This in turn then influences the extent to which wage change responds to variations in unemployment.

It is true when considering periods over which there were large fluctuations in unionisation, Hines also introduces the variable T into the wage equation. However the variable is introduced in an *ad hoc* manner simply as an additional argument in the Phillips curve, so that an increase in unionisation simply results in a uniform upward shift in that curve. In the present model, both the position and slope of the Phillips curve are made explicitly dependent on T. Equation II.5 therefore implies, given the market structure of unemployment, that an increase in unionisation results, not in a uniform upward shift, but in an anti-clockwise rotation of the Phillips curve towards the horizontal. This rotation occurs about a point lying to the right of the vertical (wage change) axis if $\gamma = 0$, but which may lie either to the right or left of that axis if $\gamma = 1$.

The market Phillips curve given a non-zero expected rate of price change

Suppose that when the expected rate of price change, ΔP^e, is zero, the market rate of wage change is given by $\Delta W_i = z_i$ and the aggregate rate of wage change by $\Delta W = Z$, these rates being determined by equations II.3 and II.5 respectively.

We define for each labour market a *threshold rate of price change* ΔP^*_i, such that whenever $\Delta P^e \geq \Delta P^*_i$, expected price changes have a definite influence on the wage determining process but whenever $\Delta P^e < \Delta P^*_i$ they have no such influence.[1] This reflects the possibility that, as the rate of wage inflation rises, wage earners become more sensitive to price changes and there is a breaking down of money illusion. Furthermore, since one of the aims of this paper is to examine the hypothesis that the response of wage change to variations in the conventional arguments of the wage equation is influenced by the level of unionisation, we now postulate that, once money illusion has broken down in a labour market the response of wage change to a change in ΔP^e is dependent on the unionisation variable T_i. We then have

$$\Delta W_i = z_i + Q(T_i)\,\Delta P^e = z_i + (p + qT_i)\,\Delta P^e \quad \text{for } \Delta P^e \geq \Delta P^*_i$$

$$\Delta W_i = z_i \qquad\qquad\qquad\qquad\qquad\qquad\quad \text{for } \Delta P^e < \Delta P^*_i$$

$$\text{(II.8)}$$

where we, again for simplicity, assume that the function $Q(T_i)$ is a linear one and we normally expect $Q(T_i)$ to lie between zero and unity.

We now consider the behaviour of the threshold rate ΔP^*_i across labour markets. There are a number of possibilities. Firstly ΔP^*_i may be a constant. In fact if $\Delta P^*_i = \text{const} = 0$, then there are no 'threshold effects'. Secondly ΔP^*_i may vary randomly across labour markets. Thirdly and more interestingly, ΔP^*_i may be a function of some relevant labour market variable(s). In the context of this paper we again consider the hypothesis that ΔP^*_i, is a function (assumed to be linear) of the level of unionisation.

$$\Delta P^*_i = P(T_i) = l + mT_i \quad l \geq 0 \tag{II.9}$$

In this model, then, there are two suggested ways by which the level of unionisation could influence the response of wage changes to

[1] ΔP^e is assumed constant in all markets.

expected price changes. Firstly, the level of unionisation could affect the threshold rate at which price changes first make their influence felt and secondly it could affect the degree to which wage change responds to price changes once such influences become operative. If such unionisation effects do in fact occur, then, in so far as the ability to bargain for real rather than money wages is likely to be positively related to the level of unionisation, we would expect q in equation II.8 to be positive rather than negative and m in equation II.9 to be negative rather than positive.

Finally, equation II.9 may be inverted to yield

$$T_i = P^{-1}(\Delta P^*_i) = (\Delta P^*_i - l)/m \qquad (\text{II}.10)$$

Using equation II.10, we may now define a *critical level of unionisation*, T^*, between zero and unity where

$$
\begin{aligned}
T^* &= 0 && \text{if} \quad (\Delta P^e - l)/m \le 0 \\
T^* &= (\Delta P^e - l)/m && \text{if } 0 \le (\Delta P^e - l)/m \le 1 \qquad (\text{II}.11) \\
T^* &= 1 && \text{if } 1 \le (\Delta P^e - l)/m
\end{aligned}
$$

and such that

$$
\begin{aligned}
\Delta W_i &= z_i + (p + qT_i)\,\Delta P^e && \text{for all markets where } T_i \ge T^* \\
\Delta W_i &= z_i && \text{for all markets where } T_i < T^*
\end{aligned}
\qquad (\text{II}.12)
$$

The critical level of unionisation is therefore a function of the expected rate of price change. Assuming $m < 0$, we have from II.11 and II.12, that if $\Delta P^e \ge l$, then $T^* = 0$ and $T_i \ge T^*$ for all i, so that all markets experience an exceptional adjustment in the rate of wage change, while if $\Delta P^e < l + m$, then $T^* = 1$ and $T_i < T^*$ for all i and no markets experience such an adjustment. Otherwise when $l > P^e \ge l + m$ only those markets for which $T_i \ge T^* = (\Delta P^e - l)/m$ experience the adjustment.

The aggregate Phillips curve given a non-zero expected rate of price change
The aggregate rate of wage change may be obtained by summing II.12 over all markets

$$
\begin{aligned}
\Delta W &= Z + \sum_{T_i \ge T^*} \alpha_i(p + qT_i)\,\Delta P^e \\
&= Z + C^*(p + qD^*)\,\Delta P^e = Z + hP^e \qquad (\text{II}.13)
\end{aligned}
$$

where Z is given by equation II.5, the summation sign is over all markets for which $T_i \geq T^*$, $C^* = \sum_{T_i \geq T^*} \alpha_i =$ the weighted proportion of all markets which respond to price changes, $D^* = 1/C^* \times \sum_{T_i \geq T^*} \alpha_i T_i =$ the overall unionisation level in these markets and $h = C^*(p + qD^*)$.

We may now examine the behaviour, *in aggregate time series*, of h the coefficient on the expected price change variable, given different assumptions about behaviour at the market level.

(1) If $m = 0$, then $\Delta P^* = l$ and is constant in all markets and independent of the level of unionisation. It follows that

$$\text{if } \Delta P^e \geq l \quad \text{then } C^* = 1, \; D^* = T \text{ and hence } h = p + qT$$

and if $\Delta P^e < l$ then $C^* = 0$ and hence $h = 0$

Since during the post-war period aggregate unionisation T has been virtually constant, we therefore have a dichotomous situation where h in some periods is zero and in other periods is a positive constant.

(2) If $m = 0$ and $l = 0$, then there are no threshold effects and for all positive values of ΔP^e we have $h = p + qT = $ const. Thus we have the aggregate wage equation normally employed in empirical work.

(3) When no restriction is placed on l or m, h is neither constant nor dichotomous but may take any of a series of discrete values, its particular value at a given moment depending on C^* and D^* and hence on the expected rate of price change. For the special case where $q = 0$ and $p = 1$, that is where the response to price changes once money illusion has broken down is identical in all markets and where this response is such that it exactly compensates wage earners for any expected price change, h may be interpreted simply as the *proportion of markets which experience a price effect*.

It is now possible to infer the form of the market Phillips curves which underlie a given aggregate equation. Firstly, if the aggregate equation has a simple single valued coefficient on the price change variable, then clearly there can be no threshold effects at the market level. Secondly, a simple dichotomous situation in the aggregate equation can only arise in the very special case where the threshold rate of price change is identical in all markets. Finally, a more general aggregate equation, with a price coefficient which is some function of the expected rate of price change, implies a less restrictive situation at the market level with the threshold rate varying from market to market. *It is important to note that this last statement holds whether or not the threshold rate of price change is dependent on the level of unionisation. All that is required is that the threshold rate should vary from market to market.*

Of the three alternative aggregate equations considered in the preceding paragraph, the simple dichotomous type seems to imply more restrictive and unlikely market equations than the other two possible forms. The choice between aggregate equations would seem to lie between the first and third alternatives.

III   The cross-sectional results

The major problem in attempting to obtain empirical estimates of cross-sectional wage equations such as II.2 and II.8 is the lack of suitable data. While unemployment data is available on both a regional and an industrial basis, data on the percentage of the labour force unionised is only available on an industrial basis (see for example P.E.P. [8]). For this reason the cross-sectional equations had to be estimated using S.I.C. industry groups, the actual choice of groups being determined by the availability of the unionisation data.

It is immediately clear that S.I.C. industry groups do not approximate closely to the labour markets of theory. The groups fall into three main categories. Firstly, there are groups such as 'mining and quarrying' which approximate fairly closely to theoretical labour markets and which consist chiefly of a single industry dominated by a single 'industrial union'. Secondly there are groups such as 'metals', sometimes covering a large number of industries, which consist of a number of inter-related labour markets and are characterised by unions whose influence is not necessarily limited to a single labour market. It is impossible to isolate separate labour markets within these groups. However, since wage levels in the inter-related markets tend to move together, with a wage change in one market having rapid, possibly immediate influence on wage levels in other markets, it seems a plausible procedure to treat such an industry group as a single combined labour market. Finally there are industry groups such as 'distributive trades' in which unionisation levels are often low and which are fairly arbitrary groupings from a labour market point of view. At best such groups can only be regarded as aggregates of a number of separate and largely non-inter-related labour markets.

Since the total number of industry groups is small, groups belonging to the third of the above categories were necessarily included in the analysis and hence any empirical results so obtained must be treated with caution. However a further analysis is later carried out using only those groups which most closely correspond to 'true' labour markets.

The next problem was to decide whether wage rates or wage earnings should be used as the dependent variable in the cross-sectional equation. Wage rates are normally determined by industry wide bargaining. Wage earnings, however, may be conveniently divided into two elements—the wage rate and a component generally referred to as 'wage drift', which is largely determined by bargaining at plant level and is hence dependent to a great extent on purely local labour market conditions. Explanation of changes in earnings is thus likely to require a much narrower classification of labour markets than does the explanation of wage rates. The unemployment and unionisation data available is by industry group—a very wide classification which corresponds more closely to the area over which wage rates are determined. It is true, as noted above, that some of these groups are aggregates of largely separate labour markets. However the extent of the aggregation involved must be less if wage rates are used rather than wage earnings. Since this paper is concerned with, as far as possible, a disaggregated analysis of wage determination, we adopt changes in wage rates as the most suitable dependent variable, given the unemployment and unionisation data available.

When data series for industry groups were examined two further problems arose. For many industries, particularly those which most closely approximate true labour markets, the official wage index tends to move in irregular jumps, plateaux of up to 12 months and more being followed by a rapid rise for two or three months, followed by another plateau. To obtain representative figures for wage change, the change in the index was measured from the end of one such rapid rise to the end of another approximately 12 months later. This change was then expressed in annual percentage terms. For industries where irregular jumps were not evident, wage change was measured over an arbitrary 12 month period—normally July to July. Details may be found in the Appendix.

Secondly, examination of the unemployment data highlighted a problem frequently met in cross-sectional work. In the conventional Phillips Curve analysis, the unemployment level is regarded as a proxy variable for the excess demand for labour. However, in an industrial cross-section it is most unlikely that the relationship between unemployment and excess labour demand will be identical or even similar for all the industry groups considered. Any estimated cross-sectional equation must be, to a certain extent 'blurred' for this reason. The best that can be done is to exclude any industry groups where the unemployment/excess demand relationship appears likely to be very different from that in the other industry groups to be considered. Two such industry groups—agriculture and construction—were eventually excluded from the cross-section. These were the two groups for which casual employment and/or seasonal variations in unemployment are most pronounced and it may well be that a given annual percentage unemployment in these industries implies a stronger excess demand for labour than does the same percentage in other industries. In fact whenever these industries were included in the cross-section, they provided outlying observations some way 'above' the estimated equation. In an attempt to obtain a reasonably homogeneous cross-section, then, the equations presented below are estimated using the remaining 12 industry groups listed in the Appendix.

Three cross-sections, 1962–3, 1964–5 and 1969–70 are examined below. These years were chosen so as to avoid periods when the distorting effects of incomes policies were most severe.

The cross-sectional equations were first estimated without the inclusion of a price change variable. Results are shown in Table 1. Figures in parentheses are standard errors. The dependent variable is ΔW_i and the method of estimation is ordinary least squares.

For all three cross-sections, empirical counterparts of equation (II.2) provide better explanations of the data than do orthodox Phillips type equations. Various forms were experimented with for the functions $A(T_i)$ and $B(T_i)$. A non-linear form for $A(T_i)$ and a linear form for $B(T_i)$ seemed most appropriate. The function $A(T_i) = a_1 + a_2 \log (T_i + 0.1)$ was preferred to $A(T_i) = a_1 + a_2 \log T_i$ since the latter implies a constant term in the market wage equation which tends to infinity as T_i tends to zero. The estimated coefficients in the 1964–5 and 1969–70 cross-sections are much larger than those for 1962–3 but it must be remembered that we have not yet allowed for price effects.

The above equations, particularly the 1964–5 cross-section, contain one anomaly. They imply that for very high values of T_i, the industrial Phillips curve has a positive unemployment slope. This finding also

Table 1

Cross-section	Const	$\log(T_i + 0.1)$	$T_i \log U_i$	$\log U_i$	R_2	$\bar{R}^2$
1962–3	5·14 (0·29)			−1·65 (0·44)	0·58	0·54
	4·20 (0·48)	−1·90 (0·84)	4·07 (2·84)	−3·96 (1·41)	0·78	0·70
1964–5	6·64 (0·51)			−1·58 (1·70)	0·08	−0·01
	4·15 (1·37)	−4·63 (2·33)	28·8 (14·6)	−17·9 (8·3)	0·39	0·17
1969–70	11·78 (1·91)			−2·20 (2·43)	0·08	−0·02
	10·98 (2·43)	−7·74 (4·22)	22·6 (9·2)	−20·3 (7·5)	0·51	0·32

held when price effects were allowed for. A positive unemployment slope is not inherently infeasible when we are dealing with industrial data which is necessarily inter-related. Unemployed workers in contracting industries with low rates of wage change may well join the queue for employment not in the industry where they become unemployed but in an expanding industry with a high rate of wage change and where job opportunities may eventually be greater. These tendencies in an extreme form make possible a positive relationship between wage change and unemployment both in the expanding industries over time and cross-sectionally across both expanding and contracting industries. However, the above results do not suggest such a relationship cross-sectionally, they merely suggest it over time for high unionisation industries. Since there is nothing in the above argument to suggest that positive unemployment slopes should occur in high but not low unionisation industries it seems more reasonable to attribute the anomaly to the not unexpected multicollinearity between the explanatory variables $\log(T_i + 0.1)$, $\log U_i$ and $T_i \log U_i$. This multicollinearity is reflected in the size of the coefficients and their standard errors, and may, to a large extent, be removed by re-estimating under the restriction $b_1 + b_2 = 0$, i.e. replacing the explanatory variables $\log U_i$ and $T_i \log U_i$ by the single variable $(T_i - 1) \log U_i$. This procedure ensures that all the industrial curves have non-positive unemployment slopes and was followed in all the remaining quoted results.

An attempt was now made to investigate the influence of expected price changes. In a cross-sectional analysis such effects can only be detected if they are 'differential' effects, i.e. varying from industry to industry. We are concerned with the hypothesis that price effects occur only in industries where the expected rate of price change, ΔP^e, exceeds the threshold rate. If this hypothesis is correct then we would expect the following pattern to emerge from the cross-sectional data. For ΔP^e below a certain limit, price effects should be impossible to detect since no industries experience them. For ΔP^e above this limit but below some second limit, a dichotomous situation may be expected to arise, with certain industries experiencing price effects and hence, other things being equal, having a rate of wage change distinctly above that experienced in other industries. Moreover, as ΔP^e rises, we expect the number of industries experiencing price effects to increase. Finally, when ΔP^e exceeds the second limit, the dichotomy between price effect and non-price effect industries should disappear and it may again become impossible to detect price effects in the cross-section.

The three cross-sections do exhibit the pattern expected given the threshold hypothesis. In 1962–3, when the actual rate of price change was about 2 per cent, no price effects could be detected. However, in 1964–5, when the rate of price change had risen to 4·5 per cent, two industries—transport and communication, and gas, electricity and water—'break away' from the other ten and experience rates of wage change which are 3·5 to 4 percentage points above the 'partial Phillips curve' formed by the observations from the remaining industries. Moreover, in 1969–70, when price inflation had risen to around 6·5 per cent, four additional industries—mining and quarrying, paper and printing, public administration, and chemicals—also break away and—together with transport and communications, and gas, electricity and water—form a partial curve over six percentage points above the curve formed by the six remaining industries.

This pattern is illustrated by the following equations in which the actual rate of price change (used as a proxy for ΔP^e) is included for those industries where price effects have been detected: [2]

[2] The estimated coefficients for the 1969–70 cross-section are still somewhat larger than those for 1962–3 and 1964–5, but it must be remembered that 1969–70 was the period during which a considerable backlog of wage increases were being negotiated after the breakdown of the 1967–8 incomes policy (see later in Section IV).

1962-3 $\Delta W_i = 4\cdot24 - 1\cdot83 \log{(T_i + 0\cdot1)}$

$\qquad$ $(0\cdot25)$ $\quad$ $(0\cdot42)$

$\qquad\qquad$ $+ 3\cdot87(T_i - 1) \log{U_i}$ $\qquad\qquad$ $\bar{R}^2 = 0\cdot74$

$\qquad$ $(0\cdot67)$

1964-5 $\Delta W_i = 4\cdot37 - 2\cdot61 \log{(T_i + 0\cdot1)}$

$\qquad$ $(0\cdot54)$ $\quad$ $(0\cdot72)$

$\qquad\qquad$ $5\cdot51(T_i - 1) \log{U_i} + 0\cdot82\Delta P$ $\quad$ $\bar{R}^2 = 0\cdot79$

$\qquad$ $(1\cdot87)$ $\qquad\qquad\qquad$ $(0\cdot14)$

1969-70 $\Delta W_i = 5\cdot82 - 5\cdot62 \log{(T_i + 0\cdot1)}$

$\qquad$ $(1\cdot22)$ $\quad$ $(1\cdot32)$

$\qquad\qquad$ $+ 7\cdot08(T_i - 1) \log{U_i} + 1\cdot01\Delta P$ $\quad$ $\bar{R}^2 = 0\cdot88$

$\qquad$ $(3\cdot45)$ $\qquad\qquad\qquad$ $(0\cdot15)$

The use of actual price changes as a proxy for ΔP^e is a less doubtful procedure in cross-sectional analysis than it is with time series data. Assuming that ΔP^e is constant for all industries, the inclusion of a price change variable for certain industries in a single cross-section is no different from the inclusion of a dummy variable. No mis-specification is involved and the only problem is that care must be taken in interpreting the price change coefficients.

There is, then, definite evidence for differential price effects and, moreover, their incidence does seem to increase as the rate of price change rises. In 1962-3, no price effects could be detected. In 1964-5, two industries representing, as a weighted proportion, 12 per cent of all industries, apparently experienced price effects. Finally, in 1969-70 price effects could be detected for six industries which represent a weighted proportion of 43 per cent of all industries.

There is also some evidence, although it is much more tenuous, that price effects tend to be concentrated in high unionisation industries.[3] In 1964-5, the second and fifth mostly highly unionised

---

[3] Since the two industry groups omitted from the cross-section (agriculture and construction), provide outlying observations above the estimated equations, it could be argued that these industries experienced price effects during all three of the periods 1962-3, 1964-5 and 1969-70. As argued earlier, consideration of the unemployment data makes this possibility seem unlikely. However, if this were the case, then, while the evidence supporting differential price effects would not be weakened, the evidence that such price effects were concentrated in high unionisation industries would become most slender.

industries exhibit price effects while in 1969–70, the first, second, third, fifth, sixth and tenth do so. However, the results are equally consistent with the hypothesis that price effects tend to be concentrated in the public sector. Unfortunately, because of the tendency for unionisation levels to be highest in public sector industries, it is not possible to discriminate between the two hypotheses.

An attempt was also made to discover whether price effects, once they occurred, tended to be strongest in high unionisation industries. However, the inclusion of terms such as $(p + qT_i)\Delta P$ in the equations resulted in no significant improvement in explanatory power. Finally, all three cross-sections *imply families of industrial curves intersecting at positive unemployment levels.* This was verified by re-estimating with $\log(U_i + 1)$ replacing $\log U_i$. The coefficient on the unionisation variable was then always negative.

So far the analysis has been performed using all three of the categories of industry group outlined earlier. This involved using some industry groups which are in fact aggregates of largely non-inter-related labour markets. It was noted above that for industries where such artificial aggregation is a minimum, the wage index tends to have a step-like character. This is most clearly defined in six industries: mining and quarrying; chemicals and allied; metals; clothing and footwear; paper and printing; and gas, electricity and water. A further analysis was therefore performed using only these six industries, under the assumption that artificial aggregation is smallest in these industries and that they therefore correspond more closely to the labour markets we would ideally wish to include in the cross-section. The six industries all belong to the first or second of the three categories discussed earlier. Problems concerning degrees of freedom make is pointless to re-estimate the individual cross-sections in this way, so the data was pooled and a combined cross-section (equation III.2) estimated incorporating all three periods 1962–3, 1964–5 and 1969–70. For the sake of comparison a similar equation (III.1) was also estimated using all industry groups:

$$\Delta W_i = 3.68 - 3.19 \log(T_i + 0.1) + 5.12(T_i - 1) \log U_i$$
$$\quad (0.40) \quad (0.52) \qquad\qquad (1.06)$$
$$\qquad + 0.90\Delta P + 0.18D_1 + 3.51D_2 \quad \bar{R}^2 = 0.92 \quad \text{(III.1)}$$
$$\qquad (0.09) \qquad (0.48) \qquad (0.48)$$

$$\Delta W_i = 3 \cdot 76 - 2 \cdot 95 \log{(T_i + 0 \cdot 1)} + 5 \cdot 10(T_i - 1) \log{U_i}$$

$$(0 \cdot 46) \quad (0 \cdot 68) \qquad\qquad (1 \cdot 77)$$

$$+ 0 \cdot 91 \Delta P + 0 \cdot 54 D_1 + 3 \cdot 47 D_2 \quad \bar{R}^2 = 0 \cdot 95 \quad \text{(III.2)}$$

$$(0 \cdot 10) \qquad (0 \cdot 59) \qquad (0 \cdot 69)$$

The dummy variable D_1 takes the value unity for the 1964–5 period and the value zero for the other two periods while D_2 is unity for 1969–70 and zero for the other periods.

Equation III.2, as expected, provides a slightly better overall fit than does equation III.1, but it is reassuring that there is very little difference between the estimated coefficients of the two equations. As far as it goes, this suggests that the problem of isolating labour markets may not be as serious as at first thought.

The combined cross-section again suggests a family of industrial Phillips curves intersecting at a positive unemployment level. For example, equation III.2 suggests that the industrial curve for $T_i = 0 \cdot 1$ intersects that for $T_i = 0 \cdot 9$ at an unemployment level of just over 3 per cent. This implies, in *the absence of price effects*, that at low levels of unemployment, rates of wage change tend to be lower in high unionisation industries than in low unionisation industries. However, the analysis also uncovered some tendency for price effects to be concentrated in high unionisation industries. Since periods of low unemployment tend to coincide with periods of relatively high price inflation, there may be a tendency for the above inverse relationship between ΔW_i and T_i to be masked in practice. That is, when unemployment is low, high unionisation industries experience additional wage increases dependent on the expected rate of price change.

Both the individual and combined cross-sections suggest that, once money illusion has broken down, the coefficient on the price change variable is not significantly different from unity. Friedman's prediction is therefore supported. However, the use of actual price changes as a proxy for ΔP^e means that such assertions must be treated with caution.

Finally, the dummy variables in the combined cross-sections suggest no general shift upwards or downwards in the family of industrial curves between 1962–3 and 1964–5, but a distinct upward shift of 3·5 percentage points by 1969–70. However, since 1969–70 covers the breakdown of the 1967–8 incomes policy and may include a substantial 'backlog' effect, it is not yet clear whether this upward shift is a permanent one or not.

IV   The aggregate data

Since the cross-sectional analysis suggested that the parameter $q = 0$, the form of the aggregate wage equation we need consider is, from equation II.13, given by

$$\Delta W = Z + C^* p \Delta P^e \quad 0 \le p \le 1 \qquad \text{(IV.1)}$$

where C^*, the weighted proportion of all markets which respond to price changes, varies over time and is dependent on ΔP^e. To obtain a version of IV.1 which is suitable for estimation purposes we must derive the precise relationship between C^* and ΔP^e. This relationship will depend on the cumulative distribution for T_i, the level of unionisation in an individual labour market.[4]

Let C be the proportion of all markets for which T_i is greater than some given level T'. A simple linear form of the cumulative distribution might then be

$$
\begin{aligned}
C &= 1 - \lambda T' \quad \text{for } 0 \le T' \le 1/\lambda \\
C &= 0 \qquad\quad \text{for } 1/\lambda \le T' \le 1
\end{aligned}
\qquad \text{(IV.2)}
$$

where $\lambda \ge 1$, the aggregate unionisation level is $\frac{1}{2}\lambda$ and the highest unionisation level is $1/\lambda$. The empirical distribution for industry groups is shown in Figure 3. The function is, of course, sharply discontinuous rather than a smooth curve, but no tendencies towards curvature are apparent so that it is well approximated by a linear function. Since the aggregate unionisation level is 0·43 and the highest industry level about 0·90 (mining and quarrying), the implied value for λ is in the region 1·1 to 1·15.

It follows from IV.2 that C^*, the proportion of all markets (industry groups) experiencing price effects, is given by

$$
\begin{aligned}
C^* &= 1 - \lambda T^* \quad \text{for } 0 \le T^* \le 1/\lambda \\
C^* &= 0 \qquad\quad \text{for } 1/\lambda \le T^* \le 1
\end{aligned}
\qquad \text{(IV.3)}
$$

---

[4] Once the cumulative distribution for T_i is known, D^* may also be expressed as a function of ΔP^e. However, since the cross-sectional results suggested $q = 0$, no attempt was made to estimate such aggregate equations.

Figure 3

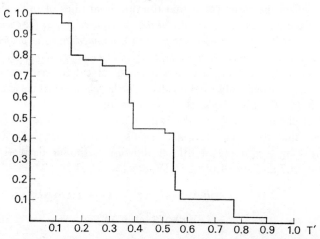

Source: Trade Union Membership, P.E.P., Vol. xxviii, No. 463.

where T^* is the 'critical level of unionisation' defined by equations II.11. Combining equations II.11 and equations IV.3, we then have:

If $\Delta P^e \geq 1$ then $T^* = 0$ and $C^* = 1$

If $l > \Delta P^e \geq 1 + m/\lambda$ then $T^* = (\Delta P^e - l)/m$ and

$$C^* = 1 - \lambda((\Delta P^e - l)/m)$$

If $l + m/\lambda > \Delta P^e$ then $1/\lambda \leq T^* \leq 1$ and $C^* = 0$

The aggregate wage equation (IV.1) then becomes

$$\Delta W = Z + p(1 + l\lambda/m)\,\Delta P_1^e - (\lambda p/m)\,\Delta P_1^{e2} + p\,\Delta P_2^e \quad \text{(IV.4)}$$

where $\Delta P_1^e = 0$ and $\Delta P_2^e = \Delta P^e$ for $\Delta P^e \geq l$

$\Delta P_1^e = \Delta P^e$ and $\Delta P_2^e = 0$ for $l > \Delta P^e \geq l + m/\lambda$

$\Delta P_1^e = 0$ and $\Delta P_2^e = 0$ for $l + m/\lambda > \Delta P^e$

Thus for $\Delta P^e \geq l$ all markets experience price effects while for $\Delta P^e < l + m/\lambda$ the critical level of unionisation exceeds the highest unionisation level and no markets experience such effects. For ΔP^e between these limits a varying proportion of markets experience price effects and ΔW depends not only on the expected rate of price change but also *on the square of that expected rate of change.*

It must also be noted that the form of equation IV.4 is not dependent on the assumption that the threshold rates of price change are a function of unionisation. *All that is required is that the threshold rates should vary over markets in such a manner that the proportion of markets experiencing price effects should be an approximately linear function of* ΔP^e. This fact is convenient since the cross-sectional analysis provided only weak evidence for a relationship between the threshold rates and the level of unionisation.

Z in equation IV.4 has the same general form as equation II.7 except that the cross-sectional results suggested that $\gamma = 0$ and $A(T_i) = a_1 + a_2 \log (T_i + 0 \cdot 1)$. Following a similar derivation to that of II.7 and substituting in IV.4 yields

$$\Delta W = \alpha + b_1 S^* + b_2 K^* + p(1 + l\lambda/m)\Delta P_1^e$$

$$- (\lambda p/m)\Delta P_1^{e^2} + p\Delta P_2^e \qquad (IV.5)$$

where $S^* = \log U - S_u^2/2U^2$, $K^* = TS^* + K/U$ and $\alpha = a_1 + a_2[\log (T + 0 \cdot 1) - (S_T^2/2(T + 0 \cdot 1))]$, α may again be regarded as constant for time series data, since T and $S_T^2 = \sum \alpha_i (T_i - T)^2$ are virtually constant for the post-war U.K.

Equation IV.5 may now be estimated by an iterative procedure beginning with arbitrary values for l and the quantity $l + m/\lambda$ and successively re-estimating until the values of l and $l + m/\lambda$ converge.

A priori considerations suggest that since $\lambda > 0$, $m \leq 0$ and $0 \leq p \leq 1$, the sign on the coefficient of $\Delta P_1^{e^2}$ will be positive and that if $l + m/\lambda > 0$, i.e. if price effects commence only when ΔP^e is above zero, the sign on ΔP_1^e will be negative. We also have from Section II that $b_1 < 0$, $b_2 > 0$ and $b_1 + b_2 \leq 0$.

Equations of the form of IV.5 were now estimated by ordinary least squares using U.K. quarterly data for the period 1961(i) to 1971(ii). Negative incomes policy dummies were initially included for three separate periods—the wage freezes of 1961–2 and 1966 and the statutory incomes policy of 1968–9. However, since the rate of wage change was measured over four quarters, four quarter moving averages of the original dummies were included in the estimating equation. Wage equations so estimated exhibited runs large positive residuals immediately after the 1966 and 1968–9 incomes policy period, suggesting a backlog effect compensating for the previous holding back of wage increases. Positive residuals were not evident after 1961–2 although runs of such residuals did occur slightly later in 1964–5. To catch this backlog effect the dummies were given additional positive values for the quarters 1967(iii) to 1967(iv) and 1969(iv) to 1970(ii). A moving average of the re-defined dummies was then included in the equation. These re-defined dummies implied that the 1966 and 1968–9 incomes policies had no long-term effect on wage inflation, an initial influence being compensated for by extra large increases a year or so later. The final form of the three dummies is given in the Appendix. The empirical version of equation IV.5 was

$$\Delta W = 9\cdot97 - 39\cdot145S^* + 71\cdot55K^* - 1\cdot04\Delta P_1^e + 0\cdot226\Delta P_1^{e^2}$$
$$ (0\cdot87) \quad (8\cdot94) \qquad (17\cdot84) \qquad (0\cdot25) \qquad (0\cdot045)$$

$$+ 0\cdot84\Delta P_2^e + 0\cdot06D_1 + 1\cdot20D_2 + 0\cdot67D_3$$
$$ (0\cdot06) \qquad (0\cdot16) \qquad (0\cdot18) \qquad (0\cdot12)$$

$$\bar{R}^2 = 0\cdot92 \quad d = 2\cdot03 \quad \text{(IV.6)}$$

where D_1, D_2 and D_3 are the 1961–2, 1966 and 1968–9 policy dummies, respectively. The actual rate of price change has, for the moment, been used as the proxy for the expected rate of price change.

The most noticeable aspect of equation IV.6 is the size of the coefficients on the variables S^* and K^* and the fact that the sum of these coefficients $b_1 + b_2 > 0$, implying industrial curves with positive unemployment slopes for high values of T_i. However, the large size of both coefficients and their standard errors is chiefly the result of high multicollinearity between S^* and K^*. The mean value of S^* is 0·59, while that of K/U is only $-0\cdot03$, so that since $T = \text{const}$ and $K^* = TS^* + K/U$, K^* is very close to being a constant multiple of S^*. Both the above problems may be resolved by re-estimating under the restriction $b_1 + b_2 = 0$, hence eliminating the multicollinearity and also ensuring non-positive slopes in the industrial curves:

$$\Delta W = 7\cdot55 + 7\cdot42K^{**} - 1\cdot31\Delta P_1^e + 0\cdot296\Delta P_1^{e^2} + 0\cdot94\Delta P_2^e$$
$$ (0\cdot46) \quad (1\cdot36) \qquad (0\cdot33) \qquad (0\cdot057) \qquad (0\cdot06)$$

$$+ 0\cdot72D_1 + 1\cdot15D_2 + 0\cdot55D_3 \quad \bar{R}^2 = 0\cdot90 \quad d = 1\cdot50 \quad \text{(IV.7)}$$
$$ (0\cdot19) \qquad (0\cdot19) \qquad (0\cdot14)$$

where $K^{**} = (T - 1)S^* + K/U$.

All coefficients now have the expected sign and the significance of the price variables provides strong evidence for differential price effects very similar to those suggested by the cross-sectional analysis. The equation implies that for $\Delta P^e \geq l = 7 \cdot 6$ per cent all industries experience price effects, while for $\Delta P^e < l + m/\lambda = 4 \cdot 4$ per cent no industries experience such effects. For intermediate rates of price change, the weighted proportion of markets experiencing price effects is estimated as $C^* = 1 - \lambda((\Delta P^e - l)/m) = 1 \cdot 37 + 0 \cdot 31 \Delta P^e$. However, while the cross-sectional results provided some tenuous evidence for the hypothesis that price effects are concentrated in highly unionised industries no such inference can necessarily be made from the time series results. The time series estimate of p is $0 \cdot 94$—virtually identical to that obtained from the cross-sectional analysis and again not significantly different from unity.

It is possible to use equation IV.7 to estimate the extent of any 'shifts' in the Phillips curve, during the 1960's, resulting from variations in S_u^2 and K. By calculating the maximum and minimum values of $S_u^2/2U^2$ and K/U during the period it is easy to deduce that the maximum shift resulting from a changing industrial distribution of unemployment was between $0 \cdot 5$ and 1 percentage points. This is very small compared with the upward shift in the 'partial' Phillips curve resulting from the increased importance of price effects.

So far we have been content to use the actual rate of price change as the proxy for ΔP^e. This is a special case of the usual procedure in this field whereby some assumed relationship is specified between ΔP^e and some observable economic variable—generally the actual rate of price change. The obvious disadvantage of this approach is that we are, necessarily, jointly testing hypothesis about both the determination of wage changes and the formation of price expectations. A direct test of the wage determination hypothesis is not possible until some method is devised of directly estimating ΔP^e and for this reason we restrict ourselves to merely considering the more general but commonly used assumption that price expectations are formed adaptively:

$$\Delta P_t^e - \Delta P_{t-1}^e = B(\Delta P_t - \Delta P_{t-1}^e) \qquad \text{(IV.8)}$$

Equation IV.8 implies that the expected rate of price change $\Delta P_t^e = \sum_{i=0}^{\infty} B(1 - B)^i \Delta P_{t-i}$, where $0 \leq B \leq 1$. Accordingly, variables of this type, for values of B between 0 and 1 were included in the wage equation. The best result was obtained for a value of $B = 0 \cdot 4$

$$\Delta W = 7 \cdot 32 + 7 \cdot 17 K^{**} - 1 \cdot 45 \Delta P_i^e + 0 \cdot 365 \Delta P_1^{e^2} + 1 \cdot 040 \Delta P_2^e$$
$$(0 \cdot 40) \quad (1 \cdot 16) \qquad (0 \cdot 28) \qquad (0 \cdot 055) \qquad (0 \cdot 06)$$

$$+ 0 \cdot 54 D_1 + 1 \cdot 19 D_2 + 0 \cdot 68 D_3 \quad \bar{R}^2 = 0 \cdot 93 \quad d = 1 \cdot 36 \quad \text{(IV.9)}$$
$$(0 \cdot 15) \qquad (0 \cdot 16) \qquad (0 \cdot 11)$$

There is an improvement in the overall fit of the equation and in the significance of the explanatory variables. It is also noticeable that the estimate of the parameter p is again not significally different from unity, implying that once money illusion has broken down, a change in ΔP^e results in an exactly equal change in ΔW.

Finally, the coefficients on the dummy variables enables some estimate to be made of the effectiveness of incomes policy. From 1968(iv) to 1969(ii) incomes policy reduced the rate of wage inflation by between 2·5 and 3 percentage points, but the backlog effect resulting from the breakdown of this policy led to wage inflation of 2·5 to 3 points higher than it would otherwise have been during the period 1969(iv) to 1970(ii). This backlog effect had expired by the end of 1970. The 1966 wage freeze reduced wage inflation by well over 4 percentage points during the brief period 1966(iii) to 1966(iv) but again there was a compensating backlog effect during 1967(iii) to 1967(iv). Finally, the 1961 freeze reduced wage inflation by only 2 percentage points. However, in this case no immediate backlog effect is evident.

V   Conclusions

The cross-sectional analysis by industry group suggests that both the slope and position of the industrial Phillips curve are influenced by the level of unionisation. Price effects appear to be differential in that the threshold rate of price change varies across industries. There is some slight evidence that the threshold rate is influenced by the level of unionisation.

Time series data support the cross-sectional finding of differential price effects. This is reflected in aggregate data by a non-linear relationship between wage and price changes. The results suggest that price effects are non-existent for rates of price change below about 4·5 per cent, but are experienced by all industries for rates of price change above 7·5 per cent. When price effects are evident the coefficient on the price change variable is very close to unity.

During the 1960's upward shift in the partial aggregate Phillips curve resulting from structural changes in the distribution of unemployment was probably less than 1 per cent. This shift is very small compared with shifts caused by this increased importance of price effects.

Appendix: sources of data

Unemployment data

The weighted variance of industry unemployment levels was constructed from data kindly supplied by Mr. A. P. Thirlwall of the University of Kent. This data gave unemployment percentages for S.I.C. industry groups for January, April, July and October of the years 1960–6. It was up-dated using Ministry of Employment and Productivity data for 1967–71. The aggregate level of unemployment used is that obtained by summing over all industries.

Unionisation data

The data used came from two sources. The P.E.P. pamphlet of July 1962 entitled *Trade Union Membership* gives the percentage of the labour force unionised by industry group for 1948 and 1958. G. S. Bain, in *The Growth of White Collar Unionism* (O.U.P., 1970), gives similar figures for 1964. In many cases there was no change in industrial unionisation between 1958 and 1964. For other industries the variations were slight and in these cases the data was linearly interpolated between 1958 and 1964 and extrapolated to 1971. The weighted covariance variable was then obtained on an annual basis and covers the industry groups for which unionisation data is available. Quarterly values were obtained by simple linear interpolation.

Wages and prices

The wage indices used are the indices of hourly wage rates published both for separate industry groups and for all industries combined in the Ministry of Employment and Productivity gazette.

The price index used is the index of retail prices.

Definitions of variables for time series analysis

$$\Delta W_t = \left(\frac{W_{t+2} - W_{t-2}}{W_{t+2} + W_{t-2}}\right) 50 \qquad \text{where } W_t = \text{average of monthly wage index values for quarter } t.$$

$$\Delta P_t = \left(\frac{P_{t+2} - P_{t-2}}{P_{t+2} + P_{t-2}}\right) 50 \qquad \text{where } P_t = \text{average of monthly price index values for quarter } t.$$

$$U_t = \frac{u_{t-1} + u_t + u_{t+1} + u_{t+2}}{4} \qquad \text{where the small } us \text{ are aggregate unemployment figures for January, April, July and October.}$$

Thus, for example, if u_t refers to April, then U_t is centred roughly at the middle of the second quarter.

$\left(\dfrac{S_u^2}{2U^2}\right)_t$ is defined in an identical number to U_t.

$\left(\dfrac{K}{U}\right)_t$ is obtained by linear interpolation of the annual series as described above.

All other variables are as defined in the main text.

The cross-sectional data

The 1969–70 cross-section

Industry group	Period over which ΔW is measured	ΔW	U	T
Agriculture, forestry and fishing	May 69 to Feb. 70	10·8	4·25	0·28
Mining and quarrying*	Nov. 68 to Apr. 71	11·1	5·55	0·92
Food, drink and tobacco	July 69 to July 70	11·3	2·2	0·11
Chemicals and allied industries	Mar. 69 to June 70	15·6	1·7	0·20
Metals	Jan. 69 to Mar. 70	6·6	1·8	0·54
Textiles†	Apr. 69 to Apr. 70	5·1	2·05	0·36
Clothing and footwear*	Sep. 68 to June 71	8·8	1·5	0·36
Timber and furniture	Jan. 69 to Apr. 70	6·3	2·5	0·36
Paper, printing and publishing	Dec. 69 to Dec. 70	14·3	1·35	0·58
Construction*	Nov. 68 to June 71	8·6	7·8	0·36
Gas, electricity and water	Mar. 69 to Sep. 70	11·7	1·75	0·48
Transport and communications	July 69 to July 70	12·4	2·35	0·77
Distributive trades	July 69 to July 70	8·3	2·15	0·15
Prof. services, p.a. and defence	Nov. 69 to Dec. 70	14·5	1·1	0·45

Arbitrary 12-month intervals used for food, drink and tobacco; textiles; transport and communications; and distributive trades.

 * Although these were industries for which the wage index characteristically showed clearly irregular jumps it was not possible to find two such jumps within the period Jan. 1969 to Dec. 1970. Wage change was therefore calculated over a period rather larger than normal but centred as far as possible about the period July 1969 to July 1970.

 † Because of an agreement in the wool industry, the index from May 1970 onwards is not strictly comparable with that for previous months (see D.E.P. gazette, July 1970, Table 131). For this reason arbitrary twelve-month period used for textiles was April 1969 to April 1970.

The 1964–5 cross-section

Industry group	Period over which ΔW is measured	ΔW	U	T
Agriculture, forestry and fishing	Jan. 64 to Jan. 65	6·5	3·2	0·28
Mining and quarrying	June 64 to July 65	4·8	1·05	0·91
Food, drink and tobacco	July 64 to July 65	5·6	1·5	0·11
Chemical and allied industries	July 64 to May 65	6·3	1·2	0·20
Metals	Dec. 63 to July 65	5·5	1·0	0·54
Textiles	July 64 to July 65	4·8	1·35	0·36
Clothing and footwear	Sep. 64 to Sep. 65	6·9	1·1	0·36
Timber and furniture	Apr. 64 to Aug. 65	6·2	1·2	0·36
Paper, printing and publishing	June 64 to June 65	6·3	0·6	0·58
Construction	Mar. 64 to Mar. 65	5·1	3·5	0·36
Gas, electricity and water	July 64 to Oct. 65	11·1	0·7	0·48
Transport and communications	July 64 to July 65	7·5	1·55	0·77
Distributive trades	July 64 to July 65	7·4	1·4	0·15
Prof. services, p.a. and defence	May 64 to June 65	5·7	0·8	0·46

Arbitrary twelve-month intervals used for food, textiles, transport and distributive trades.

The 1962–3 cross-section

Industry group	Period over which ΔW is measured	ΔW	U	T
Agriculture, forestry and fishing	Mar. 62 to Jan. 63	5·2	2·9	0·27
Mining and quarrying	Apr. 62 to Apr. 63	4·3	1·2	0·90
Food, drink and tobacco	July 62 to July 63	4·2	2·35	0·11
Chemical and allied industries	Mar. 62 to July 63	5·0	1·45	0·20
Metals	July 62 to Dec. 63	3·6	1·95	0·54
Textiles	July 62 to July 63	3·7	2·85	0·36
Clothing and footwear	Sep. 62 to Nov. 63	4·1	1·9	0·37
Timber and furniture	July 62 to July 63	2·1	2·9	0·37
Paper, printing and publishing	Jan. 62 to Mar. 63	5·4	0·85	0·57
Construction	Aug. 62 to Nov. 63	4·8	5·0	0·37
Gas, electricity and water	Jan. 62 to July 63	5·3	0·9	0·50
Transport and communication	July 62 to July 63	4·2	2·05	0·77
Distributive trades	July 62 to July 63	4·9	2·05	0·15
Prof. services, p.a. and defence	June 62 to Nov. 63	4·7	1·15	0·47

Arbitrary twelve-month intervals used for food, textiles, timber, transport and distributive trades.

The aggregate data

		ΔP	ΔW	U	S^*	K^*	K^{**}	D_1	D_2	D_3
1961	(i)	4·1	6·3	1·5	0·21	0·06	−0·15	−1	0	0
	(ii)	4·2	5·8	1·5	0·22	0·07	−0·15	−2	0	0
	(iii)	4·6	4·1	1·6	0·27	0·10	−0·18	−3	0	0
	(iv)	5·5	4·5	1·75	0·36	0·14	−0·22	−3	0	0
1962	(i)	3·7	4·9	1·9	0·46	0·19	−0·27	−2	0	0
	(ii)	2·5	4·4	2·05	0·55	0·23	−0·32	−1	0	0
	(iii)	3·0	4·2	2·6	0·70	0·30	−0·40	0	0	0
	(iv)	1·5	3·8	2·8	0·76	0·33	−0·43	0	0	0
1963	(i)	1·3	3·0	2·8	0·76	0·33	−0·43	0	0	0
	(ii)	2·1	3·6	2·8	0·76	0·33	−0·43	0	0	0
	(iii)	1·5	4·7	2·25	0·62	0·26	−0·36	0	0	0
	(iv)	2·8	4·8	2·0	0·50	0·20	−0·30	0	0	0
1964	(i)	4·3	5·5	1·85	0·43	0·17	−0·26	0	0	0
	(ii)	4·4	5·2	1·7	0·35	0·13	−0·22	0	0	0
	(iii)	4·4	5·1	1·55	0·26	0·09	−0·17	0	0	0
	(iv)	5·1	5·5	1·5	0·24	0·08	−0·16	0	0	0
1965	(i)	4·7	6·7	1·45	0·21	0·07	−0·14	0	0	0
	(ii)	4·5	7·0	1·4	0·18	0·06	−0·12	0	0	0
	(iii)	4·3	7·6	1·4	0·17	0·05	−0·12	0	0	0
	(iv)	3·7	7·3	1·35	0·12	0·03	−0·09	0	0	0
1966	(i)	3·6	6·0	1·35	0·12	0·03	−0·09	0	−1	0
	(ii)	3·7	4·8	1·5	0·23	0·08	−0·15	0	−2	0
	(iii)	3·6	3·2	1·8	0·42	0·18	−0·25	0	−2	0
	(iv)	2·5	2·8	2·2	0·62	0·27	−0·35	0	−2	0
1967	(i)	1·7	4·3	2·55	0·77	0·34	−0·43	0	0	0
	(ii)	2·1	5·7	2·8	0·85	0·38	−0·47	0	2	0
	(iii)	2·9	7·5	2·85	0·87	0·40	−0·48	0	2	0
	(iv)	4·4	7·3	2·8	0·85	0·39	−0·46	0	2	0

The aggregate data (continued)

		P	W	U	S*	K*	K**	D_1	D_2	D_3
1968	(i)	5·5	5·7	2·8	0·83	0·38	−0·45	0	1	0
	(ii)	5·5	6·1	2·75	0·80	0·37	−0·44	0	0	−1
	(iii)	6·0	5·2	2·7	0·77	0·36	−0·41	0	0	−2
	(iv)	5·3	5·0	2·7	0·75	0·35	−0·40	0	0	−3
1969	(i)	4·9	5·1	2·65	0·73	0·34	−0·39	0	0	−3
	(ii)	5·0	5·2	2·7	0·74	0·35	−0·39	0	0	−1
	(iii)	4·9	7·1	2·75	0·75	0·35	−0·40	0	0	1
	(iv)	5·7	9·1	2·85	0·79	0·37	−0·42	0	0	3
1970	(i)	6·7	10·4	2·9	0·81	0·38	−0·43	0	0	3
	(ii)	7·4	12·4	3·0	0·84	0·39	−0·45	0	0	2
	(iii)	8·2	12·8	3·1	0·91	0·43	−0·48	0	0	1
	(iv)	9·4	12·4	3·3	0·99	0·46	−0·53	0	0	0
1971	(i)	9·6	12·4	3·6	1·10	0·52	−0·58	0	0	0
	(ii)	8·8	10·5	4·1	1·24	0·59	−0·66	0	0	0

References

[1] Archibald, G. C., 'The Phillips Curve and Distribution of Unemployment', *American Economic Review Papers and Proceedings* (May 1969).
[2] Friedman, M., 'The Role of Monetary Policy', *American Economic Review* (1968).
[3] Hines, A. G., 'Trade Unions and Wage Inflation in the United Kingdom, 1893–1961', *Review of Economic Studies* (1964).
[4] Hines, A. G., 'The Determinants of the Rate of Change of Money Wage Rates and the Effectiveness of Incomes Policy', Ch. 8 in *The Current Inflation*, London, Macmillan (1971).
[5] Lipsey, R. G., 'The Relation between Unemployment and the Rate of Change of Money Wage Rates in the United Kingdom, 1862–1957: Further Analysis', *Economica* (1960).
[6] Lipsey, R. G. and Parkin, M., 'Incomes Policy: A Reappraisal', *Economica* (May 1970). Reprinted as Ch. 4 in M. Parkin and M. T. Sumner (eds.), *Incomes Policy and Inflation*, Manchester, Manchester University Press (1972).
[7] Phillips, A. W., 'The Relation between Unemployment and the Rate of Change of Money Wage Rates in the United Kingdom, 1861–1957', *Economica* (1958).
[8] P.E.P., *Trade Union Membership* (July 1962).
[9] Sumner, M. T., 'Aggregate Demand, Price Expectations and the Phillips Curve', Ch. 9 in M. Parkin and M. T. Sumner (eds.), *Incomes Policy and Inflation*, Manchester, Manchester University Press (1972).
[10] Thomas, R. L. and Storey, P. J. M., 'Unemployment Dispersion as a Determinant of Wage Inflation in the U.K., 1925–66', *Manchester School* (June 1971). Reprinted as Ch. 11 in M. Parkin and M. T. Sumner (eds.), *Incomes Policy and Inflation*, Manchester, Manchester University Press (1972).

Author Index

(*Bibliographical references in italics*)

Ainsworth, R. B., *10*
Archibald, G. C., ix, *xii*, 46, Ch. 5: 109–63, 115, 152, 156, 158, 159, *162*, 197, 198, 204, 209–10, 213–14, *226*, 227, *253*
Ashenfelter, O. C., 46, 47, 50, *59*, 76, *78*

Bain, G. S., *37*, *250*
Ball, J. R., *37*, 47, 48, *59*
Bowers, J. K., 165–6, *195*
Bowley, A. C., 127, *156*
Brechling, F. P. R., xii, 109, 117, 121, 122, 124, 156, *162*, Ch. 7: 197–226, 198, 202, 203, *226*
Brown, A. J., ix, *xii*
Burrows, P., 182, 193, *196*
Burton, J., *37*

Cameron, G. C., 58, *59*
Cheshire, P. C., 165–6, *195*
Clock, G., 58, *60*
Coddington, A., 76, *78*
Corry, B. A., 110, 111, *162*, 197, 201, *226*
Cragg, J. G., 109
Cross, J. G., 76, *78*

Dicks-Mireaux, L. A., 3, *37*, 47, *59*
Dow, J. C. R., 3, *37*, 47, *59*
Durbin, A., *60*
Dunlop, J. T., *37*, *78*

Eckstein, O., *37*
Evans, E. W., 54, *59*

Flanders, A., 52, *59*
Fisk, P. R., 61
Foster, J. I., xi, 1, Ch. 6: 164–96, 165, 166, 169, 171, *195*
Friedman, M., 111, 118, 121, *162*, 227, *253*

Galambos, P., 54, *59*
Godfrey, L., 16, *37*, 47, 52, 58, *59*, 96, *108*, 142
Goldberger, A. S., 136, *162*
Goodman, J. F. B., 52, *59*
Gordon, D. F., 121
Grant, E. K., 113
Gray, M. R., 1, 115
Gujarati, D., 165, 166, 168, 190, *195*

Hahn, F. H., *226*
Hamermesh, D., 197
Hansen, B., 79, *108*, 112, 119, *162*, 169, *196*
Harsanyi, J., 42–3, *59*
Hauser, M. M., 182, 193, *196*
Hicks, Sir J. R., 61, 68–9, *78*
Hieser, R. O., 61–5, 72, 73, 77–8, *78*
Hines, A. G., vii–viii, *xii*, 1–17, 20–1, 26–7, 29, 32, 34, 36, *37*, 46–50, 52, 58, *59*, 115, 133, *162*, 228, 232, *253*
Hobsbawm, E. J. E., 3, *37*
Holmes, J. M., 201, *226*
Holt, C. C., 125, 197, 218–20, 226
Hopkins, S. V., 156
Hynes, A., 121

Jackson, D., 85–6, 87, *108*
Johnson, G. E., 46, 47, 50, *59*, 76, *78*
Johnson, H. G., *37*, *59*, *108*, 121, 142, 162
Johnston, J., xi, 38, 58, *59*, Ch. 3: 61–78, 65, *78*, Ch. 4: 79–108, 80–1, 97, *108*

Kemmis, R., xi, Ch. 5: 109–63, *226*
Kendall, M. G., *10*
Keynes, J. M., 133, *162*
Klein, L. R., *37*, 47, 48, *59*
Knowles, K. G. J. C., 53, 58, *59*
Kornhauser, A., *60*

Kuh, E., 117, *162*

Laidler, D. E. W., 1, 79, 110, 111, 121, *162*, 201, *226*
Lipsey, R. G., ix–x, *xii*, 3, 16, *37*, 79, *108*, 109, 115–17, 123, 133, 134, 142–3, 158, *162*, 198, 204, 209, *226*, 227, 229–30, *253*
Lucas, R. E., 197, 198, *226*

Mackay, D. I., 166, 190, 192, 193, *196*
McCarthy, W. E. J., 6, 23, 25, *37*, 39–40, 53, *59*
McKensie, R. B., 41, *60*
Mortensen, D., 111, 124–5, 197, *226*

Negishi, T., 208, *226*
Nobay, A. R., *37*, *59*, *108*, 121, 142, *162*

P.E.P., 236, 250, *253*
Parker, S. R., 40, *59*
Parkin, J. M., 1, *1*, 16, *37*, *59*, *60*, *108*, 109, 111, 133, 134, 142–3, 158, *162*, *163*, 164, *196*, *226*, 229–30, *253*
Pencavel, J. H., 46, 47, 50, 58, *59*
Perkins, J. W., xi, Ch. 5: 109–63, *226*
Peston, M. H., *162*, *226*
Phelps, E. S., 110–11, 118, 121, 123–4, 125, 152, *163*, 169, *196*, 197, 201, 202, *226*
Phelps-Brown, E. H., *37*, 127, 156
Phillips, A. W., ix–x, *x*, *37*, 79, *108*, 117, 123, *163*, 209, 227, *253*
Purdy, D., x, Ch. 1: 1–37, Ch. 2: 38–60, 49, 58, *59*, 79, 164

Rapping, L. A., 198, *226*
Rees, A., 58, *60*
Reid, G. L., 166, 190, 192, 193, *196*
Reynolds, L. G., vii, *xii*
Roberts, G., 58, *60*

Rose, D., 1
Ross, A. M., 40, *60*, 208, *226*

Samuelson, P. A., vii, *x*, 122, *162*, 208, *226*
Shackle, G. L. S., 61, 69, *78*
Simler, N. J., 118, *163*
Smyth, D. J., 201, *226*
Solow, R. M., 198, 212, *226*
Steuer, M. D., *37*
Stoney, P. J., 16, *37*, 109, *163*, 198, 209, 210, 216, 223–4, *226*, 227, *253*
Sumner, M. T., *60*, *108*, 142–3, *162*, *163*, 164, *196*, *226*, 227, *253*
Surrey, M. J. C., 96, *108*

Taylor, J., 47, 52, 58, 59, *60*, 79–80, 96, *108*, 117, 118, *163*, 165, 166–8, 170, 172, 191, 195, *196*
Tella, A., 118, *163*
Thirlwall, A. P., 109, 110, 111, *163*, 250
Thomas, R. L., xii, 16, *37*, 109, *163*, 198, 209, 210, 216, 223–4, *226*, Ch. 8: 227–53, 227, *253*
Timbrell, M., xi, 58, *59*, Ch. 4: 79–108
Tobin, J., 121, *163*
Turner, H. A., 58, *60*, 85–6, 87, *108*

Vanderkamp, J., 117, 118, *163*, 201, *226*

Walton, R. E., 41, *60*
Webb, A. E., 165–6, *195*
Weeden, R., 165–6, 190, *195*
Wilkinson, F., 85–6, 87, *108*
Wilson, T. A., *37*
Wolfe, J. N., 61
Worswick, G. D. N., 61, *78*

Zis, G., x, Ch. 1: 1–37, Ch. 2: 38–60, 49, 58, *59*

Subject Index

'Addi-log' model, 115–17, 125, 126–9, 142–3, 145, 213–14
Average worker,
  growth in real net earnings, 85–7

Bayesian statistics, 155
Bilateral wage bargaining, 61–78, 80, 218
'Birth rate bulge', 164, 176–9, 184, 191–2

Chi-square test, 153–5
Chow test (F-test), 171, 176, 187, 188, 189, 190
Classical theory, 197
'Cost-push' inflation, vii, 2, 3, 38, 227

Data sources, 36, 156–62, 194–5, 250–3
'Demand-pull' inflation, ix
Dynamic market interdependence, 198, 208–9, 216, 224, 225

Earnings related insurance benefits, 164, 174, 180–2, 190
Excess demand for labour, x, xi, xii, 2, 79–80, 106–7, 110–56, 166, 168, 237–8
Expectations of inflation (see Price expectations)
Expectations of wage change (see Wage expectations)

Forecasting, 105

Gauss-Newton estimation (see also NLCLS), 212
General strike, 31, 133
Gibrat's law, 113
Gold standard, 128, 129–34, 135

'Hoarded' labour, 166–8, 170, 172

Incomes policies, 1, 38–9, 58, 59, 133–4, 142–3, 230, 243–4, 246, 249

Koyck transformation, 121, 136–8, 145–7
Moments model, 109, 110, 114–15, 123, 126–8, 142
Money illusion, 227

Neo-classical theory, 197
N.L.C.L.S. (non-linear constrained least squares) estimation, 135, 136–8, 140–2, 212–15
Non-linear aggregation hypothesis, 198, 209–16, 217, 224, 225, 227

Price expectations, xii, 53, 79, 88–91, 97–100, 106, 107, 110–11, 118, 121, 138, 156, 197, 201, 202, 228, 230, 234, 235, 240–9
  adaptive (see also Koyck transformation), 211–12, 248–49

Productivity change, 117–18, 165–6

Redundancy payments, xi, 164, 165, 174, 180–2, 190, 192–3
Retentions (taxation) rate, 86–8, 93–6, 98–100, 107

'Shake-out' (labour rationalisation), 164–76, 182–4, 187, 189, 192–3
Single equation model,
    deficiencies in, 199–200, 202–3
Stabilisation policies, 225
Strikes (*see also* General strike), 39, 45, 47, 51–6, 58, 63–78, 80–1, 96, 97–8
Strikes,
    probability, 66–7, 96–7
    length, 71

Threshold of price change, 228, 233–6
Trade unions,
    bargaining power, ix–x, 42–6, 77
    closed shop, 2, 6, 23–7, 62
    growth, 4–7, 13–15
    indices of, 47–57
    'last in first out' policy towards redundancy, 193
    level of unionisation, x, xii, 1–36, 47, 48–52, 58, 228–36, 239–49
    militancy, x, xi, 1–37, 38–60, 73, 96

Unemployment insurance scheme, 10, 158
U–V relation (unemployment-vacancies), ix–x, 164–95
Unemployment,
    'natural rate', 197–8, 200–9
    Keynesian policy for, 142
    Regional, 197–225

Wage drift, 237
Wage expectations, xii, 198–9, 201–3, 205, 208, 219–21, 225
Wage leadership, xii
Wage round, 5